The Future Generation

The Zine-Book for Subculture Parents, Kids, Friends & Others

Cover & book design by Scott Sugiuchi, revised by Jonathan Rowland
Future Generation logo (previous page) designed by Clover, age 10

ISBN: 978-1-62963-450-0
LCCN: 2017942908

10 9 8 7 6 5 4 3 2 1

PM Press
PO Box 23912
Oakland, CA 94623
www.pmpress.org

Printed in the USA by the Employee Owners of Thomson-Shore in
Dexter, Michigan.
www.thomsonshore.com

CONTENTS

Foreword

by Ariel Gore

Before *Hip Mama* and *Mutha Magazine* and *Rad Dad*, before you could Google "nursing after nipple piercing" or "gender fluid parenting," before celebrity mom rags made childrearing look glam and easy while they hid all their nannies' labor, I pushed a secondhand stroller down Haight Street in San Francisco.

"Breeder!" some punk yelled at us from across the street. I looked down at my plain cotton spit-up covered clothes from the Goodwill. "It's yuppie scum like you who are fucking up this city!" the guy went on.

But the yuppie scum at my daughter's new daycare didn't want to have anything to do with me, either. They looked down their nose-job noses at me with a mixture of pity and concern.

Maia started to fuss in her stroller, so I pulled her out, sat down on the curb, and lifted my shirt to let her nurse. A bike messenger almost got hit by a Muni bus craning his neck to stare at us.

How could it be that the simple acts of getting knocked up and having a baby had alienated me from every single subculture I had ever heard of?

Maia fell asleep sweetly in my arms there on the curb, and I lifted her back into her stroller, careful not to wake her. I pushed on through the light summer drizzle, made my way up to the anarchist bookstore, a little closet of a shop. I pawed through the zines—*EcoPussy* and *Wizard Man* or some such. I sighed. My pussy wasn't feeling very ecological these days and I was pretty sure I couldn't get into wizardry. I started to turn away, but suddenly the punk from across the street was standing right in front of us. "Why don't you go to Barnes and Noble, breeder?"

I turned back toward the zine shelf so as not to let him see the tears well up in my eyes (I was 20 years old and it was still easy to hurt my feelings). But just as I turned, from the bottom of the rows of anarchist, hippie, feminist, and punk publications, a little Xeroxed something glowed up at me, a quote from Emma Goldman: "We, who pay dearly for every breath of pure, fresh air must guard against the tendency to fetter the future." Japanese electronica burst from speakers unseen and cartoon stars floated from the homemade zine and filled the tiny store.

I grabbed issue #1 of *The Future Generation*, quickly convinced the guy behind the old-fashioned register to let me pay the $2 in food stamps, then locked eyes with the mean unpunk punk and snarled: "Fuck off."

It's a powerful thing, to find a little Xeroxed island home in a sea of alienation. Since the first issue of *The Future Generation* came out in 1990, the zine world has exploded. From *Mamalicious* to *Mad Lovin' Mama*, indie parenting mags have a whole shelf to themselves now. Alternative mothering websites abound. Even mainstream corporate publishers have gotten into the action, hoping to sell a few "hip" maternity outfits and touting a baby as the new must-have accessory. We're a *demographic* now, I guess. But in a mass-market economy, what is genuine quietly prevails. Each new issue of *The Future Generation* glows up from the shelf promising the political and philosophical resources to sustain you, the voices of the moms like you and unlike you, and the stream-of-consciousness truths only China has the ovaries to tell. In these pages, the shitty days are never glossed over and the spiritual highs never toned down for the sake of coolness. Kodak moments turn psychedelic and the impossibility of our mama-mission is put into its proper radical context. When China lays it down, it stays down. For more than 16 years, *The Future Generation* has pushed me along my path as a mom with gentle chiding and solid support.

In issue #9 China says, "I want to be the female Bukowski, the female Burroughs, instead I'm just the female." But I'll bet Bukowski and Burroughs are rolling around in their graves, wishing they could have been the male China Doll Martens.

So, welcome to *The Future Generation: The Zine-Book for Subculture Parents, Kids, Friends & Others*. Please stow your baggage in the overhead compartment. You've been invited on an adventure starring one lionhearted superhero mama and her wickedly independent and spirited girl-child. Cartoon stars should be floating up from the page right about now, and do not be alarmed if Japanese electronica bursts from speakers unseen. Prepare for takeoff.

Cartoon by Clover

Introduction
by China Martens

The first issue of *The Future Generation* came out in April 1990, soon after my daughter turned two years old, but I had been working on the idea for a while. I wanted to start a zine as a resource network for parents in the subculture to share information and help each other out. I was in new territory and felt like a total minority. Most punks weren't parents and most parents weren't punks. I knew from all my best experiences in the anarcho-punk scene that we needed to work together to support each other to create change. So much had seemed possible to me back then!

I grew up moving around each year like an army brat and then came of age in the suburbs of Washington DC (Prince George's County). Mine was the classic tale of a misfit kid. I spent my teenage years being depressed and alienated, although those feelings had probably started even before that.

When I left home in 1984 (at 18), I rapidly discovered how much was going on. The subculture held the ticket to being yourself, the information to liberate yourself. There was always a place to stay, food to eat, protests to take place in. Taking part in direct actions in DC during the Reagan Era, seeing the autonomous squatted realms of Berlin and NYC, warehouse living in San Francisco, going on the Peace March, taking road trips across America—I spent three years widening my horizons—in art, culture, possibility, social construction…in every way. There were so many little different groups of people in the "underground." And there was a history of counterculture, there was a whole lineage of revolution.

This was the world I was prepared to live in for the rest of my life. If there was a housing crisis, a class issue, a food problem, a gender/sex question, an emotional dysfunction—we took it on as a group. Wrote a zine about it, shared information to the alternatives, and created structures to build a better and new way of doing things and protested that which we felt was wrong. "Want to be free, come panhandle with me."

But after the birth of my daughter, right before my twenty-second birthday in 1988, I could no longer "keep up." I wanted to live as radically as ever, but the support I needed as a parent was not there. I found myself slipping back to an impoverished and controlled state. There was a vacuum in the subculture where issues about children simply didn't exist while The State was fully prepared—with its social workers, public indoctrination, and other mechanisms—to take over. More a freak than ever, I was unwilling and unable to navigate in the mainstream just as much as I was unsupported by the individualism in my own tribe. People in the scene were not really unfriendly to me. On the contrary, I have had many lovely experiences. But few knew what to do with a child and fewer still had one of their own. It is a lot of work to raise a child. There are a lot of places where you make life decisions and a lot of ways in which you are impacted in a physical way, that a child-free person could have easily jumped over those same hurdles

I had known about the existence of zines for some time; I had considered myself a writer but it wasn't until I became a mother that I started my first zine. It was the single issue that affected me the most, and on a daily basis. There wasn't anything out there like what I wanted to start. I was hungry for information. I was trading notes on the playground with anyone similar to me. I might have been late to join the subculture, but I felt on the cutting edge of a change in parenting values.

Having a zine on parenting was going to the next level. I didn't feel like talking Anarchy 101. We'd run that topic into the ground along with the subject of "oppression," "revolution," "freedom," or how to change the world in our late night kitchen table or bonfire discussions. It was time to concentrate on a subject. Run a bookstore, café, community center or record distribution. Form a co-op. Learn a skill, a trade. Be a roofer or an organic food farmer. Fix pipes. And if we talk anarchy, let's talk it in the details, in the practical. We have agreed that we reject the system. Now what?

My early zines were full of type-written anecdotes from personal experience and cut-and-paste excerpts from books assembled in a complementary package that aimed to see the bigger picture: The roots of societal problems and the tools we could use to build the future that we did want to see. I wasn't aiming for any kind of literary grandeur—but to share with others who could use this (hard to find) subversive information. My writing was rarely edited, coming from the "any-way-you-can-or-not-at-all" school of writing, which people seemed to respond to honestly. Others would share their own experiences and thoughts back to me, in the form of a letter or zine submission.

Each issue changed with my changing interests over the years, and I gained more contributors and included fewer theories and excerpts from the library and used bookstore books that I sought answers from. By the time the alternative parenting zine scene blossomed, my daughter was a young teen. I still was dealing with issues that barely anyone in my peer group was—while the world was opening up for radical childraising essays of young children, who was interested in the trials of raising a teenager? Which felt to me, a big as change in one's life as becoming a parent in the first place.

And now time is moving on again…

It's 2017, as I write this, and I've fought long and hard for this second "tenth-anniversary" edition to come out. *The Future Generation*, in book form, first came out with local press Atomic Company in 2007. Originally Atomic Books approached me with the idea to turn my collection of past zines into a book. It was a "for love not money" project with a humble run of 1,000 copies, which sold out in two years. It was my first book.

This compilation contains 16 years of *The Future Generation* zine history—it's spanned my parenting life. When it first came out, I was 40, my daughter was 18. Now I'm 51 and she is 29. I can think of nothing more suitable than the last word coming from her. I love you very much, Clover. Thank you for the all-new afterword. All the family tell-alls are yours to tell from here on out. LOL.

My zine always had a pretty small circulation and never did turn into the great information network or set off a squat daycare revolution like I envisioned, but it has always been really great! I mean, to find others, to get letters. To make the connections that I did—it was kind of a "small is beautiful" affair. There weren't a lot of other people interested in the topics I was, but to find them was so important. After my daughter grew up, I became an organizer for many years, until I recently pulled back from that for my own development, to support other parents as a way to make a better world, and found younger generations more interested in childcare action. I was able to engage in larger activism networks like the Intergalactic Conspiracy of Childcare Collectives, which joined together in 2010. (It still isn't a squat daycare revolution, but it's moving closer.) There has been increasing interest in such subjects every year, so I'm glad to finally have my book back in print.

Most of the writing in here has been lightly edited and tightened, but I still tried to keep true to where I was at the time. I've kept the introductions and poetry in their original typed and misspelled form to keep the zine flavor, and included a lot of collages.

So here's my zine-book: with selections starting from the beginning and going up to the present—I hope you enjoy it!

THE FUTURE GENERATION

APRIL 1990
ISSUE I
'PHYSICAL'

"WE, who PAY Dearly FOR EVERY BREATH OF PURE, FRESH AIR, MUST GUARD AGAINST THE TENDENCY TO FETTER THE FUTURE"

– EMMA GOLDMAN

I want to start a zine, for parents to communicate all over this
continent, from Canada to New Mexico, from N.Y to S.F or whereever
(mabe even other countries ?!) - I want to get something started -
for us alternative parents - to network -
Send in reality, storys, photographs, drawings, personal experiences or
philospical rantings ; storys of our actions, daycares and our desires.
Trade advice and information. Wide subject range, we have alot of work
to do. And this is important work, we can help teach each other.

    I think its real natural to want to get together with other
parents, especialy people - just a litle bit like yourself - pagans,
anarchists, skaters, long hairs, no hairs, stickin up in the air hairs,
in the scene, out of the scene, natural types, supernatural types ...
Do you know what I mean ? Do you hear what I'm saying ?

    And I hope this will interest others - besides parents - there is
such a thing as social parenting. We all have been children, have some
child in us.

    When I talk to people, my friends and see what a wide diversity of outlook there is
on childraising, when I stop to think that some of my ideas may seem radical, fanatical,
judgemental, that publishing ones work means being open to critism; I get a litle
scared, so I want to say this :

    In life , I keep my veiws to myself more, becauce then I can hang out with a wider
range of people, and be more open minded to think things over, I don't want to be pegged
as this or that, I want to to able to try things our. Sometimes I know somebody thinks
realy different than me - but I want to be able to take them , and life, for what it is -
not "think " all the time ,but just be myself.

    I really beleive we all should have the freedom to explore, to think without persecution,
to try something without finality, to be "works in progress". And to me, no morethan
in the written word do I have alot of freedom, to lay down something, I've been thinking hard about, deep stuff - to play on paper, take mytime and speak to a completely
receiving source, that which is to the best of my extent - honesty.

    Now my grammar may be bad, something may be half thought out and something mabe too
wordy, something else might be misunderstood - but well, well, I had my say -
I just realy want to open a forum for exchange on "being Parents " you know.

    I just don't want to intimidate others, who mabe think different - but similiar
enough aims if you think of the mass soceity media veiw -
instead of any rhetoric, or fussy picky this or that squabble - lets just get on with it
,give each other room when we learn to work together -

Issue One

April 1990

```
Physical
```

Long before I became a mother, I noticed children. Waiting at the doctor's office, I noticed a child's intricate dance of walk-skip singsong flip-flop on the chair upside-down. Doing unselfconsciously, and with great pleasure, the things that adults don't do. And I noticed its mother scolding, "Sit still or you will get a spanking." The impossible task of stilling a bubbly child. Why must the child sit still? Is it because an adult might trip over it, or an adult might be annoyed? Why?

On the metro, in the car, in the welfare waiting room, at the grocery store—look at all the squirming children being scolded by tired and worn caretakers. Look at the cramped quarters of many children: with small or no backyards, crowded streets, and any place they go to (besides a playground) their parents will be asked to control them and are shot dirty looks if they don't.

Look at our physical space—the space we live in, humanly-designed space—crowded space that denies freedom of movement and causes us to retreat into the imagination for the freedom to conceive of what we can not "really" do. We can go to the movies, but small theatrics in life get police attention. We can dress to express ourselves, deviate in our looks but we are legally enforced from more active alterations. Even just claiming the physical space around you—to sit or sleep on part of the earth that you have not purchased—could get you in trouble.

Babies are initiated into this world of "don't touch," especially if their parents don't have the buying power. This is the message we send to our young—don't make eye contact with strangers and don't disturb others with your noises. Expect to be picked up and put down with no respect for your own wishes. The body itself is dirty and certain contact makes it dirtier.

Scattered city plans and schedules often find children not near a suitable resting spot during naptime and parents unable to respond directly to their children's physical requirements. Our commuter society is supposed to be able to tune out time spent on the road and tune back in again when reaching the destination. Children, however, can't zone out that way.

So the infant—who is getting acquainted with this world in the rudimentary ways of smell, touch, taste, feel; learning how to co-ordinate its legs and arms; prone to intimate exploration and stimuli—is taught by modern society how to be unresponsive.

They are trained to fit into a compartmentalized power structure that is better suited for making money for the few on top than in fulfilling the human needs of the masses. We are taught to go hungry while the supermarkets are full. To suppress the body's needs under a theology of the mind—a reason, when the reason is often one developed to exploit us. (You can see how the lack of respect for the physical has reached its limit in the way we are destroying our home planet.) We are taught—and teach—that submission to authority will lessen as one climbs the ladder, "grows up," robbing our children of the years to learn about themselves (self-realization?), autonomy, and the inherent value of being no matter what transitional stage you are in.

But "dog eat dog" hierarchy is often a false condition. You can't control others as easily as you think. No matter how small a disrespect done to another is, it does effect the global conditions we all live in. You can't kill the tiniest insect without a reverberation on the food chain. Which in turn can lead to environmental disruptions.

And what is the reverberation on our souls? It is plain to see what poverty and overcrowding produce, to see some of the results of pure physical environment upon the spirit. What mental problems and alienation, what really are all the symptoms of denying so much of our body's natural needs?

I know that we must look at the communication while it is there—to forbid or manipulate it will lead you that much further in the dark and render it that much more dangerous. Suppressing behavior doesn't make it go away—just drives it underground. The mice will play when the cats are away.

When my little cousin confided in me, because I am no threat to her, that she cheated on pin the tail on the donkey to win the game—did I tell her that's bad? No—I just listened. Personally, I wonder about the kind of things that go on to make her act so sneaky, it seems she has a whole secret life hidden from adults. But really, don't most children?

I'm young enough to be almost be part of her social strata, confided in, and yet old enough to be privileged—out of school, free to move and choose for myself. She is in awe of my privilege like I belong to an upper class and I can advocate some slack for her sometimes.

Once she told me: "I don't know why they call America a free country, children aren't free. I am not allowed to drive; I hate school and my teacher put my name on the board for talking when I wasn't, and I can't eat what I want or go to sleep when I want. What's worse is my mother always orders me around. I'll make up a time of when to clean my room because it makes more sense to me and she tells me that I must do it right away or my friend will not be allowed to come over at all." And this is a seven-year-old talking! Growing up in a patriotic and semi-rural environment. I go "yeah," and talk back and forth with her. I don't think she can see that adulthood isn't really what it's cracked up to be.

Children are naturally bound to learn, expand, experiment, follow a healthy design, and to crave what they need—but when we introduce them right in the beginning to addictive compulsive things like candy, rewards, and punishment: we cloud their judgement and lessen their chances of living without submission to authority.

So, I am on the playground—and I hear two little boys telling my child (who is younger than them) "No little girls allowed on the slide—if you come up here we will hit you!" I don't know what to do, they seem so vehement, so I take my toddler away from the slide. Well, actually first I said "Yes, little girls are allowed anywhere on the playground." And that is when they said the thing about hitting her.

Another mother on the playground goes "If those were my sons, I would not allow it, I would give them no supper," like she is such a feminist or something. But the children are playing honestly (the way we learned to suppress for public—yet manipulate, fantasize, and cement into an unspoken code). I see all kinds of things on the playground.

And these little boys are absolutely products of their society, daycare and of TV watchers. They're expressing what's been expressed to them. Let's think about this—let's not break a mirror because it reflects the truth. I've seen one of those boys around and his mom goes "be nice" but she doesn't show him how. And it's not that this incident is so terrible, we all do mean things. But it affected my daughter a lot, just like it always does when she plays with kids, the good and the bad.

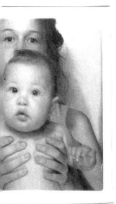

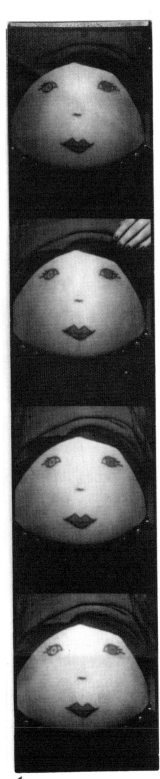

↑ clover in my belly

How am I to act, to break these cycles and those it is about to affect? What if I know some things make people pretty unhappy and while they may be a possibility of "human nature," they are surely not an inevitability of it. For I see how this behavior is transmitted from one to another, and I see how it doesn't exist at all around some very happy children. You can't shelter a child from reality they say, granted, but how much is too much, with no point but just to make you more of the same?

Children are such little imitators, we must show them by attending to ourselves. I was reading about traditional Eskimo tribes. In their culture children are allowed to run free and are fed in any house they wander in—to be watched out for by anyone who is around. And if they do something bad, something childish, the people go "It's just being a child that's all, when it grows up it will learn." And indeed it does grow into the nurturing, co-operative, and peaceful people that had gone before—socially acceptable. Of course there are always a few oddballs. But look at the numbers of the unhappy in our country, the violent, the mentally ill. Look at our Victorian heritage where children were not "childish" but "bad."

I want my child to be free to blossom into who she is, but what if she is too free for this world? Will society break her faster than those who can secret and control their desires better? Will she have problems controlling herself? Will she fight like a boy? Will she become a "brat" like some hippie kids I've seen and heard about?

I don't know. These are real fears, I'm departing from the known path and from how I was raised. But I'm not an unreasonable person, I must give her the respect and freedom I would want for myself. So society doesn't quite understand why I'm still nursing her, or this or that. All I can do is give my best and have faith in her to figure out her own solutions for her own times. I want to give that good support to her and I do believe those wild hippie children, well maybe they had unstable homes or fighting parents. I mean just because they didn't go to school doesn't mean that's the reason they got so obnoxious. I'm not a hippie anyway.

And as I respond to the physicalness of this child, reflecting back her needs as valid, real, letting her be herself, and trying not to let it worry me—for it just might be her need to be crying, taking chances, doing

"WE NEED to start talking NOT About SPARING children FOR A few YEARS FROM the HORRORS OF Adult life, but About eliMINATING these horrors."

Shulamith Firestone

"schiz - "broken" phrenos - "soul" or "heart"; a special strategy that a person invents in order to live in an unlivable situation." —R.D. Laing

"a schizophrenic episode is an initiation ceremony — A death + a rebirth — is a healing process." —R.D. Laing

The Playground

The children set up the senerio, "Im this your that"
then its Lets Go ! And they run off in their imagenation.
What are you playing ?
We are the mommies, o.k. and you guys are the babies?
    yea! screams mommmüe ! The babys all run
screamiing after the mommies wahh h
Then the momies attack the babies
bedtimes dirty dipers spankings
The children are running around with rosy cheeks
ones boys threats get very vehemt, " Im going to use
your mouth as a toleit... Im gonna...

another game I observed
" you going to join the girls club? "
"yea"
Mother asks the girl, " whats that?"
" oh, the girls have a club and the
boys have a club and we fight
The mother says " yes I guess I
used to play that too when i
was a child."

things I wouldn't (she'll learn her lessons: nature is not without discipline)—while playing the role of protector, nurturer, and trying to exist in this relationship, to have some of me and my stuff too—I see how very physical this all is. And physical is the dangerous and ultimate object of revolution. Of course it's mental, spiritual too, but we need the Bread and Butter—The Land.

Physical change is the hardest to make real. I can sit here and write about it. Imagine it. But physicality is what my child speaks of, forms with—physical love, physical survival, physical wisdom—and that means that I want to do more for her than imagine a better world, every day-to-day and nitty gritty thing has to be part of doing the right thing.

All Or Nothing?

"The period of a child's total dependency is really very short. By age 3, my daughter was in nursery school all morning; at 6 she was more thrilled about sleeping at a friend's house than staying home; by 14 she found it difficult to live with us at all—and at 18 she was gone. It's been many years since I was 'not free', and I often think about how much miss being around little children!"
—Eda J. Leshan, *When Your Child Drives you Crazy*

Leshan says this after talking about when her daughter was a little baby and had colic, and she was in the corner "crying and feeling if she went near the baby—she might shake, beat, or maybe even kill." She talked about the difference between thinking these thoughts and acting on them—it was a very helpful article.

But she leaves out big realities, like maybe it isn't natural to be raising a baby all alone and isolated in your house while your husband is at work,

maybe it is way stressful. I think mothers need support, we need to share mothering, we need society to include the child in it more, and we need to be around each other.

So instead of saying, "Oh get through it, in 3 years it will be better"—man, three years is a long time—let's try to make things better for the parents and children now.

I was in the post office the other day, listening to an older mom talk in line. She said how she had been a working mother of 6 children and how at times she thought she was simply going to die, that she couldn't do it. Older mothers would say to her then, how the time goes by so quickly. She didn't believe them, but sure enough its true. Now she is 50 and says she's free. She has her whole life ahead of her. Those kids survived. Sure, they come to her sometimes with their little problems complaining how she raised them.

The other mothers in the line all smiled and laughed, it was friendly mother talk, but it scared the shit out of me. I would be free when my skin got baggy? And why was it impossible to keep your identity and raise/love children? I "sacrifice" (as they call it) a lot for my child, it's the gift of motherhood, and that's cool. I can give out this high intensity for her young years. But there is no reason under this blue sky why a mom can't go places, do things, have some independence, fulfill her self as an individual, and have a lot more to give her child. I want me and Clover to be free now—and from what I have learned, that calls for some sharing of the children. That is what she needs to be talking about. Not how you never get to see children and wish you could, or that you are drowning under the weight of their constant presence.

PUT A LITTLE SUNSHINE IN YOUR LIFE!

. . .SPEND TIME WITH A KID TODAY. . .

(some of us are suffering from third degree burns)

from "Children and Feminism"

Is It A Cultural thing?

As I experience a life where ages rarely mingle—I look through *National Geographic* and see images of how people of all ages work together in other cultures. The child watching spear fishing, holding a fish, sleeping on the sides of fields, balancing a Frisbee on its head as its mother works in a factory, sitting in the marketplace, or walking nomads beside a camel. Visions of other countries, the past, and the future. I've always loved to read *National Geographic*, you know?

Children definitely seem to be included more in other cultures and learn through experiencing as a natural process. In the picture of the boy watching the man spear fish, I am sure the man is not thinking, "let me teach you a lesson now." But that is what is happening.

I wonder about what kinds of things we do in our culture, small, unexamined things that teach our children our values. Or maybe not even the values that we believe in, but the values of our dominant mainstream society that are normal for us.

As I strolled my baby in her stroller, I would always pick flowers for her to examine as we went along—she liked this very much. I showered her with rose petals. I played by ripping up leaves. One day when she grew into being a toddler, I saw a beautiful rose and brought her over to smell it. Without hesitation she tore the rose up, threw it on the ground, and went after another.

I was taken aback—yet I had taught her this. Later when I read in Colin Ward's book (*Eskimos, Chicanos, Indians: Volume IV of Children in Crisis*) —how Hopi Native Americans acted with the plants they treated as living beings; teaching their children to honor the land even in their play, to be thankful; that even trees can cry; and to show spiritual and psychological meaning/connection from signs in nature—I saw what a very "white" thing I had taught her.

I had been teaching her that this world is given to us for our use, to dominate, and plants don't have a life like we do. Our daily actions are unconsciously communicating many lessons, what a sensitive thing it is.

IS IT A CULTURAL Thing?
Are children happier in other cultures?

mabe " children need their community and the community needs its children"

Strength

Strength is not brute yelling or pulling. That makes everything worse. When your strength gives out you act that way. Strength is like the saying "a stitch in time saves nine." You've got to be strong or you'll suffer.

This morning I learned something from my daughter as I tried to snap one last snap on her overalls so we could be ready to go, as she kept rolling away from me. My mind was set on that last snap and getting out to keep my appointments. She kept rolling away and I kept pulling her back. You have no idea how frustrated I became because I could not finish getting her dressed. Clover kept trying to climb up, falling over, and crying. And it was time to go.

I was using all my strength against all the strength of an 8-month-old—and I was losing. She tried to roll away three times before I could pull her back and get the button snapped. She kept crying and it made me feel bad.

So I thought to myself: instead of having my mind so set on the goal and using brute strength, I should have just let her roll over and button it a few minutes later. She had been good for all her clothes changing up to that moment. Sometimes with babies, you just have to roll with it. Be flexible and forget about the bus lines and deadlines.

In fighting against her will (to be in control of her body after a time of compliance) I lost even though I was an adult and she was but 20 pounds. I could not win over a baby. I thought about adults who fight each other, nations who fight against each other. If an adult can't even win over a baby wouldn't it be even harder the bigger they get?

Now if you think getting the button snapped was the goal and that I succeeded in that, you are missing the point. Not only would I have gotten it done in less time if I let her roll over before I did it (and less anxiety for both of us) but I wanted Clover to be dressed to keep her warm because I care about her. Not the abstract button (abstract dollars etc.).

And so I knew the truth of the Tao, having seen it in action with Clover many times, and I often say to myself: have patience. Do it the right way even though that is difficult or you will wind up having an even harder time. A stitch in time saves nine. In our society we are taught to adhere to dates and order; to manipulate what we want or get mad and use force. But it solves nothing, just makes it more of a mess like Brer Rabbit kicking the Tar Baby. We are fed fantasies of having it easier. For example, it's faster to get there in a car. But the nine stitches come afterwards: acid rain, ozone thinning, working to pay off the bills, etc.

As long as you fight against a will without respect to that will; taking time to understand or to compromise—you will lose. That kind of strength is a fantasy. That kind of strength is one who would, theoretically speaking, cut off the baby's hand to keep her nails clean. The more you pull on her hand, the more she will pull back until you wind up squeezing tight and she screams as you cut her flesh. It's a delicate thing cutting baby nails. We are not doctors who put the patients to sleep, we hold the smallest fingers with gentle strength at the appropriate time and quit the job when they pull away too much, do not dwell on it but get the job done. That is strength.

It takes some wisdom not to fall victim to throwing it all away in a fit of rage. "Cutting off your nose to spite your face." Like when you're working on a car and you try to force a part in place until it breaks and you have to go buy a new piece and start all over again. Control is easing into place. You have to stay aware.

So if it sounds like you win or gain from military force, know the sound is just a mind's figment which you will now stumble blindly through the nine stitches, or perhaps endless stitches, in the cloth not meant to be under the design of your will.

—from my journal, November 1988

                    I want my muscles

not the circuirtry of controlled apetites conditioned to be
                    soft and impulsive
                    habit forming metal and buttons
                    and no education to escape it
        in the flow of paper and mutual crazyness
        I want my trees and seas and feet and muscles
          so you have offered me rent, chocolate cookies, restaurants and records , Devil-
            but I am not thankfull No I spit - You santion my nightclubs But forbid my world
        shit in the toleit, walk on the sidewalk speak when spoken too
Oh you helpfull one - you make me Homeless Then with a smile offer me the key to a
motel room Where I lock myself in with with out family - alone with a t.v. .
I don't want your zoo I don't want you. I'll take your money but Ill make my own Honey
I want my muscle I'll take your money ; you want me to use it on fueling your ways,
playing your plays, buying drugged fruit I'm not thankfull - welfare.

                    me and my child are the more   the fire
thats so meladramatic and dopey on your peptobiismo heartburn foam commercial
                    but we are alive and cackling.
                    I want my muscle
I have my body - I have a sense - I am god I won't eat your food I want my Land to grow
my own . From those actions come up the blessings of muscle
            clean smiles busy brains   liiving on the crest like a child
                we like to live up to our ability.
having it easy - like factory work or under estimatiion , makes us mean , sleepy , self -
destructive and bored.
                    we love muscle
                    I want my muscle
          You want to make it easy for me but I want to be alive.
                    My love iis enflamed.
        with the acomplishment of eating another day
        my brain is inspired withall that is here for us
                    much much much much
          Lays ahead singing screaming
        The strenght that is also crying , falling hurting doubting - the child bruising
as she learns how to walk, eating each new day clean. a spark to the paper racing.
                    The strenght of muscle that propells
                    REALISE!
Into your own self , invest, not so quick to not even know you but the you in miirrors

                not so   to look elsewhere to know
                          You are the spring
         You are the Halloween and Autum death
                    to make way for young
                    to make clean so
                        there is material to dirty and kill
              so there is a belly to be full
                     and Sedate
                 so we can Digest
                 And be hungry
                 oh yes   oh yesssss

I do not want to fight them on the streets
        but I will fight them when they come in my backyard
                        frontyard and porch
                        belly and intestines
                        brain and ears
                        skin and womb
        The power over yourself is power, Not the power over others
        serving your own interests is serving the Communiity Interests.

time when pregnant

I LOVE YOU, CLOVER

"They (the state bureaucrats) always act like we want an instant revolution. We just wanna realize our own ideas of living together. We want our own theater and our own music. I don't need no new-furniture color-TV boredom. I just want more me. We want more us.''

EAST BERLIN FAMILY AT A SHOW

crouched by my side, pale cream skin
lookat your persian slanty eyes bluish
Creature!
skin on skin - ribs across ribs
my daily hands measure the growth
of tiny legs, calfs, sineuws
Run Scream Laugh - baby from my body
physical
I chart you toenail - how your teeth
broke in, your soft breath we play, laugh
    can't say it here
But we are revolutionarys
what an intense relationship, touches glances
is the conversation between the free
Becauce - There is no world, no school, no home
 Nothing much that does right by you
I kick out the oppression in the pattern of your design
My Free mind - holds a free rein on my free horse - And I'll learn and listen
- but my baby tells me what is shit - we are born revolution
See I won't take it - Don't tell me how to Mother, Facsists !
That I'm earthmomma and got to think all good thoughts
   and have an exactly an hour bonding time to get
           the magic child

CHINA

I had a dream that the world
was a giant trampoline
made out of thin strips of
material, kinda like a cobweb.
And I was standing on it with
clover, she was on the edge,
she couldn't walk around with
out falling off. I hoped she
didnt fall all the way down to
the cement below and crack her
head, but she fell, ahh,
no its ok , she caught herself
and climbed back up where there
was sunshine and people gathered
water in cups, but she couldn't
walk, that litle todler, with
out tripping, so she feel all
the way down. I went down with
her.   We were in an underground cement, car parking lot.
That was the under world, with
no sunshine or good food,
full of misformed people.
We would live here becauce the
ground was solid and she
was safe.

Chris

Where libraries hold tapes of children being born—sperm and inner worlds of tissue—growing changing—amazing things—but no one is amazed—perhaps it's a campaign to cover up our amazement—or a desensitivity or complete stupidness and poverty.

What is reality—the teaching will stay all our life—like a jacket with undoable buttons—and if we get the buttons undone—it is our very skin that we peel off—this jacket—our guts and veins and spirits all blobbing off—we look for another jacket to put on—society's moldings is nothing but some clothes—but we do need a skin for the spirit to sit in—whatever our aims are—the flesh is up for it.

The individual born personality—instinct can be in chains—we must think Goddamn it—what we feel like evolving into.

But I don't see anybody doing this. And so "Childhood" is a Void and the old sexist violent numb dumb ways win by default. You can't simply let a child raise itself. It hangs on your words—it imitates—it jumps in front of traffic and pulls at your tit. Given such beauty and love and great expanse of inner landscape (birthing a child)—I can no long be a citizen, pay rent, to this crazy affair.

I will not put her in slavery.

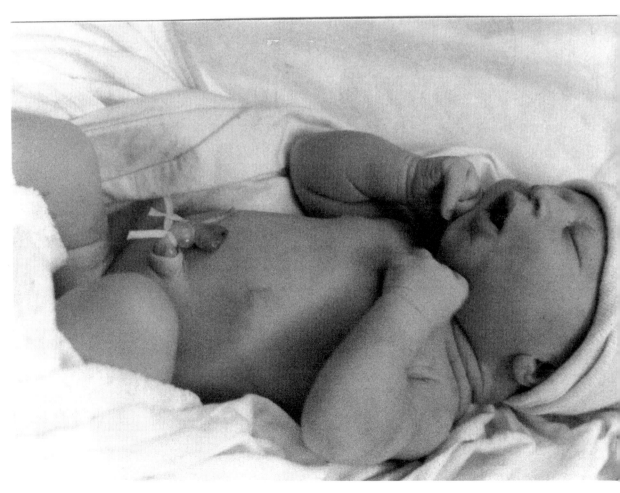

"THERE IS SOME IRONY IN THE FACT THAT CHILDREN IMAGEN THAT PA
CAN DO WHAT THEY WANT, AND PARENTS IMAGEN CHILDREN DO.
"WHEN I GROW UP ..." PARRELLS " OH TO BE A CHILD AGAIN ..."
                                          Shulamith Firestone

THE FUTURE GENERATION

the CHILD

issue #2 NOVEMBER 19

HONOUR THE CHILDREN so THEY CAN HONOUR Themself AND OTHERS.   A.M.

Issue Two

November 1990
The Child

Welcome to the second issue of this fledgling project to illuminate the situation of the young and therefore all of us. I'm a mom so a definite goal of this zine is to network with other parents and resources.

"Lay plans for the accomplishment of the difficult before it becomes the difficult; make something big by starting with it small. Difficult things in the world must needs have their beginnings in the easy; big things must have their beginnings in the small."
—Tao Te Ching

"Honor the children so they can honor themselves and others."
—Alice Miller

Involvement

The first time the baby had the strength to reach out and grab something—I was not expecting it. She was sitting on my lap when she reached for the bowl and overturned it, milk and cereal flying everywhere, all over the stranger's floor and my lap.

All my friends sitting at the table clapped "Yay Clover, you're one of us now, a Mess-maker!" Everyone smiled the first time the baby reached out.

Comfort

What feels good and is comfortable for my child—not what looks good to the mirror eyes of society. Public Inspection might prefer a toddler's clean face with the high standard of cleanliness that states un-involvement with life. Cleaning the face of a protesting child so others looking on will approve.

It is for a small time in life that humans are incredibly messy eaters—don't stress them out, they can't help it. Consider your superior force, therefore act with respect in how you treat their bodies. My little one, self-willed and messy since the time I first wrote this, has learned to wipe her own face clean with napkins. We never made it too intense, if she was spotless or not, but in her own time and observance she has picked up the desirable action through imitation. Often her messy face caused adults to bear down on her. But she hated me to wipe her face, so I didn't half the time.

Mother And Child As Mutual Oppressors

They both feel that they are kept from doing things, frustrated and restrained, because of each other. If they can not leave each other when feeling like this, their behavior gets worse. The problem seems to be in the baby or the mother's character and they receive the blame. One doesn't go "Damn it, if society were different I could finish this article"—one goes "I couldn't do it because the baby was crying."

Mother As The Middleman Of Oppression

When you put your coffee on the edge of a table, it is I who am supposed to protect the child with endless grabbing hands that have not yet learned "hot." When you leave your computer out with all its tempting buttons it is me you expect to protect them from the child. When it is up to only me to be on the alert for such examples, my child feels it is only I who restrains and meddles and becomes aggravated with me and respects my wishes less.

When it is I who is supposed to restrain my child from running 12 ft into the next door's "private property," I who is supposed to wrestle her from climbing on cars and blocking sidewalk traffic. It is I who is supposed to stop her from touching what should not be touched, eating what is not ours to eat, stepping on that which is not ours to step on, taking "other" people's things. Hold her struggling body in the bank that has no child space for living.

I Will Not Do It!

I see you grapple with the dilemma and often wind up acting generous and forming an attachment to her. I also see your annoyance and her pleasure. Her scientist activities can not be retarded by what civil behavior expects. You can express yourself to her. She can learn her own limits.

Well, yes I have done it: sandwiched between a store of "behind the counter—in the trashcan—and pulling things down" and a sidewalk crowded and full of tasty cigarette butts and stepped on french fries—2 feet from the road—our sacred cow—the road and its cars which is always welcome: black asphalt to kill any former inhabitant of the grassy earth and any toddler who knows no better than to fall into it.

I held the child. And she screamed and kicked against me. She slipped from my arms and tried to run. I was the middleman—she was hysterical—all eyes on us as we walked to find a grassy free space and still my insides hurt sitting there and still it was not over. You respect these things, child—they will kill and poison you—you have 2 inches of acceptable behavior.

I do not want to suppress her endeavors to touch and exist though.

We can't "raise" our children to be "ANARchist, conscious, intelligent, creative and free thinking"

We can apreciate our children for just who they Are, whatever choice they make - if we Agree with it or Not.

THE FUTURE GENERATIO

DECEMBER 1990
ISSUE 3

" anarchist
child-
raising "

P.O. BOX 38548 Baltimore MD 21231

Issue Three

December 1990
Anarchist Child Raising

Stanley Milgram explains in "Obedience to Authority" (about the famous Yale University experiments to see how far people would administer shocks to another when told to), how family and then institutionalized settings are the first in a series of groundwork for creating blind obedience. To the point of creating a "person who, with inner conviction, loathes stealing, killing, and assault may find himself performing these acts with relative ease when commanded by authority." This is specifically one of the points of this issue. To realize the workings of this world and see their start in childhood, thus giving us the tools to break vicious circles and love our children as they deserve to be. In focusing on children, it is also implied we are seeking knowledge about how to nurture in ways that creates health and happiness.

There is a common thread running through the literature on the psychology of oppression (be it in the educational system, state, or sexual mores); and this is that there is something opposite to our inner voice, which creates strife. It is an outside voice, meant to control us for outside interests. Once we expose these forces for what they are, then we can explore the possibilities of non-authoritarian systems.

While Anarchy, Autonomy, Authority, and Capitalism are but words we talk of and debate with others—the Health, Fluidness, Brightness, and Happiness of our children is something you can see right before your eyes, and it is that I am interested in. The more I see, the more I live with my child and research the subject, and the more I see some universal truths, if you will, emerge. And while I am not very good at defining things as the world is so confusing and always in flux, I do believe this information on Authoritarian Child-raising vs. Anarchist Child-raising is knowledge that should be widespread, for this way of being will help you in your everyday existence. Even if we cannot live exactly such, we should always have an idea of what is right and true. Take this as you will.

Nadia in NYC

A Story

At one point in my life, when we had moved into a new household and Clover was 2 and a half, something happened which definitely taught me to trust myself and Clover. She was very hard to watch, I would try to get daycare and friends to help but generally I would still wind up watching her by myself. It was really hard. Friends told me I was too nice. That I had to stop nursing her and then she would get more independent. I couldn't take her to bookstores because she would pull all the books off the shelf and run around, so I avoided bookstores instead, when I wanted to do something like that, I would get a babysitter for her. My housemates told me this was ridiculous, I was making my own problems and Clover would never respect me for it, that I must teach Clover how to behave, I must train her to be good in bookstores, after all other parents do it, don't they? Clover spilled her food on the floor so she was not allowed to eat in the living room although everyone else was there. She was not allowed to ask for food, she was not allowed to touch their things, and they got really stressed out when she tried to play with cigarette butts or with the silverware even though she was only imitating them. Obviously, I just didn't belong in this household and I left, but they were my friends before that, and its really hard to get a house on your own, and often people will not rent a room to people with kids. I was stuck there. And it was really stressing Clover out. She used to say "NO" all the time at that point. I figured she was just learning this new word and its power. It didn't bug me that she said "No" all the time. But it bugged them so much that they came to me once and said "what if we just never let her say 'No' in this house again?" Every time she said "mine", they would say "No, it's mine" or "No, it's ours" or "No, it's hers." That bugged them a lot too.

The major complaint was that I had to hold her all the time or she cried, and she cried too much anyway, they said. Once I decided I just had to vacuum the rug, which was my chore, and I would have to let her sit there and cry until I was done. It had to be done so she cried. The guy came out of his room and left the house, slamming the door, really sick of it. The other mother (with a very easy to care for baby) came down and said, "I think its good she's crying and you're

"THE MONSTER OUT there IS Realy YOU, DOCTOR,
AND all of us without the CONTROL
of GOVERNMENT AND RELIGON!"

(from a 50's SCIENCE FICTION Movie)

"OUTSIDE GUIDANCE AND INSTRUCTION ARE NOT NECESSARY
for a child to grow and flouRISH, yet they are implied in
FREUDS famous words "WheRe id WAS, there shall ego be."
The structural model (ego, id, superego) is reminiscent of the
traditional family pAtteRN according to which
ADULTS ARE SUPPOSED TO CIVILIZE THE WILD, WICKED Child
AND bring him under control, or at least "TAME" his
WICKED DRIVES.   A.M

CONTEMT FOR THE CHILDS INSTINCTUAL WISHES

Our contempt for " egoists " begins
very early in life.
Children who fufill their parents'
conscious or unconscious wishes are "good", but if they ever refuse to do so or
express wishes of their own that go against those of their parents, they are called
egoistic and inconsiderate. It usually does not occur to the prents that they might
need and use the child to fufill their own egoistic wishes. They often are convinced
that they must teach their child how to behave becauce it is their duty to help him
along on the road to socialization. If a child brought up this way does not wish to
lose his parents love (and what child can risk that ?)he must learn very early
to share, to give, to make sacrifices, and be willing to do without and forgo gratification — long before he is capable of true sharing or of the real willingness to
do without ".

Alice Miller
~ prisoneres of childhood

SPEED LIMIT 35

TIME OUT Restaurant

COACHES Corner Lounge

ALAMO

FRIENDSHIP

-11-

CITY OF CORALVILLE

doing this." "Why," I asked. "Well she has to learn. Don't you think babies will just naturally take advantage of you if they can? She's crying to manipulate you." "No," I said, I think I have to clean the floor so I have no choice, I've put it off long enough, but it's not good she is crying." What I wished for was that simply just one of my housemates could have held her for five minutes until I was done, then she wouldn't have cried, but they never would. I was trying to find another house and avoid mine as much as I could. Every time she was home, she would try to hang out with them and it always ended with her crying or them telling me to do something that made her cry. They told me I let her take advantage of me and expected everyone else to do the same. Funny when I moved into my new house, with a back yard and a really nice roommate who would share his food with her and play with her sometimes and didn't get mad the one time she drew on the wall, she completely changed! She chilled out and listened more to us.

The only thing is, at that point, I was starting to believe maybe everybody was right, maybe I had to be firm with Clover, let her cry until she learned, be stricter with her. I didn't believe that. I believed everyone should be nicer to her and avoid trouble spots that would cause us stress. I mean, I was always taking her to the playground, thinking she needs to blow off steam. I would try to solve her issues—not just make her stop acting antsy. I knew lots of moms who still nursed their children and believed if Clover wanted to nurse so much, then it must be right. I can stick up for myself, tell her when I didn't want to nurse her at that moment—but if she cried a lot, I would give in because I believed I saw her true feelings; that she was sad not manipulative. I thought I could balance it out between both our needs. But I needed free time for myself to do stuff I liked to do without her. So, maybe they are right, I thought. Maybe she will be like this for the rest of her life! God, it has to stop! (Now looking back I can say that was a high need time of her life. She's almost three now and I can take her all kinds of places, bookstores and to acupuncture. I can talk to her about something, say "not now, later," and explain stuff. It is different now she is older.)

Fortunately I met another family whose beliefs were similar to my own, but were more secure with themselves. Then, I went over their house one bad day. Clover just went in the backyard and cried, cried, and cried. I was so stressed out too, here I wanted her to come play with this nice kid and look at her—she's so hostile. The mom tried to engage her by showing her some ladybugs, and I just let her cry by herself a little, hugged her a little. Then the little child came home, Arthur was younger than she was. She kept hitting him and stealing his toys, they fought over all his toys. His parents protected him from her, but they said, "oh this is normal, you can have two sets of every toy and kids at this age will still fight over them, its part of their learning process." They were so calm, they didn't think we were bad people, although they did say I was so stressed out and like it was my problem and I was stressing out Clover not the opposite like I felt. (I didn't believe it was anyone's "fault," though.)

The thing was, we remained patient with Clover and she did unwind. After a while Arthur and her were jumping together off a large block onto a pile of cushions and laughing and laughing. And although it grew late, even past midnight, once the kids were having so much fun they let them stay up. They played some wild country music and we all ate watermelon. Clover was once again her charming self and the kids ran up and down the hallway, ate together, took a bath together. Meanwhile I was talking about the stuff that had been going on and feeling so much better. Being strict with Clover, like telling her "No, no, don't hit," stopping or trying to teach her to behave and suppressing her natural processes, it had never worked with us. We would do that at my house, because I would compromise with my roommates (four against one) and it never worked out into a happy ending. I've seen some of the ways that Arthur's dad acts with kids, because he works with "problem" children in a hospital, and I've learned a lot from him. I think he is great and wish he would write an article or a book on how he handles different situations in a positive and gentle manner, which I feel gets better results (eventually) than typical negative discipline methods.

Usually people would make me feel so bad, like I was a negligent parent because I didn't discipline her from running around or touching people and their things. Or if I didn't immediately jump on her case about how she acted with others. Oh I did it gently for the other parent's sake, and I do believe in lending a helping hand to get them out of their quibbles. If Clover had more toys she wouldn't bug us, my roommates used to say. I believe no one could say Clover isn't a healthy and bright-eyed quick and friendly child. What more could you want? Apparently a quiet, respectful and behaved one, which, at this age, how can it possibly be possible without dominating them. The thing is lots of kids are doing the same thing as her but getting hit or emotionally punished for it.

Then I moved into my new house with a nice new roommate Barry, where Clover cried so much less, and danced around the house and played, the tension in the air was gone. Barry was a Buddhist. He was older and had an almost grown teenage son who lived with his mother. This is from a conversation we had once:

"You're giving her the opportunity to be herself —to be all of it and learn her own lessons, that's the best thing you can give her," said Barry.

"The second thing I want to give her," I say, "is a sense of history, some cultural reference—so she will not get hurt as much as I was with no references, I was set up to just buy into this system."

"Yeah, but you want to give her compassion too. Not just more polarities, more war, or having a free space in the corner, away from everybody else, is that so good? Give her compassion. Tell her, when you teach her politics and all, say *those poor confused people*. Don't teach her just to hate them. Compassion, if anything, will be the thing to really change our situation."

"Wow, I never looked at it like that."

Then he said, "In your zine, you don't want to tell somebody to breastfeed or not to breastfeed. The point is to follow what you feel inside—the point is to get it themselves, to trust themselves, not to be told what to do."

"Yeah, but sometimes you need support in what you do. Like when Clover was born, my mom brought her cradle and said it wasn't good to sleep with her, but my midwife said: *She's sick, put her in your bed*, and I did, because that was what I really wanted to do, but I wasn't sure what was right."

This is what else he said, with his San Francisco Buddhist point of view, "All people, of any age, should be able to go through their life, accepted for what they are, some of them enlightened, some confused. We are born with personality. We shouldn't distinguish so much, the child category—all people are people with

Rogue and Jennnifer

separate personalities. We should enjoy our children the way we do our friends, and help them, like how anyone who needs help should be helped. Children need a lot of care, but that doesn't mean we know better than they do."

Interaction With Society: We Need Support

(Children aren't the property of adults. They need a community to be free.)

Just today, when I was at the grocery store, I saw a mother who looked so stressed and her child wanted a piece of candy; then as they stood in line, he started to thrash in her arms and cry. By the time she paid for the food, he was rolling around on the floor crying, and everybody was just standing around, giving her dirty looks. I went over and asked him, "what's a matter? Can I pick you up?" As I jiggle him on my hip, he cries, and I say "Go ahead and cry. Things suck." He stopped crying for a minute and then starts up again; then his mom takes him and goes. I had to do it, I felt better holding him. I always want to help when I see crying children and drained mothers because I know how it feels, but I'm too shy to do this most of the time; and feel like I have no right to.

Then I go out of the store and see a mom and child running for the bus; and the child crying as the mother pulls him behind her. Man it's hard for kids in this city, I think. I notice how calm and clear that I am, doing my own shopping without my child today. We all board the bus and the kid keeps crying, his face looks so sad that I almost cry too because he keeps crying and crying and his mom keeps going Shut up Shut up and pinching his face and slapping his hand. It's hard to feel compassion when you're with your kid all the time. You get worn out. I think any parent can relate to difficulties, anger, and embarrassment in dealing with a child's problematic behavior in public spaces. I think all parents feel, at least, the impulse to smack their child in certain situations, even if they control themselves and never hit their children. Perhaps instead one uses an unrealistic threat like " I am never taking you on a bus again" or says a mean word they later regret. I see this mom as much as a victim as the kid, it's all of us, just sitting like fish on the bus, all of us not helping out. What should I do? They probably wouldn't want me to butt in. Maybe I can give him one of my colored pencils? By the

time it takes me to think that, they are already getting off the bus. The kids are always getting blamed for their problems. We have to help out with the kids when they are walking by us in this city, you know, its just not right not to.

We have to help out with the kids around us; parents and children need more support. This is so crazy.

Merilee, Amra, Thor & Odin

34

Self-government in Gathering & Hunting Tribes
(I'm not saying I want to "go back" to how it was, or that we even can. But we can learn from strategies that worked before.)

!Kung

Disputes were defused by discussions that went on for hours, long into the night, in which all points of view were expressed until a consensus was reached.

"!Kung men vary widely in their skill at hunting, but different levels of success do not lead to difference in status. (It is bad form to boast, and they had a few things they would do to increase everyone to have a chance, such as hunters would share arrows; hunters would take breaks from hunting sometimes so others could make a name for themselves.)"
—M. Shostak, *Nisa*

Congo Pygmies

"Try to imagine a way of life where land, shelter, and food are free, and where there are no leaders, bosses, politics, organized crime, taxes, or laws. Add to this the benefits of being part of a society where everything is shared, where there are no poor people, and life includes: for about four hours of work per day—a steady supply of food, along with good fellowship, music, dancing, singing, and a pride and pleasure in one's family. For those so inclined, free love is openly enjoyed and even ritualized among the young people, yet marriage, when it occurs, is generally monogamous and permanent.

"...a nomadic Mbuti band will publicly criticize one of their own who hoards or keeps something to himself that others do not have. In the same way there are no chiefs among the Mbuti because to be chief means to have a power that others do not have. An informal system of community approval, or disapproval, takes the place of laws or kingly authority. Whatever the reasons, the Mbuti culture adequately survived through the centuries, while the great civilizations of ancient Egypt, Greece, and Rome, rose and fell.

"Ridicule is frequently used in small-scale societies to help settle internal disputes informally.

"When the Pygmies, who are no angels, become involved in disputes, they manage to settle them without stigmatizing anyone as a criminal."
—Colin M. Turnbull

Sioux Children

The idea of storage over a prolonged period of time is foreign. If a man has enough to keep starvation at least around the corner, has sufficient time for meditation, and something to give away now and then, he is relatively content. ...When a man's food is low, or all gone, he may hitch up his team and take his family for a visit. Food is shared equally until none is left. The most despised man is he who is rich but does not give out his riches to those about him. He it is who is really "poor".

Generosity in the Sioux child's later life was sustained not by prohibition, but by the example set by his elders in the attitude which they took toward property in general and to his property in particular. Sioux parents were ready at any time to let go of utensils and treasures, if a visitor so much as admired them, although they were, of course, conventions curbing a visitor's expression of enthusiasm. ...But all of this concerned only the parent's property. A parent with a claim to good character and integrity would not touch a child's possessions, because the value of possessions lay in the owner's right to let go of them when he was moved to do so—i.e. when it added prestige to himself and to the person in whose name he might decide to give it away. Thus the child's property was sacrosanct until the child had enough of a will of his own to decide on its disposition.

The whites, activists in educational matters, proved to consider every omission in child training, such as the complete lack of attention paid by Indian parents to anal, urethral, and genital matters in small children, a most flagrant omission with most definite malicious intent. The Indians, on the other hand, being permissive toward smaller children and only verbally cruel toward older ones, considered the white man's active approach to matters of child care a destructive and most deliberate attempt to discourage children. Whites, they thought, want to estrange their children from this world so as to make them pass through to the next world with the utmost dispatch. "They teach their children to cry!" was the indignant remark of an Indian woman when confronted with the sanitary separation of mother and child in the government hospital, and especially with the edict of government nurses and doctors that it was good for babies to cry until blue in the face. ... Beyond that there was on the Indian side the strange assumption that the whites wanted to destroy their own children too. Since the earliest contacts between the two races the Indians have considered most repugnant the white habit of slapping or beating children into compliance.
—Erik H. Erikson, *Childhood & Society*
(not a good book in my opinion)

THE FUTURE GENERATION

Jan. 1991
Issue 4 - "GETTING Together"

P.O. BOX 35570 BALTIMORE MD 21216 J

INSIDE : •WHY "MOTHERHOOD" SUCKS
• A HISTORY OF KiNShip groups + family.
AND MUCH MORE.

Issue Four

January 1991

Getting Together

Honestly, I don't have the time or energy to put out this so called zine, which is rediculous anyway becauce one person doesn't make a zine. When I hear the child next door cry so wretchedly, her face pressed to the window, I know this "zine doesn't mean anthing to her, but if I can talk to her mom, let her come over here and play, when you give kids love, take them to the park, let them come see what your doing, that means something real. I have my own life and child that I can barely handle, I could get myself free of all this shit, but I know there are so many living like this, in this bad situation, that its not right,the only thing I can think of that would be actualy usefull would be to open a childrens community center, a nabour hood thing. Use it to advocate for children, to get the community together, to get people together becauce we can do so much more when we are together, we can help each other. For example a mother who was about to abuse her child could find refuge there, could talk to other mothers while her child escaped her. It could be a soup kitchen for kids, a place to put on shows for kids, a place to put on workshops on anything a kid told you that s/he would like to learn. A garden? who knows, but I want to make a space like this for kids and everyone for when you get people participating together, its good, you know you could ask your friends to come volenteer, we could have this space to just be real ~~~~~~~ in, interaction of all ages, creating awareness. I want to create this, with a circle of others that would like to do a similiar thing so if you are interested contact me, who knows, I would consider moving to a place where its better to do this at,I'm not deeply attached to Baltimore*or anything. Anyone who thinks things suck should seriousely think about making things free er for kids, cuz it all starTs theRe. *CHINA*

* But Baltimore sure needs something good for children.

Getting Together And Breaking Up A Machine

I was listening a woman on the radio saying that black women were the lowest economic social stratosphere in America; that it went like this: white man, then white woman, then black man, then black women. But if you follow this reasoning then it's not black women that are lowest in this hierarchy, it is the black children! Children are in the lowest economic and social level with the least control of their lives and the most abuse filtering down to them.

That means we are teaching that you get no inherent respect or equality just because you are alive; we are teaching youth to taste a boot in its face from the very beginning. Teaching youth that in time, it too can gain privilege by climbing a ladder. Showing by example, how it's OK to take out your stress on others, the child can get away with kicking a dog or beating up the new kid because he's bigger. Oh sure, the superiors might reprimand him for it, again showing children the authority a superior can wield.

How many times have you heard "Together we stand, divided we fall"? Well it's true. Any exploitive government or corporation can only be maintained by military force or by dividing the people among themselves into different classes and groups who are prejudiced against each other. Our divisions are created to exploit us.

Powers that maintain this society by (among other things) pushing children out of its world until they are socialized and produced to fulfill their part in the "scheme of things".

I suggest this machine of modern life, which is like a parasite on the Earth, is AGAINST THE GRAIN OF LIFE, and that is precisely why the children hold the lowest position on the scale of dominance.

What I'm suggesting is that it's unnatural to be isolated and divided. That a single mother or family can barely help oppressing their child to a degree, and that children are naturally happier, more confident, quicker to learn and easier when in groups of all ages. That children actually have more freedom when a large circle of people feel responsible for them. That children need all the stimulation in interacting with groups of people. That the quality of a parent-child relationship can be better when it is not forced on them to be together when they don't want to be. I'm suggesting that the child's needs are too great for just one or two people to supply and so they are often suppressed instead; the child is making it too hard on the parents, so the child must be wrong.

A simple fact that deserves common acknowledgement—with more caretakers; friends; relatives; and responsible strangers in public, the child can be comforted and not be as heavy on its parents. The parent could blow off steam and not be as hostile to its child; and child abuse would go way down. Child abuse thrives in climates of stress and privacy. When other people can come to the aid of an abused child, they can play a part in helping the child. Sometimes parents need to see an example of how to handle a situation in a positive fashion.

One day I spent half the day in an apartment by myself with a one-year-old and the second part of the day in a warehouse dwelling with her, 6 adults, and a three-year-old. The difference between the experiences in my morning and in my afternoon was like night and day. When I was by myself I was at my wit's end, at a crazy point of a no win situation. I felt it was hard to explain in the sanity of the warehouse that evening. She cried a fourth of the amount as she did when we were in the apartment. She was actually happier, easier to take care of, and a joy to have in the surroundings of a community. In the apartment she was in continuous "bad" behavior and I was going crazy. Even if it was just to have someone around to hold her when she was crying as I was trying to tie my shoelaces, it would have made a world of difference in preventing a possibly volatile situation.

So—a helpful thing to me, it seems, to fit the situation I see, would be to create neighborhood community centers where we could practice some "mutual aid". Parents could get together and supply whatever is needed. Like a communal washing machine for diapers? Or perhaps surplus garden vegetables and outgrown clothes could be taken there. It could serve as a space for co-operative daycare.

The History Of The Family

"Our society is unusual for the relatively high frequency of isolated nuclear households; because the nuclear family is usually isolated from other kin, the job of caring for young children is left largely in the hands of mother. She is either the only caretaker, or she is by far the most important caretaker. Talcot Parsons points out that the isolated nuclear family, as opposed to larger kin-grouping, constitutes a small, tight social interaction system. It is an all-your-eggs-in-one-basket situation. Mother, and how mother feels—is very important, because she is the only mother you have; there are no surrogate mothers in the form of aunts, grandmothers, or older cousins. When mother becomes angry or estranged, there is no place to go, no one else to turn to.

"Mother, too, has a job which permits no rest, needless to say…there is very little 'diffusion of nurturance', Mother is the only nurturer."
—William N. Stephens, *"The Family in Cross-Cultural Perspective"*

"97% of human history was spent in Hunting and Gathering tribes where the child was a part of society."
—Alex Shoumatoff, *"The Mountain of Names: a History of the Human Family"*

Why "Motherhood" Sucks
Sadie

Rick tells me about his niece Sadie (he's always said how he loved her, but now another story comes out). She's a beautiful child, and strong, and even more of a "hell-raiser than Clover, and her mother rebels from motherhood, has a harder time and more pain than you."

"What do you mean?"

"Well, she was at the height of her career when she got pregnant, a big movie star in Australia and kind of a sex symbol. Then she had to leave her career and worried about losing her sex appeal and if she could ever go back — to have to leave her career when it was just starting, she feared she will get out of practice. She never really wanted to be a mother."

"Then why did she?"

"Because she became pregnant (unplanned) and they had the child because it was the right thing to do."

"What about her husband?"

"He's a big film producer and is gone long hours. It would hinder his career immensely if he didn't. He watches her in the evenings some. She is home alone with child during the day. She's starting to settle into it more, it seems. She used to freak out more."

"Like how?"

"Screaming, throwing things, acting irrationally, blaming her husband. They are different than you in that they are always telling their child Sadie, how bad she is."

Hmm, so this woman, so far away, I identify with and listen to these stories and see a common thread: for I know and understand what is deemed "irrational" and the "pain."

I see how childcare help is absolutely crucial; that the child, as well as the mother, wants to get away from each other sometimes, and that everything goes smoother when they get back together.

I think this blaming of the child, who is "bad," for making messes, hitting, and doing normal kid stuff—is displaced anger because you can't get away and are unrelieved in this tension. You blame people personally instead of the deficient system. There is more energy to properly handle your life with kids, and the hard times, when you can get away from them and have some time of your own.

Stories Of Struggles

I want to tell you the stories of parents all around me: neighbors, people on the street, my friends, and myself. To tell you what I've seen in the last two years, the problems I believe to be greatly caused by parents being solely responsible for their children and being isolated.

I've seen my next door neighbor struggle after her divorce, when she tried to find a babysitter, so she could find a job; how hard it was to find anyone when she had no money to hire them. I watched her make the various phone calls, the support just never came, and eventually it wore at her so she gave the child to the father in Canada. Later he gave the child back. They would both scream around their son when they fought with each other.

Once when I was visiting my parents and they went off for the weekend and left me home alone with my tiny baby, I felt so desperate. I wrote a letter to my friend, asking for her help. I told her how Clover wore me out and cried so much and was a nonstop mess and how I had no home, and no security in this world of all these worries to be bringing a child up into—Let's just say I was freaking out. I had no hope left and just wanted to be without this weight anymore, to not care, to just play, drink, and do what I saw others doing. I was writing this letter, but it was basically just letting off steam. I didn't send the letter. I knew it was too harsh, and I knew she couldn't help me, she was going to school. I knew nobody was going to help me, because I ask people all the time, and it's just not enough. Then I went out to breakfast with my parents. And this was their conversation:

"We went to the mechanics yesterday, and I saw S--. Yes, she's the one who runs a daycare, her daughter had a baby but shortly after she was more interested in running around with boys than in her daughter so her mother adopted the child from her. Now the child is 11 and her mother is more stable," said my mother.

"Well, that's not so uncommon," says my Dad, "my skating partner's sister apparently couldn't handle her child, wasn't fit to be a mother, and she gave her child to her mother to raise."

Last night my friend was telling me about her Aunt who hired a nanny to completely take over when her cousin was young. Another friend told me about her experience as a nanny where the mother wanted her to completely take over all responsibility for the child and pushed it away from her.

The point is, I feel my own thing but then I look outside of myself and I see a lot of other people feel this way, too, it's not just me. And when you feel down, there is no support to help free you.

My friend N- told me how she lost two men over her son: his father, and later a boyfriend. And now she is afraid to lose the man she is living with now, she loves him so much. She says jealousy always arises between her son and her man, and that it is so hard. I can sympathize, its true, I know how relationships can really get strained when there are children involved. I talked to another friend who was at the Haight Street Fair and she saw this man she loved so much but he was with someone new. She tried to talk to him, but her child kept fussing and wanting her, so she had to sit down to nurse her while she watched the man walk away in the crowd. And she couldn't even deal with this painful episode in her life, because there was someone who needed her, she couldn't work out her own problems. Here there are all

these people around, but society teaches the children they can only depend on their parents.

Single Dad

Talking to C-; He's physically and mentally exhausted because he has been watching his son so much. He says he needs to read everyday or he feels he has done nothing. He needs to play piano or work on a sculpture, and do these things as a person. But he can do nothing, he is caring for his child 24 hours a day ever since the mother left him. His child wakes up in the night and kicks him, his former self would be grumpy if he was woken in the night but now he must be tolerant.

He had to drop out of college because babysitting didn't work out. He has a lot of friends who help out but it's not enough. He says his child is a little boss to him. He wants to be in a communal house with other children and to find good daycare. So he's been exhausted to a state never before experienced.

I've been looking for these same things myself, for a year or more now. C-'s a good dad, loving, giving, and an idealist.

I say this because I feel it myself: it's a crime to kill a parent's love of his child. Oh we can love them—we give and give. We act "right". But how can we really when we never get to live ourselves; to grow, be nourished, and rest. It is a crime, and a useless one of that, to not allow a parent the opportunity to be all they have inside themselves to be.

People who aren't parents don't know. As parents we are in the middle of it we can't improve our situation for we are too busy with day to day survival. I think it might be similar to be a peasant or to live in a third world country. One may be a genius, talented, and capable of a million things, to create, build, and find solutions—but it doesn't matter. You cannot produce what's in you when all you can do is work day to day, busy always to survive! To eat! We can be exploited to no end, and can not be a revolutionary or follow an education. There is nothing to do but squeeze by, without the basics of life no one can build anything.

Today I see C- who is mentally and physically exhausted with the flu, at the playground where I first met him. I remember how he was so active with his son that day, before single parenthood wore him down. How he played soccer with his son and taught the boy to hold doors open for the elderly and share his food with my daughter. But today, I am the energetic one because my mother came to visit and helped me out. So I am really enjoying Clover and being patient in situations that previously would have driven me crazy—as C- lays on the park bench with a headache and a pained irritated expression on his face (much the way I did the day we met).

Beautiful Women

I have met some of the most beautiful people who happen to be mothers, and they were young, different, and still had all these problems. I met this woman who drank Absinthe and had fuchsia hair and was so cool, she had two children. She told me she had just escaped from the New Jersey suburbs, because she didn't know anybody there and her husband neglected her. Her dream was to live in a school bus and drive around the country. At least women these days up themselves out of a bad situation and they are so powerful, but I look at these women whose family life failed them and they have all the responsibilities themselves. I think of N- laughing as she eats peppermint leaves addictively—like a forest faun so slight and belching like a boy, barefoot in her warehouse, fresh flowers on the table, cooking spicy coconut soup.

Mothers, I have known the most beautiful mothers with all the shit they contained inside them, any kid would love to have one of these mothers you think. But their children are still Primitives, primitives who do not get anything out of it. Primitives who brutalize their cats (so why keep yelling at them I think), or making messes, snapping the paint brushes in two, or throwing your special stuff at the wall. Primitives—and the best thing you can give them is primitive freedom, enough people to love them so they can parasitically nurse their freedom in peace. N- said "it's like I don't have anything to offer him." What kids need is work, is to get their needs met, they need more than one person can provide—but motherhood has all this mystique around it. I look at others and keep telling myself: See, its not just me. It's not just me that is having a hard time, it's not just all my fault. We keep blaming the parents and the kids but it's not just them.

I think of this fascinating sweet punk rock mom I know. We were at a party and her baby was sleeping in a sling, she had just finished telling me how she feels left out because she has a child, when this guy said to me: "Do you think it's right that she brings her baby out so late at night to a party?" And I was like: Christ, what do you want her to do? Sit home by herself and not have fun at parties? I heard that the police hassled her once because she had her baby out at night, all close to her in the sling, and was out with punk rockers. So the policeman threatened her that he could take away her child but she yelled at him and he backed down. She said there is no respect for mothers in this culture, and I agree.

There is practically only one wild young mom I ever saw that I really admired cuz she wasn't being victimized in any big way, she seemed happy and free. Yet when I told her friend "How does Gypsy do it?" He told me that she says the same thing of me. (Wow!)

Toddlers

When I talk to other mothers of two year olds, I often hear that they are just hell when they are alone at home with them, which is what I experience too. But when we were at a party exchanging notes on our children, the children were running all over the place, playing together, playing with adults, curling up on others laps, getting take care of by others—they were so happy and independent. They were responsive to us and listened to us when we told them not to play on something, that it could break. There were no signs of their complete defiance, no signs of the terrible twos.

from "Children and Feminism"

They ate food together and watched the older people make music, then imitated. Unfortunately it is very hard to usually integrate the children into normal life. The very set up of the city or town, streets, and cars makes it difficult to get around with a kid and difficult to have any independence from each other.

Laughing Babies

I was reading about Margaret Mead. She said that when she was a child she was always treated and talked to like she was an intelligent being; treated with respect, and that she grew up to think she could do whatever she wanted to do. She became an anthropologist. Later, when she became a mother, she still worked in anthropology and her family helped her out extensively—she had all kinds of people around to help with taking care of her daughter. Her child was very happy with all these people to love it and when the child grew older she took her in the field with she and her husband, on assignment.

Mead said that a professor once stated to her that the reason women could never get ahead was illuminated by this famous black woman who once said how she wanted to write a book on slavery but she couldn't do it because her child cried too much. Then Margaret Mead said, If anything, what interrupted her studies and research was when the baby was laughing so much that she couldn't pull herself away. She said that is what she thought the state of the world was.

At first I totally resented her saying that, thought she was privileged to say that, I mean I relate to the crying baby story, it's a problem to be addressed! But then it dawned on me, she's right about the laughing baby. I mean that is how it should be, how it can be…that we can all say, "Oh, I just couldn't go to work today, the baby was laughing so much". This baby had lots of people to care for it, they didn't do it for money (daycare has its problems, like it's too expensive for a lot of people), and the baby didn't feel sad about not seeing its mom. They spent lots of time together too. It looks like a really fulfilling situation. When people are so overworked and have no support and they can not hold the baby, so the baby cries, that is something that doesn't have to be… But instead we blame the crying baby who doesn't fit into situations that don't fulfill its needs. And these babies, I don't have to remind you, do I, are the very substance of all of us, the adults of the future.

"…If we don't band together we are more easily dividable and thusly, more easily conquerable. I for one don't want to get fucked by a system I have no opportunity to be heard in and I believe that the scene is a system that won't fuck me, provided the system is composed of my friends; friends that I know and friends that know me and who I am. Friends don't usually let friends get fucked. Unless it's a safe fuck."
Rev. John, *Minn. Alternative Scene*

The unhappiness that I see in just one week is enough to convince me that the situation is really bad for children today, and to band together is just what we must do.

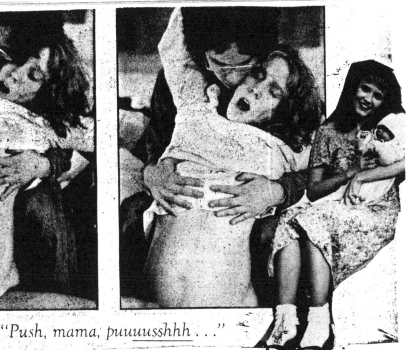

"*Push, mama, puuuusshhh...*"

WARNING AGAINST THE NEW TREND 'to ASCRIBE A MYSTIC STATUS TO MOTHERHOOD AND TO BELEIVE IN THE `NATURE OF WOMEN`. GIVEN THAT ONE CAN HARDLY tell WOMEN THAT WARSHING UP SAUCEPANS IS THEIR DIVINE MISSION.

the eternal FEMININE- `OTHER` let alone ` SUPERIOR` — SINISTER BIOLOGICAL DISTORTION- `EARTH MOTHER`

THAT IN CURRENT CONDITIONS MOTHERHOOD OFTEN MAKES SLAVES OF WOMEN AND TIES THEM TO THE HOUSE AND/OR TO THEIR ROLE. THAT WE MUST PUT AN END TO THIS KIND OF MOTHERHOOD, AND THE DIVISION OF LABOUR ALONG MALE/FEMALE LINES. AND AT THE BASIS OF THIS IS THE CONCEPT OF A ` FEMININE` MATERNAL NATURE, INVENTED BY MEN — A MATERNAL NATURE THAT IS NO MEANS INHERENT IN WOMEN BUT IMPOSED ON THEM BY THEIR EDUCATION.   S. BEAUVOIR

" So even within these groups, whose theoretical aim is to liberate everybody, including women, even there women are still inferior" What I have been able to establish is class struggle in the strict sense does not emancipate women. Liberation on an individual level is not enough. There must be collective struggle, at the level of the class struggle too. (This was written by a women who opposed an autonomous women's movement, and beleived that the socialist revolution would automaticaly resolve the question of womens' oppression untill she wrote this in her 60s)   S.B

US CHILD POVERY, INFANT MORTALITY AND SCHOOL ACHEIVEMENT ARE AMONG THE WORST OF ALL INDUSTRIALIZED COUNTRIES.

NATIONAL SECURITY

Dollars vs. Needs of Children

More teenage boys die from gunshots than from all natural causes combined, and a black male teenager is 11 times more likely to be murdered with a gun than a white counterpart,

" BEHIND EVERY SERIAL KILLER IS A PROFOUNDLY ABUSED AND NEGLECTED CHILD. WHEN YOUR MAKING A MOVIE LIKE THIS YOU THINK ABOUT WHY THIS WHOLE COUNTRY IS FUCKED UP, WHY CHILD ABUSE AND FAMILY VIOLENCE, ANDVIOLENCE TOWARD WOMEN IS TOLERATED. .... THE WAY WE PRACTICE IT (CHILD ABUSE) ON A SOCIETAL LEVEL, ON WHOLE SECTIONS OF CITIES, ON THE VAST MAJORITY OF KIDS IN HARLEM AND IN BROOKLYN.

- DEMME ,Filmmaker of "Silence of the Lambs"

THE FUTURE GENERATION

ISSUE 5

PART I

inside: questioning p@rental @uthority

Included in the next 2 parts of this 3 part series:

health and commercialism, preventing child abuse, sex-economy

home- birth, letters, and much more !

Issue Five

April 1991: Part 1
Violence

"You can not have a good humanity by treating it with hate and punishment and suppression. The only way is the way of love."
A. S. Neill

Violence, said Stokely Carmichael, is as American as apple pie. Our hierarchical capitalist government promotes violence through exploitation while it obscures the root causes of injustice. War, politics, jails, economics, laws exploit the masses for the gains of the elite. Is this the way it has to be? Is this human nature? Not necessarily so.

INTRODUCTION

Becauce of all the violence going on in our cities, homes, and wars, I decided the topic of this issue should be exploring some of the causes of violence. Once I was done doing that, I had 70 pages; too much for one zine! So I broke it into 3 sections and will put it out as three parts of issue number five, one each month.

The emphasis, as always, is on the kind of topics you are not going to find in the newspaper, or on the telivision. That media reports the effects but rarely the causes. When you read about mortality rates in southeast D.C, child abuse,drug abuse and other things like famine; you really are not getting all the facts or a clear picture.

In here, I included some information on famine next to a child asking her mother why people starve while she has so much. In your newspapers it will be called a natural disaster. But most famines are the result of exploitation of people by their governments. This is the topic of part one; how exploitation by government and authority causes violence. That all governments, all over the world are corrupt and just successful gangsters. That being bossed around causes violence to our systems, and equality and co-operation to exist in a soceity without government is a possibility of human nature.

EQUALITY

TO TREAT CHILDREN AS EQUALS. BY AND LARGE,TO RESPECT THE INDIVIDUALITY AND PERSONALITY OF A CHILD JUST AS WE WOULD RESPECT THE INDIVIDUALITY AND PERSONALITY OF AN ADULT,KNOWING THAT THE CHILD IS DIFFERENT FROM AN ADULT.

Equality is a funny thing when you think about how someone will struggle to be treated equal and then not beleive another person deserves equality too. What I mean can be illustrated by the examples of black revolutionarys that created free african states while leaving behind their wives in the village with the children, leaving behind their wives for good when they got famous. Slowly the freed countrys became neo-colonized, not free at all! Perhaps thats why revolutions fail; for their was not equality for everyone, really. Or look at that point in history when women and blacks were ataining the right to vote, women told the white men,"Let your own white women vote before those niggers" while the blacks were telling the white men,"Come now, let us men have all a vote before those bitches". Yes its true, and of course divisions are created among people to benefit those who wish to rule them both.

But equality, really means equality for all. How can we have it when we raise our children like we know everything in the world and they must obey us ? The molding under with most children grow up leaves them with an unflexibility to understand what equality really takes. People can join causes of "social justice" and ect. but still treat that issue, act out in that issue, as rigid and dogmatic as those they feel to be unjust, and join up under that banner as they once did under a overwhelming controlling parent. Can we trust our children to make the right choices and tell them the truth ? Trust them with their very lives and parent without "owning" them, love without condition ? To have the relationship of parent-child in freedom might just be part of the fundamental parts missing in creating the truly free soceity.

Violence In American Culture

"Basic instinctual impulses have a biological origin, and most of the goals of all pleasure-directed impulses are rational, with an inherent capacity for self-regulation. Anti-social impulses are caused by repressing natural biological needs. This results in secondary, pathologically anti-social impulses that have to be inhibited out of necessity. For example, the suppression of the natural gratification of hunger led to theft; this in turn necessitated the moral condemnation of theft. In a free society—there would be no obstacles in the path of the gratifi-cation of natural needs. And thus—none of the secondary pathologically anti-social impulses like murder, rape, robbery, etc.

"Many people believe if we eliminate 'morals', the 'animal instincts' would gather the upper hand and this would "lead to chaos" but it is evident that the formula of threatening social chaos is nothing more than the fear of human instincts. People can work and live out of their own independence and really voluntary discipline which cannot be imposed from outside. Of course it would be a slow path for society to get back to natural regulation once a society was hooked on compulsive moral regulations."

—Wilhelm Reich

"James Demeo became interested in Reich's work on the source of human neurosis and destructive aggression, took his findings and tested them systematically— looking for a developmental as opposed to an instinctual or innate origin. Demeo analyzed anthropological data on 1,170 subsistence level cultures and found that people in cultures around the world did not behave similarly. Some were far harsher in their behavior, particularly towards children, and more violent and warlike. He called their culture's patrist. Others were gentler in their behavior, protective of children, and peaceful. He called their culture's matrist. Patrism in a political system comes from people who have been raised with a great deal of suppression, and they duplicate politically what they have experienced in the family during childhood."

—from Utne Reader

I think the public is generally psychology-savvy with a vague feeling, even in American Pop culture, that something is wrong. American Kids, wrote Stephen King in Rage, labor under a huge life of violence, both real and make-believe. And Demme, the filmmaker of Silence of the Lambs, couldn't have said it better when he reflected: "Behind every serial killer is a profoundly abused and neglected child. When you are making a movie like this you think about why this whole country is fucked up, why child abuse and family violence, and violence toward woman is tolerated. The way we practice it (child abuse) on a societal level…"

This isn't just the exception for the worst case scenarios that explode into the news, however. Violent practices in child raising are actually something quite ordinary in most American families.

"'Poisonous Pedagogy' is the viscous cycle that is handed down from parent to child to parent, of abuse of children while claiming the adult is always right. … adults have all been children; questioning the naturalness of adult power questions not only their present status as adults, but their view of their own past. Most adults are still trying in some way or another to please their own parents, some of which takes the form of identification with them. This can effectively silence forever the legitimate voice of the child within them. It would appear that adults themselves are still afraid of being bad."

—Wendy Ayotte, *"As soon as you're born they make you feel small…"*

Government

"It is our work to form individuals in the full possession of their faculties, while politics would subject their faculties to other men".

—Ferrer

"Anarchists mistrust all governments as an abuse of power and believe in voluntary cooperation with freedom to do what you want to as long as you don't infringe on someone else's freedom. However even a refresher course in democracy shows a healthy skepticism towards government and belief in the rights of the individual. The belief in liberty that to suppress even one person's viewpoint could mean suppressing a vitally important truth. That there is no danger to have everyone free to express themselves but to the contrary, it will bring innovation. That variety and opposing debate keeps ideas fresh. American was begun, in part, on these ideals. "The determination to squelch every attempt of those entrusted with power to encroach upon the sphere of individual action".

—Voltaire De Cleyre

A WORDS(PIERRE JOSEPH PROUDHON 1848 PARIS) VISUALS(CLIFFORD PETER HARPER 1981 LONDON)

To be governed is to be watched over, inspected, spied on, directed, legislated at, regulated, docketed, indoctrinated, preached at, controlled, assessed, weighed, censored, ordered about, by men who have neither the right nor the knowledge nor the virtue. To be governed means to be at each operation, at each transaction, at each movement, noted, registred, controlled, taxed, measured, assessed, licensed, stamped, valued, patented, authorized, enadmonished, hampered, reformed, rebuked, arrested. It is to be, on the pretext of general interest, taxed, drilled, held to ransom, exploited, monopolised, extorted, squeezed, hoaxed, robbed; then at the least resistance, at the first word of complaint, to be repressed, beaten, disarmed, garotted, imprisoned, machine gunned, judged, condemned, deported, flayed, sold, betrayed and finally mocked, ridiculed, insulted, dishonored. That's government, that's justice, that's morality!

The states were separate and there were checks and balances. No one was expected to blindly believe their governments knew best for them: that is what they rebelled in the first place, against governments that were like wolves over sheep. Elected representatives were to be held answerable to the people who had the right to bear arms and overthrow a government that didn't serve them.

Is it in our ideals of democracy that people do not know what is good for them, that people cannot rule themselves, that choices and questions are dangerous? Who but a King, Queen, or Slave master could disagree with the principles of equality?

But too often we have the illusion of free choice but in actuality very little free choice and a lot of bureaucracy. Do not forget the struggles of the past, of serfs to escape from serfdom, of workers to make unions and struggle for a ten-hour work day, for safer conditions and an end to child labor. Do not forget the not distant past of people struggling for equal rights, the fight is not over but in mid-stream. The propaganda of the powers-that-be are against people-power like they always have been in the past.

Knowing what man can do to man when he rules above, isn't it suicidal to give your liberty up? National security is the security of the wealth in the pockets of the elite. It is out and out corruption but also it is our problems, all of us, which allow this.

"The curse of humanity is the external compulsion, whether it comes from the Pope or the state or the teacher or the parent. It is fascism in toto."
—A. S. Neill

The School System

Our educational policy as a nation is that we must force children or they wouldn't learn. We persuade through fear and punishment.

Let's take literacy for example since Baltimore has one of the highest illiteracy rates in America. So, this city has a problem; how do they handle it? The city declares itself "The City That Reads" as if one can change reality with a marketing slogan and paints this slogan on every bus bench. (But then we have billboards proclaiming: *Virgin: teach your child it's not a bad word* in response to the high numbers of teenage pregnancies. Its more like "The City that Breeds" as my friend puts it.) Child abuse is reported at the highest frequency each time report cards come out. Education becomes

Seth Tobocman, World War III

not an enlightening opportunity but a punishment. A special issue of Spider-man comics is put in the classrooms where Spidey explores the adventures of how "fun it is to read"—just another gimmick.

Of course I believe people mean well as they start these programs that are supposed to help everyone, young and old, who wants to learn to read. And for some, there probably are genuinely positive results. Yet, reading is merely the issue of the day, stemming from a sense of embarrassment, and aiming for some kind of higher score on some report or other. To force everyone to be literate is infinitely more important to them than for children to be exposed to the kind of ideas contained in books. The problem of illiteracy, like most, is not treated at its roots because solving social problems threaten vested interests! The city's response to any problem with school children is stricter state control.

Stop shoving things down children's throats! Don't you know people have to get it on their own, you can't force them to find reading interesting. If anything it is the attitude of force that is what is creating illiteracy, children are simply rebelling from boring and mandatory choicelessness. They deserve a lot better. Now they have a mental block when they try to read because it stinks too much like school.

Punishing The Youth

Today, the kind of attention given to youth is that of an increasingly punitive nature with continuing losses in civil liberties. When over fifty percent of high school students drop out in North Virginia (about the same amount as Baltimore) - does the school think to ask itself: "Why do all these children find no interest or promise in school?" No. Instead they come up with a law to deny High School drop outs a driver license and enforce a new law that arrests the parents of kids under 16 that skip school too much. Parents have also threatened to be arrested or fined if their children stay out past curfew (11 on weekdays and midnight on weekends) in such cities as Detroit, Newark, Atlanta, and possibly Annapolis. We will make sure the children listen to authority! And we will punish the parents if they don't help enforce it!

Children are considered troublemakers who if left to their own devices will only vandalize, do drugs, kill each other, and make babies. Should we ask them why or how they feel, what they want? Don't bother, they have criminal minds and don't know what's good for them. Listen! More law enforcement is not the solution, we already have one of the highest, if not the highest, percentage of our population in jail out of all the countries on the planet. We have no one to protect us from the police as it is.

"Children are wise. They will react to love with love, and will react to hate with hate. They will respond easily to discipline of the team type. I aver that badness is not basic in human nature any more than it is basic in rabbit nature or lion nature. Chain a dog and a good dog becomes a bad dog. Discipline a child and a good social child becomes a bad, insincere hater. Sad to say, most people are sure that a bad boy wants to be bad; they believe that with the help of God or a big stick, the child has the power of choosing to be good. And if he refuses to exercise this power, then they'll damn well see to it that he suffers for his contumaciousness."
—A.S. Neill

Yet, how are we going to keep the children from burning down their schools like how two Bladensburg Maryland 10th graders tried to do this month, simply because "they were disgruntled with the school in general"? I'll tell you—stop building schools children want to burn down.

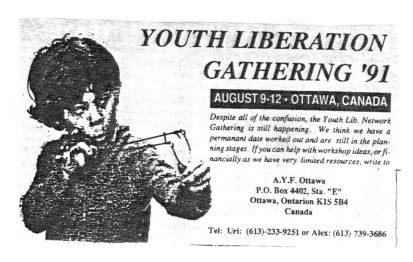

Let children follow their natural curiosity, supply them with the nutrients they need, talk to them with honesty and intelligence, but listen as well as talk. Allow them areas to create music, art, and pursue other interests in. Recognize the pursuit of happiness as a right. Provide opportunities to apprentice and learn real skills, to travel, and to take part in running and having a voice in the schools they go to.

"This is hardly 'running wild'. Rather than waiting for adulthood to be responsible, they are doing it now. It is participation in one's community, in the decisions which affect one's life which fosters respect for collective decisions, for others and for one's own worth, not coercion and submission to other people's rules 'for your own good.'"

—Wendy Ayotte, *"As soon as you're born they make you feel small..."*

Equality & Peace

Change is a continual process. And how we pass down our traditions and how it begins anew is with our youth. We must treat the children with the values we want to be found in society.

"What is the child's reaction to freedom? Children clever and children not-so-clever gain something that they never had before — a something that is almost indefinable. Is chief outer sign is a great increase in sincerity and charity, plus a lessening of aggression. When children are not under fear and discipline, they are not patently aggressive. Only once in thirty-eight years at Summerhill have I seen a fight with bloody noses."

—A. S. Neill, *Summerhill*

"Wherever you find movements for liberation, opposition to colonialism, dictatorship and fascism, you will find children involved from an early age. In the Spanish Civil War they were active and under Franco's regime the legal age of torture was 14. In Nicaragua, the majority of those killed in the fight to topple the Somoza dictatorship were under 20. In Algeria they were message carriers, decoys and ammunition runners.

"In Uganda, Eritrea, Guatemala and countries other places you will find them actively involved. In Chile a sit-in by 500 school girls (aged upward from 8 years old) to protest against Pinochet, the dictator, resulted in their mass arrest, detainment, and sexual harassment.

"In South Africa children and youth are at the very heart of the resistance. In 1976 in Soweto, their protest against the teaching of Afrikaans in their schools, erupted into mass protest against apartheid and thousands of children were killed. Today in South Africa they organize boycotts of schools, of white businesses. In Port Alfred they run street committees which replace the racist municipal organizations. When funerals take place it is they who run about to ensure maximum attendance. They display impressive discipline and organizational skills. Many children cannot return home because they are police targets and must effectively live underground.

"Children in South Africa are detained, tortured and murdered because they are the centre of the anti-apartheid movement, not because they are accidental victims of widespread police and army violence."

—from *"As Soon As You Are Born They Make You Feel Small..."*

Classmates pick on 8-year-old opposed to war.

By Melody Simmons
Evening Sun Staff

When his third-grade class was ...ed to write letters to U.S. soldiers ...Saudia Arabia, J. Alesandro Ken-... declined.

The freckle-faced 8-year-old also ...d his teacher at Brehms Lane Ele-...ntary School in northeast Balti-...re that he didn't want to donate ...ndy or food to a gift box the stu-...nts were readying to send to the ...ops. He politely explained that he ...a pacifist and does not support the ...rsian Gulf war.

Soon, a rumor about Alesandro ...rning an American flag started ...nong his schoolmates.

Then fellow students started to ...ick fights with him.

"One boy has been trying to fight ...e for three days," Alesandro said. ...his has made all the other people ...my class have violence toward ...e. Really, all I'm asking is to give ...ace a chance."

"I have my own opinions," said Alesandro, whose parents live in Belair-Edison. "The teacher wanted us to write a letter to the soldiers and thank them for defending us. But to me, the only thing she's promoting is war.

"My father has been telling me all my life that no war is moral un-less we are defending ourselves, our families or our homes. He taught me to never use violence. Now every-body in that class is against me."

ALESANDRO KENDALL
Joins peace demonstration

OLM
Stop th...
racist
U.S. war—
by any
means
necessary.

McFarley said Zachariah's father, Stanley, had his own hair cut to show his son that "it was no big deal," McFarley said. "But Zach... still wouldn't cut his ponytail and his parents can't think of a reason to make him."

School officials have remained rigid in dealing with the situation, September Toungate said. "We said we would pin it up, stick it inside his shirt, even put a wig on him," she said. "But they insist that he cut it. They say he can't come to school until he conforms to the dress code."

BY ASSOCIATED PRESS FOR THE WASHINGTON POST
Zachariah Toungate, 8, was isolated by school officials because of nonconforming hairstyle.

Joseph Kendall, Alesandro's fa-ther, went to Brehms Lane last week to speak with the principal about the problem. The father said Principal William Koutrelakos told him he re-spected the boy's pacifist views and asked Alesandro to report any fur-ther problems to his office.

Kendall also said he has written Mayor Kurt L. Schmoke protesting the "promotion of war" in the schools by teachers.

"This is causing a great deal of stress for him," Kendall said of his son. "It's hard to be on an unpopular side. The other parents who have not taught their kids the difference be-tween right and wrong, their kids are looking at him in a different way. He's pretty tough, but I can see that he's not as anxious to go to school as he used to be."

Wherever you find r...
tion, opposition to col...
and fascism, you will f...
from an early age. In t...
they were active and u...
the legal age of tortu...
gua, the majority of th...
to topple the Somo...
under 20. In Algeria...
carriers, decoys and a...

In Uganda, Eritrea, ...
tless other places you ...
involved. In Chile a sit...
(aged upward from 8 ...
against Pinochet, the ...
their mass arrest, de...
harassment.

In South Africa chil...
he very heart of the ...
Soweto, their protest ...
Afrikaans in their scho...
protest against aparth...
children were killed. T...
they organise boycott...
businesses. In Port A...
committees which rep...
pal organisation. Whe...
it is they who run abo...
attendance. They dis...
pline and organisatio...
dren cannot return h...
police targets and ...
underground.

Children in South ...
tortured and murdere...
the centre of the anti...
not because they are ...
widespread police an...

Zachariah has had the "ra...
all of his three years in th...
Bastrop, a town of 5,700 ...
miles southeast of Austin. ...
however, his mother said...
told her that Zachariah's ha...
met regulations.

"He just didn't understa...
"And he is adamant that he ...
cut his hair."

The Future
Generation
wants to be a
real & vital
resource
network.
Your verbal
donations &
artwork,ect.
will be pub-
lished if sent
  xxoooxxxx
    China
P.S. I'm
moving from
Baltimore to
Minneapolis.

Letters

Dear China,

Thank you for the package of information inspiration. I should have written to you right away with input and support, I read every page as quickly as I could, but I have been too busy moping/celebrating/experiencing motherhood and student-hood.

I'm almost afraid to write because I love writing so and I'm so rusty, but here goes!

[On Edna Leshan's essay] *Getting Mad Is Quite Okay*: I rebel against therapism and the culture of popular psychology, but I do find out things that help, or reinforce me and my ability to deal with motherhood.

For example, I read that "spirited" children need transition time between modes of being, they can't deal with being suddenly yanked out of one place and brought to another without warning or time to make the transition. That explains why Rosa, my daughter, freaks out screaming and kicking at very inopportune times — getting off the bus going into a new place. When she does it, I try to prevent her from hurting herself and wait, saying: "What!? What can I do?!" Well now I have a strategy for preventing the freak-outs — tell her in advance what's going to happen, keep talking, and follow her lead as much as I can. Which should be a given, she should have the right to decide what we're going to do half the time (safety permitting) but I don't have the luxury of being able to treat her as an equal human being, I try, but she is my prisoner when I absolutely cannot avoid washing the dishes any longer, or when the laundry must be done so she has diapers to wear to the park. The point is: a lot of Psychology would be stupid and unnecessary if people had the space/ environment where they could treat each other with respect as equals. *Getting Mad Is Quite Okay* shows how psychology has taught parents that they are bound to fuck up because its normal for a jealous little boy to hit his baby sister but sister will get hurt if normal behavior is allowed, but suppressing normal behavior makes you sick. . .

Psychology doesn't address the fact that parents are bound to fuck up because there's too much isolation of the nuclear family and it's a sick system. Oh yes, parents are bound to fuck up. But psychology puts a band aide on the sick psyche, gives a language for expressing the feelings you're repressing, but does not address the root cause of repression.

Still, the article says great things, it's still pretty radical to say emotions are good and powerful, isn't it? Yes even a child's emotions are good and powerful. Sometimes I envy Rosa's rage when her desires are denied. I only remember being able to express that kind of rage a few times in my life—only to lovers. Psychology can be a kind of trap—leading you deeper and deeper into the maze of the nonsense collecting in your brain. For example, I was a quiet, well-behaved child—my mom said she was worried there was something weird about me because I was too good, no temper tantrums, etc. According to the article, I'm likely to be one big violent act waiting to happen, it could be. I believe in a romantic ideal (in my heart, not in my brain) of loving so strongly you become one with the loved one and that is more important than anything and it's inexpressible.

Therefore, I don't talk to Rosa that much, I feel for her, feel for her hunger, pain, delight. . . I don't talk about stuff that much and this psychologist with her "magic" (yes words are magic) words recommends you inundate your kid with words as you take away the hammer. It probably works but I feel offended by the tactic, maybe mostly because the words are condescending—"you're normal, you're OK, you're just like many other people, and I know exactly what you are thinking" . . . We are not normal.

The obsession with normal and above average statistically and socially is dangerous for me. I'm always worried that Rosa's not up to par because I fucked up—I drank a bit too much beer while nursing her, she fell off the bed when an infant, (separate crimes by the way) and she almost drowned and I gave her CPR when she was 13 months old. . . So if I have an idea that a "normal" child should be able to talk more than she does, I feel incredible guilt. But I know she's smart and

strong and agile, she just doesn't talk. Maybe she will agree with me one day that words are magic, and they don't just appear to be magical to children (as the article says).

Well, I'm getting a lot off my chest, it's hard to communicate about these things because we need to read and write about it—conversations tend to be too short and business oriented when babies are around. (I just reread the ending, I guess Edna's very radical for a psychologist and we have a lot in common.)

I guess you said it all on page—20—sunburned by 20 hrs of sunshine, too much of a good thing.

I think motherhood sucks.

Not the biological function but the social function.

The biological function is great, it inspires the most beautiful perfect love, but when Rosa's grandmother took her for a week, I did not miss her at all. I thought of her happily and wondered if it meant I was a cold mother. Then I had a realization. I wasn't really afraid that I was cold, I was afraid that Rosa was getting old and independent. She is not my whole life any more. Even though I'm supposed to be responsible 20 hours a day, I'm gonna try like hell to get other people to help so I can get my life going.

I want other people to be with Rosa because she needs variety and adults need children and I hate my life if I don't do anything just for me or as an individual rather than a mother. A lot of people (who don't have children!) say, "Why don't all you mothers get together and raise your children together?" Well, that might be good, but I DON'T WANT TO BE CLOISTERED—Why should mothers and children hang out with only mothers and children? Well, it's 3 a.m., gotta get up in a few hours, so Write Back!

Anne Ness

P.S. Enclosed is *FightBack*, just a few punx writing anarcha-feminist propaganda and shit. (I wrote "motherhood is a social disease") I could write a lot more if I went thru every article you sent . . . Thanx again!

Communicate!

Are you parents, or a single parent, with an "alternative" life style? Would you like to be put in touch with others like yourself? Just to write or even visit? This is where we would like to help out. It is our aim to build up a list of names and addresses of people with children, circulate them, and hopefully build up some kind of network where people can write each other for advice, help, ideas, and friendship. People bringing up vegan or vegetarian children might have a bit of difficulty knowing what to feed them, especially with young babies, or baby lotions, talc, toothpastes which are cruelty free, or people concerned about putting their children through the State education system might like to find out more about the alternatives, eg: free-schooling, education at home, etc. By being in contact with others you would be able to share your knowledge or learn from them.

Also, you may feel a bit isolated or cut off, so this way you will be able to feel that there are others with children who feel the same at times, and who knows, you might find someone near you who you can help get out a bit by looking after their children for an evening, and vice versa. It's up to you really what you want to get out of it. Maybe you would just like someone to talk or write to. If you are interested please contact us at the address below, with some details, eg: name, address, how any children you have, their ages, etc. and wife will add your name to the list. Who knows, you could receive letters from all over. But for this to be a successful venture we need your support and co-operation. So please, if you are interested, write soon so that we can get this idea off the ground!

We hope to hear from you soon.

Love, peace, and friendship
Paul and Elaine
London

Or

Graham and Debbie
Essex

I want freedom, the right to self-expression, everybodys right to beautiful, radiant things.

Emma Goldman

MRR:Two words; The future.
Vic: I would want my children and my children's children to live in an environment where they feel they belong. When you're born, all these layers of shit are piled onto you; to actually get anything done you gotta cut through all the bullshit.
Al: We have to strive to peel layers of conditioning and oppression that have been piled on us since birth and strive to . .
Amy: . . .create . . .
Al. A ..
Amy: ...better, truer,freer...Regime! (laughter)
Al: We almost had it! We almost had it!

(FROM AN interview with NAUSEA)

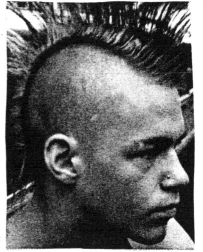

The Future Generation

$1

A u t o n o m y

INSIDE:

EXPLORING the REASONS children are punished + Alternative suggestions.

#5, part II

QUESTION AUTHORITY

Preventi
Violence

E

FIGHT POWER NOT PEOPLE

City streets AND Health

IDEAS

self-determined

AND

Actions

Kid

power

Issue Five

Part 2

Discipline

INTroductioN

The FuTuRe GeneRation is an attempt by me (ChiNA) to stARt an Alternative PARenTs CommuNication-NetwoRk. This zine is 'bout being A pARent + About ChildRens LibeRation. want to contRibute?

ISSUE FiVE: "Violence"
(a thRee pARt thing)

Last week, a child about to turn seven was hit in the crossfire and she died. She had been playing on the sidewalk when two men started to argue and shot at each other, hitting her. That was on the otherside of town. But just two blocks from my house, another pointless death happened last month. Three kids, ages fifteen and one thirteen, beat to death a young man with his own baseball bat. Some kids from their school stood around and chanted, "kill, kill, kill,". Not too long ago, a similar thing happened. People sat in front of the telivision with glee, shouting "kick ass America, Americas number one" as they watched the bombs drop on Iraq.

So, becauce of stuff like this, I decided issue five would be about understanding some causes of violence and suggesting ideas on child-raising that would reduce violence in this society.

ISSUE FiVE, PaRt II: "Discipline"

Most Modern institutions in our Country today teach it is wrong to hit children and recomend other forms of dicipline. The "Gilmartin Report" says that children who are spanked tend to be nervous and be slower in learning things, that harsh punishment leads to a decrease in family comunication and is strongly associated with the development of a low self image in children. That violence begets more violence. But on the other hand, it can also create chronic passivity in children, a "follower" mentality.

But the "progressive" discipline recomended over spanking tends to be a kind of mindfuck instead. It is intended to get similiar results through creating an established order around the person, the atmosphere of submission. This mind control is always backed up of course, ultimately with force if the first technique fails. Franz Fanon was the person I read which said something like that. He added in colonial countries, the agents of government speak the language of pure force, after he said Americans are mindfucked into being controlled, and it is a lighter task that way. Still as I look around me, seeing children being hit everyday, it would appear the lower classes still use physical punishment over rationalizations. As Colin Ward suggests, the child born into the lowest social bracket has everything stacked against him including his parents' principles of child upbringing.

"Discipline is a branch of Religion. Lack of trust in ones own self; an outside force will compel goodness and truth."
—A. S. Neill

"A child learns quick, from the hatred they find. The children are bred with your pain. Soon they'll destroy, your domain."
—Septic Death

Punishment:
There's Never A Need To Punish Children!

If one wanted to not just prevent abuse but actually do good for a child, one would suspend all punishment. There is no reason to punish children. Time-out (making a child sit on a chair by her/himself to think over what s/he has done wrong) is as different from spanking as wage-slavery is from bond-slavery. Different all right. But not good enough, not freedom. Time-outs are inefficient and they operate on the same principles

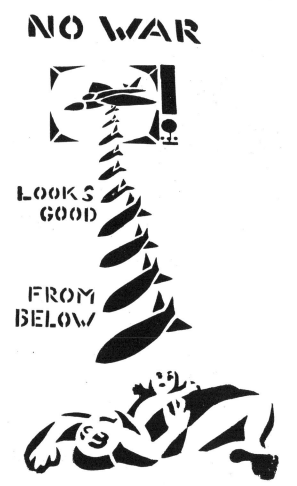

Sabrina Jones, World War III

as spanking: to guide a child through fear and obedience. What constructive pattern does it teach?

I was reading a paper from a college student who volunteered at a woman's shelter where she watched children. She wrote that discipline was the only part of her job with the kids that made her uncomfortable but that it was necessary and done in the peaceful method of Time-outs in order to protect everyone's security. The children, many victims of domestic violence, were told that this was a safe place. Yet I feel the two examples she gave of using this form of discipline could have been handled much better.

One reason she gave time out was to a child who wouldn't share crayons, after she told him that everyone must share. This is ridiculous to me. To dominate someone into sharing when true sharing comes from a honest feeling to do so—not because someone bigger makes you.

Another reason she gave to use time-out was because a child hit another child. When you remove a child to be punished by sitting on a chair by itself, you can bet that child is not going to be feeling compassion or sorry that it hurt another. No, most likely the child will feel a little angry at you for putting it there. The child hasn't learned a better way to deal with conflict and probably will go on feeling justified in it's aggressive actions. You have robbed the child of the opportunity to learn and feel compassion and tried instead to make fear of punishment by a higher power the motivation to not hurt others. In addition, you have reinforced the lesson that the most important thing is just not to get caught, not that you shouldn't do things that hurt others.

I would prefer to treat this incident as a fact of life and just deal with it. For example: we were at the playground and my daughter wanted to play with a slightly angry older boy who was building sand structures. She came up to him and he was not receptive to her. He threw sand at her. My first reaction was to let them deal with it themselves. She throws sand back. He then takes a lot of sand and throws it at her face and into her eyes. She cries out in pain. "Oh Clover", I crouch by her side with one arm around her and my other hand wiping the sand out of her eyes, nose, and mouth until she is all cleaned up. I comfort her until she feels better. The boy watches this. Then I turn to him, "The sand hurt her." She sees me tell the boy this. She resumes playing in the sand, this time he doesn't bug her. She doesn't get as close to him but in the course of the next hour of enjoyable play in the sand they sometimes comment to each other and look at the structures each other build. I give the boy a little attention, because a little is about all he wants from me, over the pyramids he is building. When we leave we wave goodbye to him and I sense that he is slightly less angry then when we arrived; he's had a good time in the sand; and no one has attacked him and blamed him for things. He obviously must be having a hard time so I feel it is important for us to be calm and decent to him.

The children were able to resume their play, troubles were moved through. He had the opportunity, to perhaps, feel compassion for what his actions caused in Clover. He saw my nurturing behavior rather than my first reaction to be with punishment, telling him he was bad, and the extraction of my child. Children need to deal with the realities of conflict. They have us on their side looking out for them but one day they will be on their own with no parents to intervene. The sad thing is when small incidents are treated with big reactions. The situation I just described to you is common, many problems are on this scale. Can you start to see why I believe in completely suspending punishment?

My motivation is parental love and to get results. I learned how to handle this playground problem by watching another parent's reaction to a similar incident when my daughter was younger (a toddler) and the situation was reversed. She pulled another toddler down three feet to the ground, as she scrambled to get over him and up the monkey bars. The parent comforted their child and then told my daughter how falling had hurt him. Obviously, from the look on her face, she did think about the harm that she had caused when she saw his tears. What is more, as they played together, she never did that to him again. She was bigger than him and had learned about her own strength. (Toddlers can act with a youthful egotism and not be aware of consequences of their actions on others. This is what we help them learn.) Meanwhile we didn't treat the smaller child as more fragile than he was. He was comforted and able to resume his playing and was fine. Kids take their bumps and mishaps in stride. That is how

it is with little kids on the playground. My child was that little when she was hurt senselessly by older children once in a while. But you must deal with the situation and not completely shelter your child. Let them step out on their own a little bit. As a whole, I believe there could be a lot less violence in our culture, yet we have to deal with the reality of it.

Violent Physical Force: Culturally Unacceptable

If spanking children was culturally unacceptable, adults who go over the accepted amount of physical punishment and land their children in the hospital, would know it's not ever alright to hit children, so the line of a spanking and a beating would not be as easily slipped over.

I've read that corporal punishment is devoid of constructive education value, since it cannot provide a sense of security and non-arbitrary authority. Rarely, if ever, is corporal punishment administered for the benefit of the child, for it serves the immediate needs of the attacking adult who is seeking relief from his uncontrollable anger and stress. Physical attack by an adult on a weak child is not a sign of strength!

Not a day goes by that I don't hear something of the likes of "I'm going to bust your ass" or "If you don't be good for grandma she will give you a beating". No—laugh the children—We will run away. It is just normal threats and doesn't even scare the kids; its not even uttered with malice.

Yet I can see it is a major preoccupation for children, as in their games they often reenact adult's treatment of them. They gather together and beat a doll—saying it has been bad. Then when they see me they suddenly stop and hug the doll, calling it good. They talk of good, bad, and monsters often.

Spanking perpetuates dependence on spanking for discipline. The child will run carelessly in the absence of the person who spanks it, the child will not listen to words of warning or common sense. This I see just from my own experience. You have lost the opportunity to reason with each other.

When I was in Jamaica, I saw a child whose mother sells fruit in the market playing around and annoying a passerbyer when the man goes to whack the child in annoyance. The child crouched and picked up a stone to hurl at him. Then the man picked the child up in the air and was going to beat him—the boy's mother wasn't there to defend him. It all escalated so fast I was yet to utter a word when a Rastafarian came forth and pulled the boy back down. He said "Don't hit the child, you are like the white slave master beating a slave in days of old. Reason with him."

Stories Of Our Past

How much do we define ourselves from the stories our parents told us about what we were like as children? A man who was beaten for breaking the television as a child, says he believes children need to be yelled and spanked so they can learn right from wrong. A girl is told that she never was any good—and wonders if it's true. A woman told me she always has gotten mad a lot—she threw many temper tantrums as a child. "Well, you were just strong willed," I say. My child is strong willed. But I don't ever really remember her throwing temper tantrums, not kicking on the floor and all that. Of course I've seen her rage and she's cried a lot. But if I was saying no to her needs and not respecting her she would have lots of frustrated temper tantrums.

Many people do not know they contain self-motivation for they have never been given the opportunity. They think the authority of their parents saved them from getting in trouble, and therefore, from their experiences, they will use authority over their children.

Every Mother Is A Single Mother

Don't put all the blame on mothers when they yank the little ones arm up and pull him along from the "magical crack in the sidewalk filled with life he was exploring. A verbal barrage of abuse sputtering from her wicked lips, possibly scarring him for eternity, robbing him of all of the precious wonder found in every tiny human life." (As I read in a children's rights publication)

Yes, I have heard a mother call her kid a brat for kicking a clod of snow; another tell her son that "You can't get through this life without a beating, you have to learn right from wrong" as she hit him for getting tired on a bus ride.

But I have also been there. Been a mother as well as a child. Have you? And it hurts like hell to be turned into a bitch, hurting your child on top of the hurt you feel for being in an overwhelming situation.

I don't think the abuse done to children can be lessened until there is more support for mothers in this society and responsibility taken for including the children in this society.

Class-Conscience Children's Liberation

Once you believe in respecting a child's decisions and in laying off them—you find there is more to it than just a frame of mind and getting the old harmful patterns you grew up with out of your soul. You find your environment may be making you act in ways you don't want to and giving you stress. If you don't have the money to buy respect, space, and attention for your kids— you're out of luck. If you do have that kind of money you should consider the walled garden you're living in and that we are all in this together and affect each other. Of course I am talking about the city living that I am familiar with. Here in Baltimore, Head Start programs for poor kids have

been cut completely in the summer and reduced to half days in the fall. I really wonder what I am supposed to do about Clover's environment. A friend told me that the ratio of funding for a rich white school in the county compared to a poor inner city black school is 6 to 1. Their schools get six times as much funding, while even in South Africa the ratio is 3 to 1. So you don't have to look far for apartheid, do you?

I've read A. S. Neill—saying "I agree, I agree" but I can't let both of us be free. I can't when she is screaming at me in the supermarket and when I am tired walking home. I can't when she demands more than I can give and keeps me from writing. It seems then that she is oppressing me although I know it's not her fault. And then I'm oppressing her. I think I have it a lot better because I am in the "subculture". Some people have said, "How can I let my child run free when you know the mortality rates for young inner city black boys like my own?" A. S. Neill was working in a privileged situation, but children's liberation ideals still work for us here, its just everyone's specific problems must be dealt with. When we talk of changing how we raise our children and of changing society to be more just and inclusive, we cannot ignore the differences in class, gender and race. We are not all alike, and we do not all have the same amount of privilege—this is important to recognize as we set about the task to make this a more free and less violent world, for everyone.

sunshine

fresh
air

CLEAN
WATER

uncontaminated
soil

PLENTY OF FRESH FRUITS AND VEGTABLES

EAT WHOLE, NATURAL FOODS AS MUCH AS POSSIBLE, FRESH, IN SEASON, ORGANIC AND
   AN EMPHASIS ON GREEN LEAFY VEGTABLES.   EAT RAW OR SLIGHTLY STEAMED.

WHOLE GRAINS   NO DAIRY   NO FACTORY FARMED MEAT
   (INTERPRETING SYMPTONS OF PESTICIDE POISONING AS "THAT BUG GOING AROUND" HAS BEEN
VOID SUGAR : REFINED SUGAR CONSUMPTION WEAKENS THE IMMUNE SYSTEM AND HAS BEEN | GOING
LICATED IN A NUMBER OF SERIOUS DISEASES SUCH AS CANCER AND MENTAL ILLNESS. | ON FOR
                                                                              | 30 YRS)

ID ALCOHOL,TOBBACCO,COFFEE.   GET ADEQUATE REST AND EXERCISE.
ID DRUGS AND VACINATIONS WHEN POSSIBLE.
       HAPPINESS WILL BOOST YOUR RESISTANCE TO DISEASE.

   TAKE SUPPLIMENTS AS NEEDED:GARLIC,AFALFA,VITAMIN C, ECT.

The Future GENERATION

OUR BODIES OUR SELVES OUR BODIES OUR SELVES OUR BODIES OUR SELVES OUR BODIES OUR SELVES OUR BODIES OUR SELVES

OUR BODIES   OUR SELVES

ALTERNATIVE CHILD-RAISING

iN Their public ENTER-TAINMENT For ALL AGES, THE MBUTI

ISSUE NUMBER FIVE, part 3: "EXPLORING THE SUBJECT OF VIOLENCE AND SEX"

SEE NOTHING WRONG OR IMMORAL WITH THE DEPICTION OF COPULATION AS REP-RESENTING A NATURAL PLEASURE TO BE OPENLY APPRECIATED AND ENJOYED. IN THEIR SENSE OF VALUES, IT IS ACCEPTED JUST AS WESTERN SOCIETY ACCEPTS VIOLENCE AND KILLING IN ORGANIZED ENTERTAINMENT THAT HAS EXTENDED FROM ...

CONTINUED ON NEXT PAGE ▶

Issue Five

Part 3
Sex & Violence

"*In their public entertainment for all ages, the Mbuti see nothing wrong or immoral with the depiction of copulation as representing a natural pleasure to be openly appreciated and enjoyed. In their sense of values, it is accepted just as western society accepts violence and killing in organized entertainment that has extended from the earliest Greek plays to modern cinema and television. An outstanding difference between our moral attitudes is that the Mbuti look on any form of violence between one person and another with great abhorrence and distaste, and never represent it in their dancing or playacting.*" – The Forest People, Colin Turnbull

-FILM AS A SUBVERSIVE ART-

THE PREVAILING "ORDER" SANCTIFIES VIOLENCE AND GENOCIDE

BUT DENIES THE BODY AND ITS FUNCTIONS.

- commic from THE REALIST -

RATED NC-17

Look at Saturday morning cartoons – think of all the violence and murders a child see's on t.v. – yet to see the Ninja turtles making love would be obscene, wouldn't it?

My little cousins can explain any murder plot to my young child yet when she asks whats going on in a love-making scene on the television, they blush and don't answer.

Introduction: Sex And Violence

Crime Dog McGruff says in his pamphlet for kids, "Say 'No' and go tell a trusted adult if someone tries to touch you where it makes you feel uncomfortable." Yet if you are a child and let's say, for example, being spanked on the butt or going to school makes you uncomfortable, no adult is going to listen to that. Children are often told "be good and do everything the babysitter tells you to do," and they are often ignored when they express what is uncomfortable to them. So I think the real message in the McGruff pamphlet is your genitals are not to be touched and there is a lot of perverts who want to touch them so don't talk to strangers. This is not very helpful advice. I like what I read in a zine called *Body Memories: Radical Perspectives on Childhood Sexual Abuse* much better:

"Child abuse will never be stopped until all children have control over what is done to them and are respected as the human being they are. Even young children, who are dependent on others for much of their physical and emotional needs know what they do and do not want, though adults do not always know how to listen to them. …while it is vital that children be treated with respect and get taught that no one has the right to abuse them, the first and foremost fact is Adults have the responsibility and the power to end child sexual abuse—kids don't."

Adult invasion and abuse of children is rampant. Children are threatened to be quiet—thus the rule— "if you don't talk about it—it doesn't exist" (no one can know). The voice of children needs to be heard, believed, acted on. Abusing and non-abusing parents are caught up in the same problem of relating to the children from a position of pure power. "We do not teach our children the freedom to express what they feel and know, and we often fail to respect their place among us. Children are unable to tell us what they experience precisely because they are considered to be our property, and as such, have no option in the family to be heard, particularly when they want to tell us things we do not want to hear." (I forgot where I got this from.)

We need to protect our children from abuse. But sexuality is also wonderful and we need to protect children from sensual repression too. When an "expert", moralist or educator moves to help children but gives information that uses AIDS and pregnancy as agents of fear proving sex's sinfulness, it is no help. When an "expert" gives information that is twisted by hypocrisy, ignorance, shame, prejudice, ageism, conformity or submission—it is no help. There are a lot of people afraid of sex and they want to repress information, punish desires. Keep things quiet. They want to expel signs of sexuality from the domestic field of vision—childhood "innocence" is supposed to de-sexualize the child's world.

"Among the damaging sexual attitudes in our families, and a form of violence, is the perpetuation of our cultures personally debilitating negative sexual attitudes. Few parents feel comfortable with their own sexuality. Verbally, and physically expressing themselves, their feelings, and their experiences makes parents uncomfortable. Children learn that parts of the body are touched and stroked in a loving and caring way while others are not to be displayed or talked about. The touching and curiosity about these body parts is forbidden and shameful—innocent curiosity or exploration can lead to over reaction in family members. We are estranged from our sexuality as a culture. And the silence is awkward. When sex is brought up with children it is more to establish rules rather than engage in an open dialogue.

"Sexual violence also includes denying children the right to their own bodies, the right to learn about them, to touch and enjoy them, to share them when they choose and to live wholly and delightedly within them."

—*Conspiracy of Silence: The Trauma of Incest*

We are sexual beings, and sex is part of our life. Young children all over the world often play sex, hump their stuffed animals, etc. just like how they play other things. They are curious about everything. It is natural for them to play sex with their friends if they want to and preferable for them to be in touch with their feelings to know what they do and do not want. Desire is the life force of a human being—and I do not mean, but do include, sex as desire. Desire to live, to be, to do, to achieve, and to feel: Desire is the "Yes" inside us. But in America sex just seems like something "dirty" to smirk about and be used as a marketing strategy to sell products.

Kids often grow up in a world where there is the "acceptance of the powerful abusing the less powerful" and this colors their experiences of sexuality. A friend told me that he thought playing doctor was really sick, because as a kid he saw some friend put pliers into his little sister's vagina to "pull out her baby". And another friend told me when he was in boarding school, older boys would often torment him, but if he told anyone he would be made to jack off the ringleader in the bathroom. Children who are tormented and subjected to their elder's abuse often take it out on those younger than them. There is a lot of sadomasochistic play going on with children. This is not rare, but rather the norm, the American Way:

"The pattern of dominance and submission is repeated in every facet of a child's social experience."
—*Children and Feminism*

Parents—most probably because of their own childhood experiences—can have a hard time dealing with their young child's budding sexuality and sexual curiosity. I've known two mother friends that reacted in the same way when they found out their child was playing sex with another child in the neighborhood They told their child it shouldn't be doing stuff like that, it was much too young. They expressed to me it was the other child's fault, a bad or sick child, a child that must have been abused to know how to do such things. And they put a tense feeling onto their child about the experience. But when I listened to all they said, all I heard mentioned was that the children were found pretending to have sex, not that any child was upset or anything abusive was going on, but the fact that they were pretending was seen in a horrible light.

Often in our culture, even a young child's knowledge of sexual matter or a young child's nudity is seen as wrong and met with strong reaction. Once my aunt said when discussing abuse in a day-care, that young children would not know about sex so graphic in their pre-school years, that white middle-class children are not exposed to such things unless they have been the victims of abuse. (yuck) And my mother worried about my child when she was three and was using words like "penis, yoni, clitoris, condom" and talking about making love with pretend friends because

she thought somebody would think she's been abused and take her away from me. But I found with her, just to answer her questions and live with her, lead to this young fascination at such things; she was learning about life about her own speed, nothing was pushed on her. But this could be seen by somebody in authority as wrong, I know, just like even a child's nudity can be wrong. Remember some years ago when a photographer was arrested for taking pictures of naked children in a "tasteful, arty" way with consent of parent and child? A little child's body is not pornographic!

Another time when she was even younger (and had messed her underwear since she was just getting potty trained so my mom took them off and was taking her home), she flashed some basketball players and threw her dress up in the air laughing. My Aunt was there and was horrified: she said, "Those guys could be convicts, rapists, and Clover is going to give them ideas!" How sick, that the child provokes rape? That's not true, it's in people's twisted minds to see that.

It's really upsetting to me that the most innocent kind of things are taken so badly, and I really am only talking of the most innocent things, nothing radical, that could lead to a paranoia that if you open with your child and answer her questions without shame, people could take your child away or something. But on the other side of this really skewed system—is that when people are sexually abused—do we run to help them? No—it's likely as not that Society always seems to punish the victims. Everything sexual is all clouded over, and ignorance certainly isn't bliss.

Sex Doesn't = Violence
Violence = Violence
We should put the blame on those who abuse, not on the victim.

An article I read by Gail Pheterson on the Social Consequences of Unchastity brings up some very interesting points, such as identifying abuse with female unchastity (rather than female oppression) maintains the illusions that surround violence against women. One illusion is that female behavior causes male sexual violence.

"Any woman whose virtue is called into question can be blamed for any abuse they suffer from male violence. A wife's sexual infidelity can be used as a justification to abuse or control her. A girl-child is held responsible for preventing male sexual assault: she maybe blamed for being too provocative (even a 5 year old!) or her mother may be blamed for giving her too much freedom. Supposedly, a whore can not be violated because she is already in violation of chastity norms."

—*Sex Work: Writings by Women in the Sex Industry*

In 1990, a San Diego police officer was quoted in the *Sacramento Bee*—in response to a string of murders—as saying "These were misdemeanor murders, biker women and hookers…we call them NHI—no human involved".

"Since we are conditioned to believe that violence and death are known occupational hazards for sex workers, we respond to their demise with apathy of a resigned willingness to blame the victim, to accept the murder of the prostitutes as one of life's harsh realities. At the same time we are relieved that such brutality could never be visited upon those of us who comply with societal mores. But the lines separating 'good girls' from 'bad girls' are mutable and any one of us could appear to be a 'bad girl' at any time."

—*Critical Conditions: Women on the Edge of Violence*

It makes you think, doesn't it? I mean abuse has nothing to do with sexiness, but even if a girl was "strutting her stuff," does that mean it's an invitation to abuse her? Why is the idea of sex and violence so connected in the minds of many, that they can't see what is the sex and what is the violence? To be sexual is not to be asking for violence, it is not meaning you are disowning the other parts of yourself, it is not meaning you are giving up your human rights.

People are definitely talking back against the nonsense going on. Like how the Gay Mans Center put forth all kinds of information on how to protect yourself from AIDS when the government's message was just that sex equals death and they could not deal openly with sex—or gay people—their worst fear. And there are a lot of people analyzing and spreading the facts of what is this psychology of abusing and using people. Boy children are sexually abused as well as girl children, that's a fact … but I wanted to put down this thing on violence against women as another example of how to look at this from a different angle than from blaming the victim:

"Once in cabinet we had to deal with the fact that there had been an outbreak of assaults on women at night. One minister suggested a curfew: women should stay home after dark. I said, "But it's the men who are attacking the women. If there's to be a curfew, let the men stay home, not the women."

—*Golda Meir,* former Israeli Prime Minister

This has been a difficult article for me, I apologize for my bad skills of article writing. I just wanted to share some information. Everything depends on the context it is taken in.

THE SEXUAL OUTLAW by John Rechy

"A man emerges staggering out of the brush in a park, his face smashed in blood. Yelling 'Queer! Queer!' four thugs kicked and beat him with sticks. The cops are called. No one shows up.

But tell them two men are fucking, and they'll storm the area in minutes."

Sex Positive Childraising

Wilhelm Reich said that knowing who one is; feeling authentic emotions; and not falling into Fascism — comes, in part, from being raised with trust in your body. If you don't have the freedom to feel your most basic feelings then how can you have the freedom to have your own mind. Or something like that.

George Dennison said (in the '60s as a response to people talking about sexual repression all the time), "It is the whole child we are interested in. We can increase his security, treat him with justice and consideration, respect his pride of life, value the independence of his spirit, be his ally in a world that needs to be changed. ...sexuality permeates everything. ...when in the classroom, the child is allowed to speak freely and experience the creative unity of feelings, hunches, thoughts, humor, etc.,

we are in fact supporting a positive sexuality. When we create conditions that do away with shame and self-contempt, we are supporting a positive sexuality. And so on."

Freud used the term sexuality in a much wider sense than is common to include all manifestations of striving for pleasure. He assumed a basic instinct, Eros or Libido—generally speaking an urge to live—as the source of all motivation. Sexuality in the infant is: satisfaction in bodily sensations, sucking at the breast when no longer hungry, mouthing, sucking and biting at objects with his mouth, the enjoyment of peeing and pooing, the enjoyment of genital sensations. (There's the definition—gee) There are articles in this zine about birth, nursing, potty training and holding because I see them as the building blocks of sexuality, the first experiences we have.

"Today - people want to KNOW how to make the baby accept OUR RULES!"

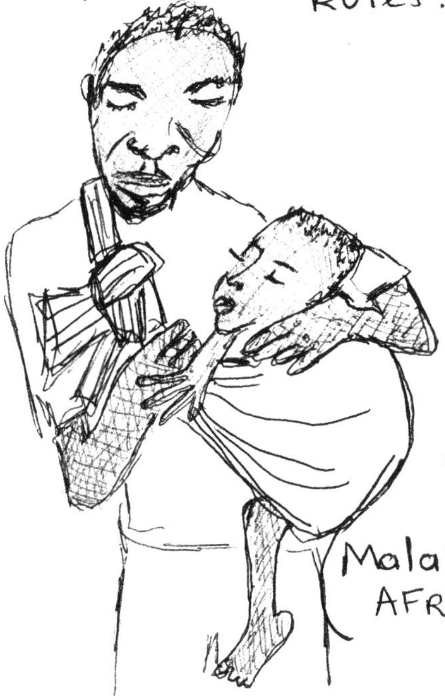

(Nepal)

"The innate expectations of infants are not what we in our society, have been led to believe they are"

Malawi, AFRICA)

BABES IN ARMS

from "NATURAL HEALTH"

(child carying baby in Uganda)

"Yequana Indians (S. Americans) Babies are in constant contact w/ adults, or older children. (Untill about the age of 6-8 months). At night they sleep w/ their parents. By day they are caried on the hip or in slings on the body, and sleep when they become tired. While the women, man, or child carying them wold carry on their normal activities. Yequanna baber in arms almost never cried. They did not spit up unless they were ill, and they did not suffer from colic. Yequanna Indian infants behavior + temperments were remarkably different than ours. This behavior sharply contrasts with the desperate discomfort of our own infants, tucked in cribs or carriages and left to "scream."
                                    — Jean Liedloff

Birds and Bees for Lesbians' kids : ASK FANNY

excerted from the special issue: Lesbians, Sex and Motherhood
of ON OUR BACKS Mar/Apr 1994

Dear Fanny: As a single mother, I look forward to more discussions in *On Our Backs* about children and sexuality. What I'd like to know is: how do we raise them to be free about their sexuality without embarrassing us at daycare by talking about dildos? How much sexual information, and at what age, do they need? Are there erotic images that we enjoy but don't want our kids to see?

—*Single Mom*

That issue of on our backs had
some really beautiful pictures
of pregnaut woman in it-
naked .
I think pregnaut woman can
look so hot , ya know.

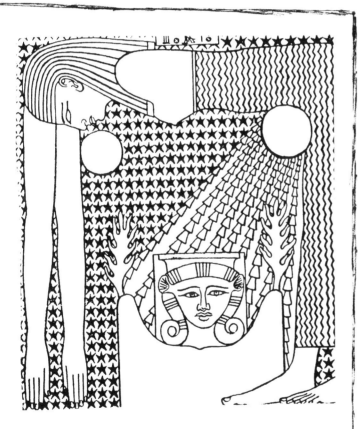

Dear Mom: If being embarrassed at daycare is all you have to worry about, then simply don't be. If you let the children see your sex toys, and you feel comfortable with that, then don't contradict yourself by displaying a negative reaction to a daycare worker's remark in front of your children. Both the worker and children will immediately assume you have done something you don't feel good about, and their attitude toward you and/or your behavior will mirror your own shame. Considering the paranoia over anything sexual that parents and daycare workers are experiencing due to recent media coverage of sexual child abuse, count yourself fortunate that embarrassment, rather than hysteria, is all you have to contend with.

Children are not going to understand sophisticated sexual knowledge anymore than they can understand calculus or modern dance. Little kids just wanna have fun, so let them! Your child may ask, "Mommy, why do you laugh when Sarah slaps your butt, pulls your hair to bend you over backward, and then kisses you?" You could respond, "Because it's fun, and I'm going to slap your butt, too!" while you chase her into the living room with a few love pats to the bottom, and collapse on the floor in a giggling ball of roughhouse. Or, perhaps you see her try Sarah's trick on her playmate, complete with the amorous look in her eye! No need to say anything at all, unless she pulls her friend's hair too hard and hurts her!

As your children grow, trust your instincts. You will know how much they are ready for. Ask them what they learned in school about sex, and fill in the gaps as pertains to your family views and lifestyle. When your daughter begins menstruation, or your son develops pubic hair, use the opportunity to bond with them by acknowledging their first step into adulthood with warmth and excitement. If your children see an unruffled, interested mom when sex questions are raised, you'll create a trust and openness that will serve you well through the teen years, when individuation causes them to seek sexual information elsewhere at a time when they most need guidance from you.

If you feel comfortable letting erotic images lie around the house along with computer manuals and fashion magazines, then do so, and the children will grow up thinking it's natural. But be prepared to put them away when they get older and are highly sensitive to what their friends may think. Respecting their sexual boundaries means they will do the same for you.

–Fanny Fatale

All The Arms We Need

Dr. James Prescott, an experienced anthro-psy-chologist, doing a vast cross-cultural study of the causes of violence compared dozens of violent and peaceful cultures. He found a high correlation between the affection and sexual freedom in children and the peaceful life of that culture's adults. Children given lots of affection and touching early on and allowed to sexplore themselves and peers grew up more naturally and much more peaceful. The bonding at birth is so important that it deeply imprints a baby now and lifelong. The other deep cause of violence is the anti-sexual activities by parents and others, which stresses the natural needs for love and touching, which makes kids crave touching, more repressed and thus open to war toys, tuff-sports and secrecy games to act out or release the tension.

"Generally, it's axiomatic that wherever you have a culture that's punitive toward its children, that manipulates and dominates them, and where the sexual feelings of those children are suppressed—those kind of cultures are invariably very violent. In fact, you can't find an example of a culture like that that is peaceful. They are always, always violent.

"On the other hand, in a culture where the children are raised with a great deal of love, breastfed to the child's satisfaction, allowed to toilet-train spontaneously, allowed and even looked favorably at the sexual play and expression of children, which also allows their unmarried adolescents the full rights to a private sexual life, in those societies, always, always the people are peaceful and don't have any interest in warfare."
—James Demeo

I believe it is important to note that raising children with warm physical contact and an open "sex positive" attitude does not promote incest, rape, and sexual abuse—no, those things come more from the uptight and moralistic set. Those who feel justified in beating children, writes Reich in *The Sexual Revolution*, also feel justified in using them for living out their unsatisfied sexuality. Reich started as a student of Freud's theories in psychology but challenged and expanded on them substantially.

"Freud's cultural philosophical standpoint was always that culture owes its existence to instinctual repression and renunciation. The basic idea is that cultural achievements are the result of sublimated sexual energy, from this it follows logically that sexual suppression are an indispensable factor in the cultural process. There is historical evidence of the incorrectness of this formulation; there are in existence highly cultured societies without any sexual suppression and a completely free sex life.

"What is correct in this theory is only that sexual suppression forms the mass-psychological basis for a certain culture, namely the patriarchal authoritarian one, in all its forms"
—Wilhelm Reich, *The Sexual Revolution*

Breastfeeding

Nursing, why would I want to write an article about that? It's just something that I do, no big deal. I think I've written a few poems about it for myself. It's something wonderful; very warm, close, and special. It's something my little titty-monger of a child has been enjoying for some time now. I've never had a problem with it but I know it can be something women need advice on sometimes. Fortunately there are many good books written on the subject and a Le Leche League exists in most towns (look them up in the yellow pages) that will answer your questions and give you support.

I have been surprised how much and how long my child has nursed, and after a gentle weaning attempt now and then, and advice from friends, "you really have to get your child to stop nursing", I've decided that if she wants it, it's OK. I'm still going to try to let her wean naturally. I know people in other cultures have nursed their children this long and longer. I know people in this culture do too; I've met a lot of them. My child is still nursing at three years old, you can think what you like, who knows, but this suits us just fine. It's just our decision, I don't know what's "right" for you. I know before she was born, I imagined a year was good enough, I thought she'd wean herself then. At a year old I knew there was no way we were ready to quit. A friend had weaned her child at two, which sounded like a good age. But then at two, I had the confidence from seeing a another friend who nursed her child to three and they liked it a lot. So she would probably stop

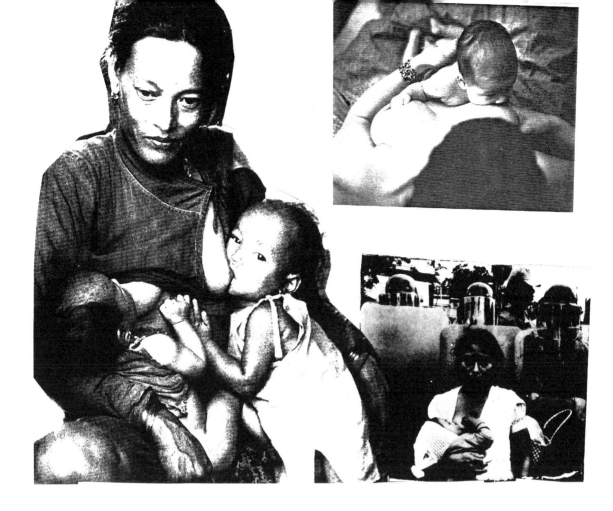

then, I thought. And now, I don't know when she will stop, but I know it will be a decision we make together, and I'm really not worried about it.

At two years old I stopped nursing her in public. I didn't do this out of modesty, Clover has thrown my shirt up over my tits in public before and I just laughed and pulled my shirt down. I don't wear a bra and I kinda like that punk rock thing about not worrying what people think about you, just be yourself. It sure has come in handy with giving my child her liberty; I'm seldom embarrassed. And it's come in handy with avoiding a lot of costs of trying to keep up appearance. But anyway, I stopped because since then I've lived in cities where I never saw anybody nurse their infants even, and it made me feel vulnerable to nurse her outside if I wasn't around friends. I know of instances where my friends have been harassed and bugged by guys for nursing their children outside. I just didn't want to deal with it, and she was at an age where she didn't have to nurse all the time anymore so it was ok. That's part of our relationship. Taking my feelings into consideration too.

I've dealt with having people question the fact that my child nurses so much, but it's not a big deal, just the stuff you deal with; sometimes people are kinda shy cuz you're nursing around them, but they get used to it. I tell you something that was great though: walking down Haight Street and seeing this mom (Merilee) sitting on the sidewalk with her shirt pushed up and her two year old nursing on one breast while twisting the nipple of the other and standing up on her back legs doing little nursing gymnastics. She was just hanging out with a bunch of punks. Well, I went up and met her; sat down and talked and got to be friends. It was really nice nursing our children together, there were two of us so I didn't feel shy. I felt like, *wow, she's just like me.* She told me all the moms in Oregon nurse their children until they want to stop on their own and they let their kids so whatever they wanted to and at the County Fair they announce over loudspeakers: "Remember, we all look out for the kids here." Wow, that's pretty cool, I said. It was great hanging out with her. Her child used to play nursing games with my child. "Come here and nurse me," she would say as she pulled up her shirt but my daughter never did for they would both collapse in giggles over their two-year-old humor. And yeah, sometimes their presence would encourage each other to nurse too much and we wanted to be freer and would tell them to stop, or nurse irritated, but that's all part of it, you know, the good and the bad, which I wouldn't have given up for anything.

I knew another great mother friend who wanted to wean her child at two and he definitely did not want to, just like Clover. So she left him with his father and weaned him by going on vacation. Then later, she gave him a bottle at night, and still he would not fall asleep but to lay next to somebody and hold their tit. I think she felt a little sad once, looking at me and Clover, still nursing. And I was very glad I hadn't forced my child to stop nursing yet, it would be too hard to do that. And it's so nice to give her titty when she's sick or grumpy; it's so nice to curl up together. But mostly, it's just what she wants, and it's just ordinary for us. I have less milk now because Clover sometimes leaves me for three or more days so we can enjoy some time away. She nurses less, so I have less milk and it doesn't hurt me at all when she is gone. Maybe this is our weaning process? I've heard of kids nursing to four and five. People have told me that they met them. It kind of scares me that Clover could nurse that long. I always thought I would wean her before then, I just couldn't take that! But we will see. I know it will be kind of sad when we stop nursing, a time in our lives, a time sometimes I was so sick of, will be over with finality.

I think Clover has received a lot of security from nursing, from me being there and listening to her, believing in her. No one could say that she doesn't look healthy. She's extremely outgoing and independent.

I guess what motivated me to write this article was I got to thinking about problems women can have with nursing. Some mothers can't nurse their children or don't enjoy it so much, and so it makes them feel uncomfortable hearing people say how great it is. I definitely don't want to make anyone feel weird about their experience. Sometimes there are problems, everyone has some part of the parenting experience that they have trouble with, that doesn't just come "naturally" and easy—like I had a very colicky baby, for instance. Like my grandmother comes up in my mind, for instance. She had wanted to nurse her child but her milk just wasn't "good", her infant was crying, not getting enough nutrition. She supplemented feedings with a bottle as the doctor told her too. (Which we now know to be a big no-no) And things went downhill from there, her body didn't work, and she switched over to bottles. With her next two children, she didn't even try to breastfeed them, she had no confidence in it. As we talk now, she can't tell me why her "milk was bad" yet after all these years I hear a tone of insecurity in her voice about the whole thing.

And even my own mother, although she was really siked to nurse me, and it was a wonderful experience, weaned me suddenly at 6 months old when a neighbor made a comment to her. The woman said it was really weird she was still nursing her baby and implied it was like sexually perverse. It made my mom feel embarrassed and she weaned me on the spot. I started sucking my thumb then.

And even I, I recall now, had my doubts. When I was pregnant and discussing stuff with my midwife, she asked me if I planned on breastfeeding and I said I didn't know if I would be able to. "Why not?" she asked me. I told her because my breasts are really small. "Oh, everyone can nurse," she laughed. "Look at the midwife assistant and me—we nursed our children and we are small-breasted like you." She told me it was actually more difficult for the woman with large breasts, which they had to hold up their breasts sometimes, so they didn't press down on the newborn's face. But that there were no difficulties associated with having small breasts.

Then when I nursed her for the first time, I didn't know what to do, but my baby sure did! She latched right on. Wow! God I was blown away, in love, and amazed with it all. It hurt until my nipples toughened up—infants nurse so hard! It was so beautiful, it really was, the look of ecstasy on her face when she nursed, I think I'll always be able to remember that pleased peaceful little face with her eyes closed. And my breasts were like, my breasts, useful, not too small, not something to be hidden away that just boys like.

Stop Hypocracy.... stop to think... stop false morality!

PRostitutes deserve equal Rights as any person... not to be blamed for violence against them + to be "fucked over by the law because" they "fuck", everybody else gets off scott free while injustices are committed against them, their Rights and their children.

JUST WHAT KIND OF LIFE IS THIS ANYWAY?

A child is born out of a warm uterus (37°C), experiences a sudden drop in temperature and is exposed to light.

In most patriarchal, obstetrician-influenced hospitals the child is immediately taken away from its mother, often given the famous slap on the buttocks,

sometimes prodded with tubes and generally regimented to serve the schedules of the hospital.

In the very beginning the child's spite against the world begins.

Call off your tired old ethics

Designed by Judy Sickle
Written by Tom Donaghy

SAFER SEX IS FOR EVERYONE

Here's Why

Anyone who's sexually active is at risk of getting the AIDS virus, syphilis, gonorrhea, hepatitis or chlamydia.

Here's How

You can have all the great sex you want—just be sure to make it safer. In vaginal, anal and oral sex, ALWAYS use a latex condom.

HOW TO USE A CONDOM

Condoms are easy to use. Before you do anything, take the condom and lubricant out of this stylish package. Then...

1 Place the condom against the head of the erect penis (or have a friend do it for you) leaving some space at the tip. We suggest using a dab of water-based lubricant inside the tip of the condom. You'll both enjoy increased pleasure.

2 Hold on to the tip of the condom and unroll it completely to the base of the penis. If the penis is uncut, pull back the foreskin before you put it on the condom. Once it's on, take a deep breath, smile and go do that voodoo that you do so well.

3 Use plenty of water-based lube, like KY* or ForPlay* during penetration. Don't use Crisco*, baby oil, hand lotions or Vaseline*—they can break The make the condom lubricant in this package is water-based and A-OK.

4 Immediately after ejaculation, hold the base of the condom and pull out. Don't ever reuse a condom. But don't worry; we gave you two 'cause we knew you'd want to practice using a condom again real soon.

Condom illustrations courtesy of San Francisco AIDS Foundation

And remember: it's true. Drugs and alcohol impair judgment, and worse, weaken the body's ability to fight off infection so be smart! Stay healthy!

ENJOY SAFER SEX!

There's no need to deprive yourself or take chances anymore.

For further information call the
HOTLINE 212-807-6655
TDD 212-645-7470(hearing impaired)

GMHC

© 1990 Gay Men's Health Crisis, Inc.
129 West 20th Street, New York, New York 10011-0022

"Safe+Sexy"

This↑ enclosed condoms + came in a pamphlet called "Kids Fuck too"

YPSL 514 W. 25th St. New York, NY 10001

-22-

"Fascism is the Cancer of the Body Politic."

"Kids Liberation involves having power over one's own life. It involves power never being removed from it's source in the individual."
Su Negrin

I made up my mind that when I was older I would never forget that a five-year-old is a complete individual, a character in his own right. But this was precisely what adults refused to admit and whenever they treated me with condescension I at once took offence.
-Simone de Beauvoir

The Future Generation
#6
APRIL 1994
$ ONE BUCK
For homes like yours, with little folks
PUNK ROCK IS MY LIFE!

Issue Six

April 1994

For Homes Like Yours, With Little Folks

INTRODUCTION

Hi!   I haven't done this zine for a while ... so I'm
going to plunge right into this. I've amused myself
alot this year with trashy magazines,like Cosmo, and really
all kinds of magazines, and taken glimpses at the Weekly
World News,so its kinda influenced the slant of this zine,
when I said to myself , I want to have a "fun" issue.

I wanted to do a parody Womans day with all kinds of cross-
word puzzles,psychology quiz's,recipes and gossip...something
good for taking to the laundry matt,or reading in your trail-
or park,sitting on your fire escape,ect. I'm burned out on
trying hard to write serious stuff, right now. I wanted a fun project,with
interesting articles too. So I'm reaching in my box of recipes,coupons,
and clipped out articles i've saved to put this zine together of a litle
this and that. Its basicaly a Hi, Im back (I put my last zine out 3 years
ago) lets get re- aquanted thing. I'm starting up. I want to put out a zine
for subculture parents concerns,communication,networking,artwork,all that
stuff,+put it out more regular. And be damned my mispelling.whatever.

Eeks,I feel stiff on this typewriter. Anyway back to the idea of magazines,
The woman in my family always read them;and beyond just my cheap amusement
of their rediculous content, their realy is something to the idea of a
womans circle,even if mines more a terrorist sewing circle.Comic books
were fun for me. And when Clover brought home XXXXXX from school one of
those book club order forms, that you get to order books from.(Do you remember what I mean?)¢ it was so cool,free sticker,stuff like that, printed
on great colourfull paper,it was a 70s childhood flashback and I wanted my
zine to look like that, be fun to have like that. I hope I haven't lost you.

In the past my zines been about stuff like, oh, kid lib,childraising in
various tribes,anarchist stuff,personal experience,home birth,sycology
kinda shit,all kinds of stuff, this zine , I'll try to define it for you
again, if you don't know - is for sub culture parents of the various
cultures to communicate ,express feeling,share communication. What all was
in those old zines ? radical stuff,redesighning cities for human needs,
anarchist stuff, ok. I'm sorry,i've got a litle hang-over, 24 hours,to do
this project,of freetime (kid-free, yippee!) before i got to work on packing to move and parenting and stuff. AND for some reason I'd like to shirk
even this project which is very important to me, and sit in the sun with my
dog on the fire- escape. The zines gonna be great tho-so contribute. Back
orders available. SO,heres my explanation of xx why I haven't put out this
zine for the last 3 years ; parental burn-out,absorption in personal life,
failure,stress,depression,apathy,poverty,obsession with the ooposite sex,writers-
block,self doubt,questioning my belief system, and being a mom is hard!
But springs here and I really want to get active in alot of stuff,I'm
ready to try again   China   /

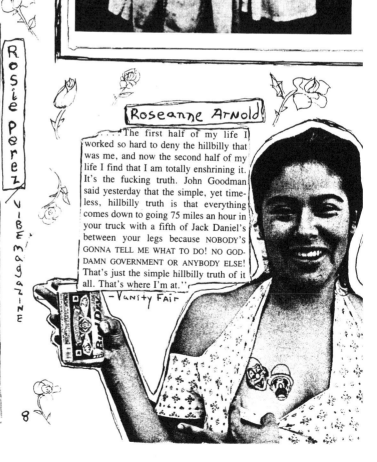

The observation that *"even your children do not know how to play"* was directed at both the seeming absence of artistic creativity in mass culture and its tendency to homogenize its young according to formalized school norms. The dependency of American children on manufactured toys, the rigid scheduling of childhood hours, and age grouping and its concomitant discontinuities appeared to them to rob our children of free play and spontaneity. Segregated in the world of childhood, they asked, "When do your children learn to be adults, to know life?" *"In America, children and adults are too far apart. It seems they do not like each other."* The direct experience of Gypsy children with their cultural heritage, a heritage communicated verbally, through the folk arts, and largely in an intimate face-to-face milieu, was not, in their opinion, mirrored in American culture. Seeing our children as "victims" of an impersonal school system, isolated from the adult world, they saw them as failing to acquire that sense of being linked to the past which, without benefit of written history, strongly unites each generation of Gypsies one to the other. "We want just a little schooling. . . ."

Watching news telecasts of the Watts racial riots led one young *gitano* dancer to state, *"You have many laws, but no law. Gypsy laws are few, but we live by them. This does not seem to be your way."* Working on the assumption that rich and poor people are subject to different legal norms, Gypsy visitors identified closely with racial problems in the United States, an identification based primarily on what they viewed as inconsistencies in the application of law. "You say this, but you do that. How can this be?" We have been similarly questioned in subsequent field trips to Spain concerning violence in American culture. "You kill all of your best people. Los Kennedys, Martín Lutero King. *Es una locura* [it is a madness]. *What you do not understand, you mistreat."*

-from "Que Gitano!"

I. LATINA

Carmen's house, in Ridgewood, is small, immaculate, and has a front room dominated by a three-piece living-room suite covered in plastic and a chandelier that would remind you of your grandmother's. This is, according to Rosie, "very Puerto Rican." The list of very Puerto Rican attributes, according to Rosie, includes, but is not limited to: "Being very loud. And when you come off the plane from Puerto Rico with a leaky bag of *pasteles* wrapped in banana leaves, that's a very Puerto Rican sight to see. And also—this is why I made my company Ten in a Car Productions—oh my god, when my family used to pile in a car I used to bury my head and hope nobody from school would see me. And saying certain things in English the way you would say it in Spanish, so if I want to

say, 'Could you walk me to the store?' the very Puerto Rican way is"—she smacks her lips and whines—"'Can you give me the walk to the store?'"

Rosie and Carmen are sisters and partners in very Puerto Rican-ness. "Me and Carmen went to the premiere of *Spic-O-Rama*," says Rosie, referring to John Leguizamo's one-man send-up of Latino stereotypes, "and there were all these high-class Spanish people, and we had like the *boricua* crew. *Boricua* is like the real, real native Puerto Ricans. So we had a table, and everybody else was like: ha, ha, ha, ha. And we were like : AAAAAAAAAAAAAAH! screaming out family members' names when he went into different characters, and Daisy Fuentes was looking at us like: 'Oh, please.' And we were like: 'Aw, shut up, honey, you know you got a family just like that.' Afterwards, John Leguizamo's family came over and thanked us, and I thought that was so cool. I thought, yo, they down, they down for theirs."

Rosie Perez / VIBE Magazine

8

Roseanne Arnold

. . . The first half of my life I worked so hard to deny the hillbilly that was me, and now the second half of my life I find that I am totally enshrining it. It's the fucking truth. John Goodman said yesterday that the simple, yet timeless, hillbilly truth is that everything comes down to going 75 miles an hour in your truck with a fifth of Jack Daniel's between your legs because NOBODY'S GONNA TELL ME WHAT TO DO! NO GODDAMN GOVERNMENT OR ANYBODY ELSE! That's just the simple hillbilly truth of it all. That's where I'm at.''

-Vanity Fair

Sister Immaculate Conception

Alright, get funky with me, Sister!

The other day when I was thinking about what to write for this column, I was in a bookstore looking at the about a thousand different books written about children by adults and thinking about how I was about to add to all that. All (or most) of these books claim to know just how kids are and how and what they think and want. Conveniently enough, it's usually what makes things easier for adults. Some books claim some pretty ridiculous stuff, like this book my mom has called "Your One-Year Old". It says that one-year olds love it when you set limits and control their actions because they can't control themselves yet. This seems like pretty blatant propaganda and bullshit as well. I'm pretty sure that Isadora, my daughter, doesn't like it at all when I set limits (like not let her climb in the stove). I can tell because of the way she screams and freaks out. People like the womyn who wrote that book must completely ignore the signals kids are sending them, and I bet people think she's an expert too! Anyway, everything I write isn't some big truth about kids, it's just the way I interpret my experiences with Is. I try to do it while remembering how I felt about things when I was younger, and how I think now, because it's not like we're totally alien beings just because there's 17 years between our ages.

Isa is 18 months old now and she is changing a lot in what she can do and understand. She is getting more independent, but at the same time she doesn't understand about some things like electricity and getting squished by cars in the street. She wants to be in control of her own life more but I still need to stop her from doing things pretty often so she doesn't get hurt or destroy other people's stuff, and she still wants me to be right there when she's in unfamiliar territory or if she needs something. She gets frustrated with my interference a lot and sometimes she pulls my hair or hits when she is really mad. Sometimes she does stuff just to bug me (I think) like lick her shoes (which she only does when she knows I'm looking and not just whenever she can get away with it like with things she really wants to do that I won't let her). My mom says that she's "testing authority" (strangely enough she sometimes says that's what I'm doing too). This is a generic adult excuse to get more authoritarian just "to show them who's boss". In my opinion, kids doing things to defy authority shows even more how important it is to respect their choices and to not make more rules then necessary.

It can be hard when a kid is growing up as fast as Isa is to remember to respect their will and space. Even though I try to treat Isadora with as much equality as possible, sometimes it's really easy to space the fact that she is a real persyn. The other day I found myself trying to grab this thing that wasn't hers out of her hand and she was freaking out, and then I realized that I was being a complete jerk, so I put out my hand and asked her for it and she gave it to me. Why didn't I ask her and give her a chance first? Partially because not too long ago she wouldn't have understood, but I need to keep remembering to show her respect and not treat her like she's nothing. I also try now to compromise what I want with what she wants as much as possible, like if we're at a friend's house and I want to get going but she is having fun and wants to stay, to compromise like I would if she were anyone else and stay for a while. That's something that I and most people don't do because kids are little and you can physically drag them where you want to go, even if they are kicking and screaming.

There is one thing that people do that I want to say really annoys me, and probably Isa too, and that is when people see Is and right away ask "Who does she BELONG to?". Usually this is the first thing a grown-up will say when they see Is, whether she is just hanging out with a group of people or if she just goes up to them to say "hi". Isa doesn't belong to me, she's not my property. It's fine if you want to know who her mom is, and the language we have doesn't give any better words to ask, but deal with her and acknowledge her first. It's especially stupid when complete strangers ask this question, because it's not like it matters to them or they'll ever see us again, they just can't deal with Is as a humyn being and have to switch to talking to someone older when she trys to talk to them. By the way, kids under about 12 or so almost never do this, they usually communicate with her first and then maybe they'll ask me if she's my daughter.

Off the subject a bit, this is an actual real- life scenario at our house the other night:

joel: *Izzy, say anarchy. Can you say anarchy?*
Isadora: *Momma!*
joel: *No, no, can you say tyrant?*
Isadora: *Dole!* (That's joel in Izzy-speak)

exerted from *Profane Existence* summer 1993

Philadelphia
MOVE; black commune of back to nature anarchists, with their own religon based on the writings and teachings of John Africa

1977

MOVE has non-violently endured multiple killings of their members since 1970. This includes children and babies (and an estimated 35 dogs). Women in MOVE who were pregnant, on 2 occasions, were kicked in the stomach and vagina, and on both occasions had miscarriages.

MOVE wanted supporters, relatives and friends to have their children. But the children were placed in new homes throughout the city, with a gag order concealing their location. Sandra Davis, who was new in MOVE because of her recent marriage, is one of the prisoners. She too is kept from her baby and children. Some of the children whose locations are known think their parents are dead. The shock is so deep that they cannot talk to their imprisoned parents on the phone. The children are also undergoing haircuts, diet changes and school, all of which are against MOVE's beliefs.

1985 - Move house bombed
11 people killed in the fire
4 of them children

BALTIMORE, 1991, 'TAKE BACK the Night' MARCH AGAINST RAPE
Another woman who had her young son with her was arrested and the cops took her son to turn him over to Children's Services.

I usually try not to dwell on my personal experiences, but in this case it may help to show a real example of the government using children as weapons. Last year I was promoting underground shows each week and putting out my zine in a small city in Arizona. The cop continually tried to have our drug free all ages shows shut down, but they could never bust us for anything. Well as you might have guessed they began to dislike me. One day we had a party with about twenty people at our house. The police illegally entered the place and arrested about a dozen people bringing them to jail. Although they tried to bust us for dealing and drug offenses, they could not because basically we were just a few friends drinking together. So they ended up charging us with child neglect because we had a child. Our child had been asleep in her bed for hours, until the police busted in and woke her up. How could we have been neglecting our child by letting her sleep peacefully in her bed. What are any young children doing at midnight? Frankly I saw this as a last ditch effort by the police to gain control over our lives, and bring down upon us as much hardship as possible. Striking at someone through their children is as low as a man can get and when governments condone it, perhaps it time for a new government (or maybe no government).

exerted from
Alex Bone
IN
Civil Disturbance

" Blacklisted News/Secret Historys" by the yippies

In Montgomery County during the fall semester of school over 300 students had been arrested on pot-related charges under former Chief of Police Robert DiGrazia's dope war. Students were arrested for tobacco smoking, for standing near people smoking pot, for having papers or pipes, etc. Finally on Oct. 17 at the Bethesda police station, about 10 students from Walt Whitman High were arrested for peacfully protesting the arrest of a known non-potsmoker.

On Oct. 31 people returned to the same police station, unintimidated by the earlier arrests. By one o'clock about 40 people gathered in front of the police station to protest the use of undercover police, the laws against marijuana and to call for the ousting of DiGrazia.

At about 3:10 a smoke-in broke out across the street. The riot squat came out and ordered people to disperse. The crowd had grown to about 75. The cops charged in as undercover cops in the people's midst carried off 3 people. Then for a half hour the riot squad chased the demonstration through downtown Bethesda. During rush hour, the police fell back and folks returned to continue the smoke-in after about 10 minutes.

At about 3:45, Rupert Yippie and Leatrice Urbanowicz were carried off; her kid, Gabriel Yippie, was confiscated. After the arrest of these supposed

Leatrice and Gabriel—*Froggy Smith*

leaders, the riot squad chased the remaining crowd back through Bethesda again; **most came back to the smoke-in site a second time, and then a third time, on their own.**

The last 10 arrests occurred at 7:00 PM, bringing the total to 27, mostly on charges of loitering and/or disturbing the peace. Other charges included possession and one for concealed weapon for carrying a pocket knife.

About two and a half weeks later, a mounting wave of parents' protests combined with the usual editorial controversy set off by the smoke-in, and Chief diGrazia was sacked. The raids were discontinued, although police are hinting that new raids are set for the spring.

Charges are still pending, however, against Rupert and Leatrice, and no one will forget that police tried to have her child, Gabriel, taken away permanently, and that a judge is still holding that as a threat against further political activities. Unless all charges are dropped immediately (including unconditional freedom for Gabriel) Yippies by the thousands will invade Montgomery County July 3rd.

Bethesda, we will bury you.

OVERTHROW, April, '79

9

MOVE

1977—MOVE has non-violently endured multiple killings of their members since 1970. This includes small children and babies (and an estimated 35 dogs). Women in MOVE who were pregnant, on 2 occasions, were kicked in the stomach and vagina, and on both occasions had miscarriages.

MOVE wanted supporters, relatives, and friends to have their children. But the children were placed in new homes throughout the city, with a gag order concealing their locations. Sandra Davis, who was new in MOVE because of her recent marriage, is one of the prisoners. She too is kept from her baby and children. Some of the children whose locations are known think their parents are dead. The shock is so deep that they cannot talk to their imprisoned parents on the phone. The children are also undergoing haircuts, diet changes and school, all of which are against MOVE's beliefs.

(In 1985—MOVE house bombed by police and 11 people were killed in the fire, 4 of them children.)
From *"Blacklisted News/Secret Histories" by the Yippies*

In Montgomery County during the fall semester of school over 300 students had been arrested on pot related charges under former Chief of Police Robert DiGrazia's dope war. Students were arrested for tobacco smoking, for standing near people smoking pot, for having papers or pipes, etc. Finally on Oct. 17 at the Bethesda police station, about 10 students from Walt Whitman High were arrested for peacefully protesting the arrest of a known non-potsmoker.

On Oct. 31 people returned to the same police station, unintimidated by the earlier arrests. By one o'clock about 40 people gathered in front of the police station to protest the use of undercover police, the laws against marijuana and to call for the outing of DiGrazia.

At about 3:10 a smoke-in broke out across the street. The riot squad came out and ordered people to disperse. The crowd had grown to about 75. The cops charged in as undercover cops in the people's midst carried off 3 people. Then for a half-hour the riot squad chased the demonstrations through downtown Bethesda. During rush hour, the police fell back and folks returned to continue the smoke in after about 10 minutes.

At about 3:45, Rupert Yippie and Leatrice Urbanowicz were carried off; her kid, Gabriel Yippie was confiscated. After the arrest of these supposed leaders, the riot squad chased the remaining crowd back through Bethesda again; most came back to the smoke-in site a second time, on their own.

The last 10 arrests occurred at 7:00 PM, bringing the total to 27, mostly on charges of loitering and/or disturbing the peace. Other charges included possession and one for concealed weapons for carrying a pocket knife.

About two and a half weeks later, a mounting wave of parents' protests combined with the usual editorial controversy set off by the smoke-in and Chief DiGrazia was sacked. The raids were discontinued although police are hinting that new raids are set for the spring.

Charges are still pending, however, against Rupert and Leatrice, and no one will forget that police tried to have her child, Gabriel, take away permanently, and that a judge is still holding that as a threat against further political activities.

Unless all charges are dropped immediately (including unconditional freedom for Gabriel) Yippies by the thousands will invade Montgomery County July 3rd.

Bethesda, we will bury you.
—*OVERTHROW, April, '79*

Baltimore, 1991, Take Back The Night March Against Rape
"Another woman who had her young son with her was arrested and the cops took her son to turn him over to Children's Services."
—Baltimore Newspaper

"I usually try not to dwell on my personal experiences, but in this case it may help to show a real example of the government using children as weapons. Last year I was promoting underground shows each week and putting out my zine in a small city in Arizona. The cops continually tried to have our drug free all ages shows shut down, but they could never bust us for anything. Well as you might have guessed they began to dislike me. One day we had a party with about twenty people at our house. The police illegally entered the place and arrested about a dozen people bringing them to jail. Although they tired to bust us for dealing and drug offences, they could not because basically we were just a few friends drinking together. So they ended up charging us with child neglect because we had a child. Our child had been asleep in her bed for hours, until the police busted in and woke her up. How could we have been neglecting our child by letting her sleep peacefully in her bed. What are any young children doing at midnight? Frankly I saw this as a last ditch effort by the police to gain control over our lives, and bring down upon us as much hardship as possible. Striking at someone through their children is a s low as a man can get and when governments condone it, perhaps it is time for a new government (or maybe no government)."
—*Excerpt from Alex Bone in "Civil Disturbance" zine*

When you are angry, depressed, and/or guilty, there are good reasons why! So-called negative emotions are like physical pain; they let you know what is going on inside of you.

Mothers isolation and total responsability for child's well being

Motherhood is full of impossible behavioral expectations

can lead to insanity and destruction !!!

The truth of the matter is that it is an impossible job for all women as presently defined.

"MOTHERHOOD" SUCKS!

Parents should continue to have ultimate responsibility for their children ,but society has an obligation to integrate parents and children into everyday life ...

CONSUME + DIE

however SOCIETY SUCKS! We have to do it for ourselves, improve our communities on a grass roots level. They say, after all, "It takes a whole village to raise one child"

I don't Think so! There was more I wanted to say but oh well. I got P.M.s. #!@*¢! Geena Davis had a 77,000 $ wedding & I got a 25¢ back of cheetos for my daughter, she's sick and theirs thiis alcohol criple trading bus tokens: this is a memmory.

The Future Generation

february 1997

Issue # 7

inside:

MOTHERHOOD

pirates

welfare reform

prostitute rights

industrial slaughter

industrial revolution

Industrial Mary

Issue Seven

February 1997
Industrial Mary

China Reads a bunch of Goddess books: Summary of what I learned + some thoughts about it.

It has been affirmed that in all countries, from the Euphrates to the Adriatic, the chief divinity was at first in a woman's form. The Goddess figure in human thought is a direct outgrowth of the primacy of the mother in individual experience and also because biological fatherhood was (perhaps) unknown until fairly late in the development of civilization.

When I read of older belief systems (than Judeo-Christianity) I see the creative powers of woman are more honored. When I look around I see more dishonor done to woman than I'd like to see. Especially on the subject of female sexuality in all of its cycles.

Patriarchal Judeo-Christian culture created the diabolization of the female principle. They equated sex with sin. Why did they do that when belief systems before Christianity equated sexual love with the source of life? Clearly for political reasons. Some new guys wanted to be on top. They came to rip down the goddesses' temples and put their own institutions to rule. So they made up stories against the current ones. Patriarchal God wanted to take over the Goddess's powers of fertility; an invading army wanted to turn over the belief systems of the people it wished to conquer. Ishtar, the Goddess of all nourishment, Queen of Heaven, River of Life, Star, had her sexual character belittled by being called "Whore of Babylon, Mother of Harlots" by the Christian writers of history.

The time-honored drama of the death and resurrection of Ishtar's son/lover Tammuz was reworked (as conquering tribes are apt to do) assimilated into the death and resurrected son. The agent of Osiris's resurrection was not the heavenly father, but the Goddess, Isis. The image of her suckling her child Horus under the sacred tree of Hathor became the archetypal model for similar images of the Virgin Mary. Maya Kali — the dancing creatress—danced on the body of her consort, Shiva—who lay in his "dead" phase. It was believed only mother could give birth, rebirth, and new creation of living worlds.

To us now living in a culture that degrades "mother," making the typical television joke over and over again, of the pregnant woman on her way to the hospital to have her child delivered by the male doctor expert but she's stopped by traffic in the backseat of a taxi and the taxi driver gives us that "oh my gosh" look supposed to bring on our ha ha laughter, or the sitcom ice cream eating pregnant woman with her "hormones out of control" and the husband looks at us as he cracks his ha ha pregnant woman joke—do we see the power of creation in pregnancy as awesome as then? Certainly the power of the act of birth is still very apparent but also often tampered with by negative societal influences and practices. But, yes, there is great power and awe in the existence and miracle of life during birth.

So then it makes sense, in a twisted way, that these (now) dead Christian men decided to assimilate potent symbols like the metaphorically uterine blood—call it His, the Redeemers', "the boundless soul-suffering of the heart of God whose blood flows over all Mankind." Their flowery language, however, could not conceal the fact that it is woman's blood that flows over all humanity born of mothers. God borrowed from the Goddess the term "children"—calling his flock, his humans "his children". But in truth he was no father but a manufacturer—he MADE his children. Fucking was no longer important to Creation.

"Man is not of the woman, but woman is of the man"
—Paul

The contempt of female qualities seems to be part of a war like dominant attitude; where creative powers mean less than who can dominate and control them; and the ability to nurture life means less than the ability to take away life.

To hold the female principle in esteem is to treat women with more respect in our society. (Not as a dominator but as an equal. Duh!) Cunt deserves respect! For a while it seemed feminists wanted to get away from being defined by biology (and for good reason) but consider the power of motherhood in a self-respecting, self-determined way. The unique fact of what is female and our choice over how we govern our biology. What each of us gives to the world, in part due to our sexuality.

But for so long, motherhood has been degraded. The liberated woman, Simone de Beauvoir philosophized that with children you are not capable of anything artistic, intellectual, or of pertaining to having freedom; that with a child, you are exploited and made inferior—that it is a better choice not to have children. Yes—but is this good? That our human race was born, not out of original sin but of original exploitation, inequality, and inferiority?

This damages what we are as humans. We should then do everything we can to support mothers and children, with equal rights and with full human needs and freedom, as respected members of society. To free motherhood frees the human race.

The mother-child relationship is the prime relationship of all life—not the "caveman hunter and his prey, that's how civilization began" theme. You know it's true when you remember your early feelings, how prime and important a mother is, your first love. Even the people who were mistreated still remember their early love of her in the beginning, how mother was so important.

"I remember, since I wasn't able to hate my mother, especially when she hurt me viciously, I hated everyone who was alive in this world as viciously as possible."
— Kathy Acker, *Empire of the Senseless*

To support mothers supports children. To support communities supports children. They can not stay healthy in isolation. Mothers need to be mothered. Mothers sometimes need to take the choice not to mother. They need improvements in civil society like we all do. They need help with the children from the fathers, grandmothers, grandfathers, aunts, uncles, cousins, neighbors, and friends, or some combination of the above. This is because they are not completely independent entities.

While sex brings a connection between two people, children bring an interconnection of the whole community.

I think women need a source of united power so they never have to be completely dependent on a male, even in motherhood. I think what is our most significant differences (in this case, as the female sex) should be mostly, also our power and our glory—not our downfall or degradation. Women need power, real power, over women things, and in reality it is women (as a percentage of our society) who do the majority of childcare and romantic relationships can be tempestuous; mothers need back up besides their lovers. In the old days it was the tribe or extended family.

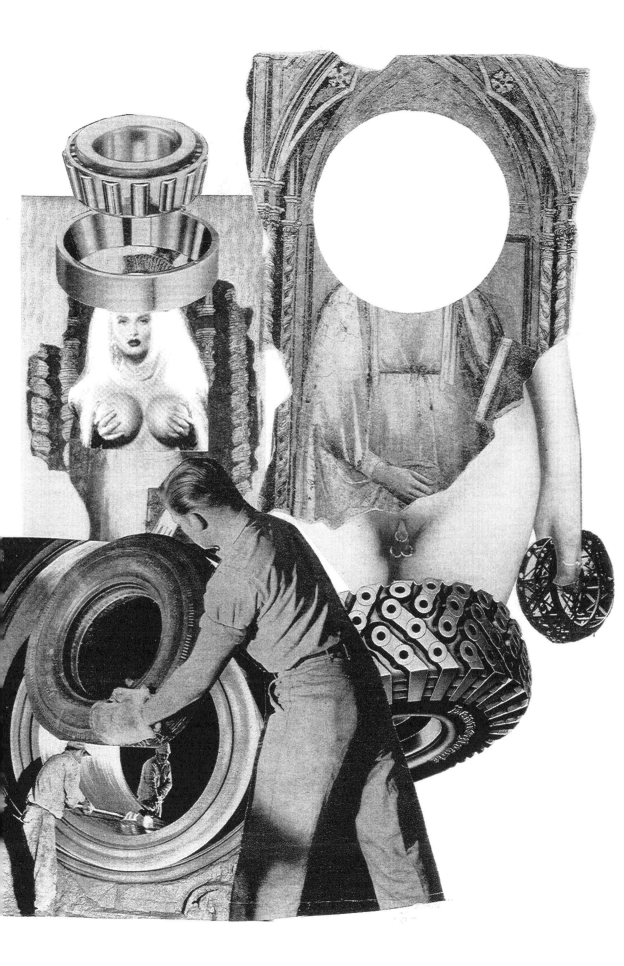

I believe that all the conservative outrage over single mothers is because they can not stand to see a woman who does not belong to a man. The man is the head of the household, disciplinarian, and the paycheck that motherhood is sponsored; made respectable with. Without that, it means you're a poor bitch burden on society. Man needs woman to maintain his control and his lineage and his passed down patriarchal structure. Fatherhood is so sacred to those conservatives but the women still do all the work without the power due to them.

BOOKS READ AND HEAVILY QUOTED AND PLAGIARIZED IN THIS ARTICLE:

When God Was a Woman by Merlin Stone
Chalice and the Blade by Riane Eisler
The Wise Crone by Walker
(I might have left some book out, I can't find my notes, eek, but those were the major books I used)

You can probably feel what I wrote and what I didn't. The last section is all my own, most stuff stolen is goddess facts and theories. I just didn't want to keep putting quotes around everything I wrote in this little "book report" for you

P.S. I don't know everything or say that I did.

Afterthoughts: Fathers + Single Mothers

Personally, I've always felt there was something special about single mothers, in that some of the most beautiful, interesting, strong and complex beings I have ever met were women with a baby on their hip, or a child trailing behind. They were beautiful young women doing interesting things, with this energy, this knowledge—not somehow the image I was raised to know as "mother". (Undesirable, weary, no power—yet always loving and patient) Just, when I looked at some woman I was like "wow'. I wanted to be a single mother. I didn't really think of the word "single" for single was what I had always been, a single independent entity, just plain old me.

I think I wanted to be a single mom, perhaps, for two reasons. (1) I was raised in an environment were most fathers were oppressive and didn't share in the parenting but more in the discipline and financial support. We felt free when

dad was out of the house. (2) It's a complicated world where one has so much to learn growing up and we don't rely on tradition. I felt ready to have a child (because I could count on myself and desired one very much), but I did not feel ready to form a partnership with a man. I hadn't much experience yet—or not enough—with men, sex, relationships, traveling, exploring my world and myself. How was I to be ready to "settle down" with someone? How was I to know who was this one person, who was right, to form this serious commitment with? I believed to have a father in our lives would be an equal 50/50 or not at all. Looking back, working on an equal marriage and raising a child with another person seems way too complicated when I hadn't even enough experiences with relationships yet.

I did a lot of changing and independent moving with myself as the sole decision-maker, when I was a young mom. I thought that all couples fight and I was lucky to not be in such a situation. Looking around me, most of them did. I grew on my own, and in relationships, and learned about love, after I became a mother.

I was a somewhat young 21-year-old in this respect. Yet I felt fully capable to be a mother and wanted to have my child at a younger age rather than an older "settled" one.

Her father and I talked about all these things before her conception. Having a child was my idea and I expressed my ideals and ideas on the subject. There are other factors in this and everything wasn't a big plan. But I remember thinking about freedom and what a free child would be. That this was my child, and whatever would be would be, he would be known as the father and their relationship would be between them, no obligations if we didn't stay together. (A distinct possibility since we had only known each other for a few months.) I left a few months later. It was not a bad thing, we are still open with each other and friends—but looking back, it seems so far away, we were still young and didn't know all this would bring, exactly. (But who does?) She just felt like my child to me: no big deal, no sad story. But maybe I made her father sad, I don't know really, I was far away.

I thought there are biological parents, who one owes their conception to—but parenthood is made by actions, not name alone, and not limited to birth. I believed she wasn't really "my" child either, she was not a possession to be owned but an individual.

Now, nine years later, I see there are critical periods for a father to experience with his child, and will he ever be as bonded and sensitive if he misses pregnancy, birth, infancy, toddlerhood? I thought bonds should be made freely, not on conventional obligation, yet in a way I have made a child that has no father. (Not a participating one, but a loving one to see once in a while so she knows who her father is.) Now suddenly I think about this more.

It is very normal for me to be a single mother. Most of my mama friends are single mothers. As Clover grows up, most of the friends she has made come from single mother families. I think we most believe that all is important is a loving family and family is who you make it. Nobody feels "deprived". I haven't even questioned it. I think variations in the family unit are fine and widely accepted today—there are lots of variations and different reasons for how they came to be.

But now as I think over this more, as over the years I have had friends whom are fathers, real parents not just in name alone. I have seen some really good dads: cool fathers in partnerships that support each other in raising children and include the love to cover all the family members. I've seen some single dads, separated dads, split up co-parents—and I'm more impressed. I think I needed to see these dads as role models of what a father can be. I've seen some sexy family men who are interesting people and also nurturers with responsibilities. I like that wholeness in men as well as women. I guess these happening papa's aren't the image I had of "Father" when I was growing up. They have opened my eyes to the possibilities.

And Damn! It can be a good thing, well the work of being a parent could be a lot easier. It could even be 50% easier. Imagine that for a minute! I do the best I can for my child and that's the bottom line. But my best isn't always good enough, if there were two of me that would be so amazing. A better life perhaps.

The fact is anybody can play a meaningful 50% in her life but keeping a meaningful connection with a child that is not your flesh and blood doesn't happen to the extent I thought it would, in my life.

So all I can say is I think society should totally encourage fatherhood because of all the beautiful fathers (and some of the just OK, funky, not perfect, but good enough dads, too) I have seen. They have something to offer, something good, something to make a better world. Parenthood can make deeper more interesting people out of men as well as women. I value commitment more now that I am 30, I'm also taking a new look at marriage and seeing some beauty and happiness to it where before I was repulsed.

But to narrowly define and institute fatherhood or nuclear families—doesn't sit well with me.

My generation lives in a changing world where they need to re-define some roles for themselves. We need some flexibility. Yet people need to be able to rely and count on each other in Real Ways. This is important. We also need to examine the power dynamics in how we work together.

Now that my child is older, I'm not totally absorbed in the wonder of her and theories of child development anymore. She is part of my life, but I don't feel like talking, or writing, about her all the time. We are two developing people, more independent of each other, and within a committed lifetime relationship.

I am not enough for her, by far. The days of all she needed were her mom's love and attention is long, long gone. Her peers are really important to her. Just a mother alone—is not what she needs. She needs the World!!! (A world of things and people are going to effect her development and life as much and probably more than I am.) I haven't changed my viewpoint at all. This is just one of the few times you will ever hear me say something is hard because I'm a single mom—I'm just exploring that topic. I still believe what is wrong is the decline of the tribe and the community, that's what makes it really hard to be a mother and is a more substantial problem than the decline of the two parent household. Raising children with two parents can still be incredibly hard, alienating, and as unhealthy as anything else. Mothers need support, company, and liberty, regardless of their marital status.

I can't be Mother Mary -
calm and gentle - I'll take in all your ills and concerns unto me
and sooth them - I'll take in your carbon dioxide and breeth back
oxigen like a tree - self sacrificing and loving.

And because I can't be Mary, and mothers should be Mary - I'll
be crucified and you'll see me in tomorro's newspaper.

I wake up to plunge the ever rising tide of my Own Shit,threat-
ening to flow over. I plunge the toleit. I stand in a long line,
shuffeling inch by inch to receive rotten brocoli from the pastors
truck. In line, I rub two pennies in my pocket and contimplate
that phrase about rubbing two coins in your hand - that it actually
stemmed from somewhere.

As I get close to the boxes of vegtables - they run out of milk,
and suddenly I get dizzy. I sit down in the line because my vision
fades out - till I can't see anything but black - close to fainting
- I regain my sight but it's in this weird black and white while my
ears ring. I hold my childs hand - suddenly she comforting me now.

When I tell my boyfriend - he tells me that I'm crazy and he is
mad at me.

I yell alot that day - how I don't want to live with my man - I
want to desert my child - how they all want from me and I can't
give. I need comfort,I need taking care of,I need affection. I have
no-one. I can't,can't,can't give anymore. I've reached that break-
down area.

He wouldn't put her to bed and read a book to her. I couldn't
stand,just couldn't give of myself - a bit more - while ignoring my
own needs.

I said,"I've skinned catfish, (something alien to me but not to
him) so why can't you put her to bed?!

He said,"Thats different - thats a survival skill."

"If No one took care of children, the human
race wouldn't survive",I said. But he didn't
buy it.

That constant tending I do to her. The litle I ever get taken care of or acknowledged. I
don't want to turn into my mother. "I'm not a
robot",I yell. Everything, I yell. Once in a
while I break down and go "crazy". When ever I
insult instead of compliment,need instead of
give, When ever the pressure grows in my head
and I just can not do it.

OH Mary, Mary, Mary Mother of Jesus
        I am not.

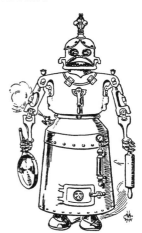

-20-

1997, Ink on paper by China

Anger

As mothers,we try to surpress the anger in us,
some of us even learned how to express anger in "healthy ways"
without it coming out in a terrifying pent up explosion -
by letting it out a little here and there and just
expressing the anger in words that don't neccecarily
take it all out on the child.
But this anger/stress/depression issue is hard.
It's not the devil making us do it.
I know for a fact some support and community
can help alleviate alot of stress.

Who is this Crazy haywire Medusa Mommie ?
The woman screaming at her toddler
and everyone giving her bad looks,nasty looks -
Why is she like that?
Why did maddonna mommie turn so terrifying?
The anger is coming from somewhere -
I wish it could get together with all the other
dissatisfaction in the world
and make a better world.
The craziness is coming cuz somethings wrong -
and I wish we could make something right!

The Anger in us - is coming for a reason.
And so is the despair.
The children shouldn't have to suffer for it.
We as mothers don't want to take this out on our children,
at All!
It is just that we can't escape doing so, we can't escape
our children. We live with them day in and day out.
We are responsible.

It drives us crazy. Angers,a natural emotion after all.

China

*"Our father, who art in heaven—remain there!
We for our part shall remain here on earth; for
earthly life can be quite beautiful."
--Jacques Prevert*

The Future Generation

$2

Generation M.P.

#8

the zine for subculture parents, friends + others.

"Resistance means vigilance in protecting one's own spirit from

the forces that would break it." M.P.

Issue Eight

August 1997
Resistance

Summertime and the livin's easy. (kinda) Out of school—Yay! I like doing stuff and sharing my life with my daughter—I have a job as a waitress a couple days a week and I take her with me on Sunday brunches. She busses tables and helps out. We chat with people and hang out together.

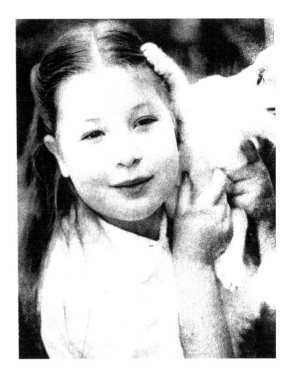

We moved into a house in Hanover, outside the airport—we live with Faith, baby Malila, Gunar, and his brother. Well, there is a bunch of biker dudes always hanging out. We got dogs and cats, 10 acres of woods, ticks and lightening bugs, fleas, low flying planes and motorcycles. Lots of motorcycles.

Malila is cool! She is Clover's li'l spit sister. It's cool living with another mom! It's been a good summer. Clover is nine now and doing real good. We are out of the suburbs and (10 minutes away) into the boonies.

Most of the essays in this issue were written from last year when Clover and I lived with my grandmother for a year and a half—after we left Minneapolis.

Community Or "How Clover And I Came To Live In The Suburbs"

My community is big and diverse, and it includes people that I barely know. I can go to any city and meet the people in my community, I'd recognize them. One could refer to this as the subculture. When I was young and disgruntled and didn't fit into the general culture and society at large, I found out I didn't have to fit into the things I hated. I could live closer to my heart; there were alternatives. And I found that other people felt this way too.

Now, like most parents, I want to raise my child with a sense of my values and what her culture is all about. (Of course I want her to know about many different opinions and choose her own path too). While I do often struggle in my own isolated issues, especially after I became a parent, I continue to find resources and inspiration in the wooly cobweb of interconnection between the radical and artistic.

Like when I took her to the Pow Wow (it's an annual Baltimore spring music and freak festival on a desolated and polluted peninsula) this spring and there is a bunch of bands playing; people I haven't seen for a long time; and kids running around—that's my community. (There's always a lot of picnic blankets, dogs, and kids—more than you will ever see at any other alternative event, at the Pow Wow.) When a guy comes up to my 8-year-old daughter and tells her that he remembers when she was little and would dance up front to his band—that's really sweet. She doesn't remember way back then anymore, but all these people are a part of us. She sees Amanda sing with her most amazing voice and then is told by her how she is growing up beautifully. That means something. It counts. My daughter's spirit gets fed as well as mine by going to such an event.

I've been away for a while, but I still feel like a part of Baltimore. It's not like I know everyone, but I always know someone who knows someone—and sometimes that interconnection feels like it stretches out to points infinite. You know how this works—it's a cobweb. Information is shared, favors are traded, and when your friend knows somebody who knows somebody, your community can get pretty large.

Now we live with my grandmother in the suburbs and my daughter goes to public school. But she could see from the large group around us that day, that others besides her mother have an attitude of respect, tolerance, and acceptance towards what is generally unaccepted in her daily school day—from small things like having a knot in your hair or a rip in your clothes to larger issues like expressing one's individuality or having a broader,

more open mindset. For me it feels like liberty.

When I was at the Doggy Drool show (whose singer is 11 by the way) at a my friends' collectively owned bookstore I saw more kids than I have ever seen at a show in Baltimore before. It was good music, good vibes, and bouncing on the sofa time. All my time in Baltimore, well I've never seen many kids and parents at a show, it just didn't happen. Usually events were later at night, smokey, and I used to be the only parent pretty much, as far as I know, back when I lived here. I really missed not having any peers who were parents in my daily existence. I left this city to look for a better place to raise a child in Minneapolis, just as Uni Ki's family is leaving to move to Portland, for better schools and a healthier more alternative environment that hopefully will be more supportive.

I've made that move to find better for my child a lot of times! But I bottomed out in Minneapolis, and bottomed out hard. It was the poorest I've ever been in the coldest climate. And so I returned to the East Coast. When I left Minneapolis, I felt that sad feeling of seeing all the good things now that you are leaving. Of missing suddenly, even the people I hadn't met, or people I had just seen around. To paraphrase Holy, who paraphrased Jenna: "Cities are like jealous lovers, they are so bad to you but once you want to leave them they give you gifts and act so very nice to you."

Anyway, why do we leave and look for better? Why do our experiences as parents stress us out, burn us out, depress us to the point that we move back in with our families in the conformist suburbs and the conservative small towns, the boondocks that we left? (I'm not just thinking of myself here but also my friend Cari, a very rad single mama, who moved back home to her mother's because of how hard it was to pay the bills on her own.) Well, because our communities are not strong enough to take care of the future generation, its children. It is a loosely tied knot of inspiration and support, but not strong enough to really help you out as a parent. You're on your own with that.

Case in point, to me, is that my child goes to public school. I don't believe in the school system, don't like it, and I have my reasons. But there is nothing in my culture that's going to help me raise and educate my child, it is just me. I personally do not have much support with her, friends or not. In Minneapolis she went to a free school where you had to participate in your own education. It was more aligned with what I believed in and I felt comfortable there. It was run with democratic weekly school meetings and discussions, K-12, and non-compulsory. One problem was that it had very few younger children in it and my daughter didn't like that. She decided the next year (second grade) that she wanted to ride the school bus with the neighborhood kids. That is the year I looked at my life and her experiences: in school, the neighborhood, and at home—and I saw how bad things had gotten. I was simply impoverished, not alternative by any means. I bottomed out, emotionally and financially and couldn't pull myself back up. It was a personal issue—but the point was I felt really alone and life sucked.

I decided to better myself by gaining a trade, to make sure I would never be that powerless again. (I'd been on welfare for years and now that my child was older I could work but found I had no skills.) A lot of people around me found a way to earn a living in an independent subculture way, but I just didn't. I looked at the niches' I'd seen people find, construction, cooking, etc. and I was interested in none of it. So I just tried to think in the most practical way that I ever had. No useless English and Art degrees for me! (I thought following my own interests didn't pay, since they never had before. Also plenty of my friends had English and art degrees and they were poor just like me.) One of my radical mom friends was a nurse and she worked part-time, it seemed to work well for her. It looked like a solid field, and if I had no interest in it—quite to the contrary, I hated Western Medicine, was rarely sick, and not good around sick people or medical emergencies—it seemed the best option. My new motto was a woman has to do what a woman has to do and I was dedicated. I thought of all the ways I could make this cool, I could use this skill no matter where I went in life. I thought I could use my radical ideas and knowledge of holistic medicine within the framework of being a nurse—but that to train in holistic medicine would lend towards my job being elitist, limited, and less financially promising.

Make no mistake, the motivating factor for my choice to become a nurse was poverty and the desire to take care of my daughter. I came up with "Plan Z" after the Landlord told me he was going to evict us for all the back rent we hadn't paid; but really I had known for a while that I had to leave. I had to leave my alcoholic boyfriend, if not for my sake then for hers. He was really at the heart of this problem, the one that never financially contributed his part and basically had been living off me for the last two years. I got down to barely ever having much food most days of the month, going to food banks and stuff, with no phone, no bus fair, often not enough money to buy the most essential things. There was gunfire on the streets that weren't safe to play on, verbal conflict in the school halls and at home; my daughter was developing a nervous twitch in her eye.

So I left him and enrolled myself in nursing school, and I really dig it. I live with my grandmother rent-free; she has given me the support and peace to be a person who can accomplish more in life, to be a happier person, not totally burnt out and stressed. My dad bought me a car, a necessity for life in the suburbs. It's weird to be back after I haven't lived in the suburbs since I was a teen—with the event of commonplace MTV fashion, now kids complement my artificially bright colored hair, nose-ring, ripped jeans and boots (same old look to me) more often then they laugh at me. Even the bag boys at grocery stores are pierced these days. It's really strange how things change. I remember a time when people would stop their cars and try to beat us up for looking weird. Yell hostile things and laugh hysterically, or pull their children to their sides in fright. Looks aren't very important to me anymore, or I don't think how a person looks signifies all too much. Truthfully, it's become meaningless. These days just because you look different, doesn't mean you actually are. I'm a live and let live, relaxed and polite kind of person. Still, how I look is completely different than how any of the other parents look like in the suburbs where we live.

I'm an "A" student now, ha ha, after dropping out of school at age 15. I've always believed learning is self-motivated and admired people more who did something on their own. I have always valued education but not schools. Entering college I saw my assumptions were mostly correct. While some people use school for their own means, the majority of young people there have never been out on their own and are going to school because they believe they have to be there, their parents want them to do it, and they don't have the guts to do any differently. So their actions are motivated for grades and not interest; and they get by with the least effort possible or jump through hoops to get the high marks. These are not independent interesting people.

School for me was an alien place, but since I'm good at book learning I knew I would do fine. I just needed to get a practical trade. But I found out I had a love and aptitude for science, the Latin, the poetical witchy learning of how the body functions. Studying human anatomy and physiology reminded me of my old boyfriend's gory art—he was into horror. It's just cool.

But anyway, the point of all this, is my place in the community. In order to get support and peace so I could accomplish what I wanted—I took Plan Z, my last option, and moved in with family. There really weren't that many options. I was about to turn 30 when I decided to "play it straight", to do what my parents had always told me I should and merge that with my normal concerns and way of life.

It all turned out good and it's a long story really. But, what I'm saying, our subculture isn't strong enough to offer support with raising children so therefore Clover and I are in the grips of stuff more mainstream. I live how I am, no different, because I have no choice. And we are making the best of this because I am struggling and I believe life is a struggle. There is a saying that brought me comfort: Ideals are like stars, you can't reach them but you can navigate by them.

I want to do my little part to increase connections in my community by putting out this zine for subculture parents. As parents, we can be isolated and have a hard time. The mainstream is everywhere. But I want to build the things I believe in! A lot of it is personal. What do you have personally going on for you? I guess I didn't have a lot. But don't you think a lot of it is political too? (About what sucks in your life.) We are all in this together. I want to hear what's going on with you!

Life In The Suburbs: Ponytails And Popularity

I don't pick on people—it's hard for me to understand it. I was a shy child. I don't know how to fight back; how to be aggressive. I avoid stuff, trying to work on what I have inside and not care what "they" say. I moved a lot as a kid, and I didn't have a big family—just like my daughter— but I was less social.

As a pre-schooler, my daughter was so robust, strong, brave, self-expressive, and socially adept. She could make friends anywhere we went. I was so proud of her for doing all the things I could never do as a child. She was a playground queen!

But that was the years before school started. Before kindergarten. Before I had one very dominant boyfriend. Now things have changed and I wonder …would she still be as strong if I hadn't made some of the choices that I did?

Some pain and complexity is part of growing up. How much can be avoided? But I worry that the changes I brought her through took away some of her self-esteem and courage. She's still so young but at age 9, the unselfconscious freedom of girlhood seems to be behind her. I want to nurture her freedom, her confidence, her security, but the seeds of doubt and fear have been planted. She is vulnerable. She cares too much. Some people don't like her. School nurtures these negative experiences. Beautiful people are picked on. Everybody gets picked on, it seems.

I tell her stories about all the movie stars and all the cool people who were called geeks or called ugly. Neve Campbell had to eat lunch all alone— declared the ugliest girl in school! John Goodman couldn't play outside because of all the bullies. He spent his time watching TV and reading comic books.

My daughter knows my feelings about equality, individuality, and body image: Chubby is fine, tall is fine, we are all different; self-hatred is not fine, being mean to other people for how they look is not fine. She rebels when my grandmother tells her she'll get fat if she eats to many graham crackers. She yells, "I want to get fat! Ha ha!"

I tell my daughter that she's beautiful—like Xena the Warrior Princess in build. She's not skinny, that's all. She is beautiful. We are all beautiful in our own ways.

But when people pick on you, you need someone besides your mother to tell you that you're alright. I tell her everybody feels bad about themselves sometimes. During teenagehood she might go through an ugly duck phase as her body fills out into a swan—it's natural. Lots of kids that are different grow up to be artists and fabulous people.

Still, she doesn't want to be different. She wants to be popular. What's popular? I don't understand the world, I say. You just need two or three good friends. Everything and everyone has someone who doesn't like them. I had a cousin who didn't like chocolate.

But she is sensitive. At this stage in her life, peers are so important. We all need to feel a sense of belonging. Who wants to be made fun of and not included?

But weight! Weight is an issue I want to talk about—I felt strongly about it before I ever knew she would have to deal with this. I felt strongly about it because I am "skinny" in a family of "overweight" women. My grandmother told me as a child to watch what I ate; if I kept eating so much, I would get fat. Obvious to me, since I never did, is my body type is due to genetics, the metabolism I inherited from my dad's side of the family—since I eat a lot and can't gain weight even when I want to. I've seen my mom and her sisters go through sporadic dieting for the last 30 years and I've seen a lot of meanness and fat-phobia. I've seen how people can develop problems with their relationship to food—restriction, compulsion, guilt, fixation. The binge and purge morality where you fear your own desires and lose your natural sense of balance. I've seen the way people can feel bad about themselves, not even let themselves wear pretty clothes until they "lose the weight."

My mom's weight looks nice on her. She's voluptuous. But yeesh, she got picked on for being overweight even back in her twenties when she was just 5 or 10 pounds over the ideal. And yeesh! What about her other attributes? And damn, I hate those Jenny Craig commercials. NO, being skinnier will not bring you happiness, men, and better jobs!

No matter who we are, we have to struggle with our own bad days and troubles. And beauty is not a surface level thing. Beautiful people come in all shapes and sizes. This fixation on weight is ridiculous. A pretty face or eyes can count for more. I mean, I just don't understand why a little belly on a beautiful young girl makes her feel ugly and fat—when it's a nice belly dancer's belly. What's the deal? The more a person feels free to be themselves, the prettier they are.

But the majority of 9-year-old girls actually think they are overweight! Nine-year-olds! Clover tells me that some of her friends wish they were skinny like me—but I'm extremely tall and lanky. When I was growing up, skinny was not a good thing; we wanted to be more "womanly." I like how my body is now, but hey, I'm kinda freaky. Anyway, the point is that most of us are not happy with our bodies and there are so many eating disorders going on with teenagers. We know this! So how dare we put this crap on our young girls— that they should watch their weight!

These are the suburbs. We moved here after one down-and-out urban winter where we had nothing to eat but beans and rice. We went to food pantries. Our food stamps for a mom and kid were stretched to include my boyfriend. So I took plan Z: to go to college was the only way I knew I would get family support. I was tired out and needed refuge. We moved in with my grandmother.

So, we came from an environment of food shortage, an environment that was unsafe—gunfire on the streets and bullies— to an affluent suburban one where it's safe and food is plentiful. We even have a car to bring the food home in. But suddenly everyone is hyper-conscious of eating too much.

My grandmother, because of her own lifetime fixation that thin is good, that cake and cookies and "goodies" are divine, but that fat is disgusting, says, "Here, have a cookie. Now don't eat too much. Oh we are bad, we ate too much!" Because of her lifetime of watching her own weight and that of her three daughters, she feels it's perfectly fine to tell my daughter to "loose that tummy." She pinches an inch on her.

It makes me so angry! I have a hard time dealing with the situation, however, since my grandmother took me into her house and she is a respected matriarch. So I tell Clover it's wrong for someone to pinch your belly and tell you to get rid of it. That she never has to get rid of any part of herself. We were not meant to be Barbies.

I explain to Clover, this is a chain of self-hating behavior that is passed down in this family. I try to talk to my grandmother about weight and eating disorders. But still, I see my daughter then pinch the inch around her waist and look at it sadly.

We women pass this down through generations. A skinny blond popular girl spent the night one night. I heard her speak vehemently against fat. I wondered why she would be concerned about it. "Oh, I Hate fat," she said. When her mother picked her up, I saw she was pretty and chubby I wondered—is the mom, through her own self hating remarks, teaching her child that fat is bad?

When my mother talks of dieting, I reminded her that she is a role model to her grandchild; to watch what she says; not to imply any disgust toward herself. Clover thinks of her grandmother's body as a soft comforting one to hug.

My daughter looks at me in the dressing room. "Oh, you are so thin," she says. "You are so beautiful." I laugh and say, "Thank you, I feel beautiful, but not everybody would think that of me." I tell her how everyone made fun of me when I was in Junior High School, I tell her how terrible I felt. We talk, I tell her pro-giant stuff. I tell her it was my chubby friend who got all the positive attention when I was in school. We talk about how it felt for me to develop late and how it feels for her to be developing early. These are our conversations. A lot of it she takes to heart 'cuz I practice what I preach. Sometimes she just says I talk too much.

Clover has made a new friend today, an 11-year-old on a diet. She tells me she barely eats and can only eat nonfat things. She is a very beautiful girl of medium build who used to be thicker. She is completely serious about her diet and tells me how many steps it takes to loose a calorie as we walk around the zoo. She exercises to loose weight. I tell her that her body is not even done growing yet, that she should just eat how much her body tells her too. Instead of dieting, I say, she could focus on eating healthy foods. I make her a stir-fry and a smoothie, which she enjoys very much. I tell her that most women do feel bad about some part of their body, so why fall into it and be so self-criticizing? Besides, I said, they are all beautiful. The girls smiled.

Roller Skating Girl

I'm sitting here with tears in my eyes
trying hard to not let them start dripping.

Why am I so sentimental? —
In the Laurel rolling skating rink, with the walls painted mustard
and the little poodle running around the edges of the rink
the DJ playing Donna Lewis "for Clover" she dedicates the song

I watch my daughter roller-skate in her shimmering skirt
and I'm seeing this little light starting to shine
she's pulling out her dance moves, tenuously
skating to the music

She looks so pretty—but she is all held back inside
afraid when a new friend shows up with someone else
afraid to be left out and get her feelings hurt.
speeding girls, her age, but smaller,
twirl around, smooth, fast with grace.

I watch her be taught figure skating: how to jump, how to spin
for the first time in steps—
sometimes she just stands there, sometimes
she follows the steps, around and up on one foot—
learning, as the other girls fly, that she wanted to be with
but I see she is learning and committed—and
I'm like (inside) Don't give up, you're gonna get it!
I'm like—don't be afraid, just go hang out with the people you want to
don't be all insecure inside. So tied up, you can't get out.
She's a sensitive person.

She's alone on the floor and I see her dance to her song
I see some of her lessons, grace, and a bit of her self come out.
It's the music. It's this white trash retro poodle skating rink,
it's the DJ, and the song. It's the children and all the people,
they are so sweet—and the good teacher
that is making me tear up.

She's not having a lot of support, no hand to hold or friend,
she's on her own teetering self confidence. While I know
she is stronger and braver than that. At home, when she dances,
she dances wildly, beautifully, fluid, free.
The dances she does here are held back, stiff recreations.
I see my daughter's held back spirit—while
she puts scarves in her hair, pretty skating outfits, and nylons on,
her inner beauty is held more in. Shyness they call it.
fear

She looks at the quick popular girls and misses out
on the opportunities to make friends with other
girls who are more at her level—misses the
opportunities to make friends. Her natural friendliness—
she does not feel secure but fear. She is not at ease—
to make the first move, to speak up.
They are shy too, don't make the first move either

Then the DJ dedicates her favorite song to her and she dances
She puts up one leg—puts out her hand—
and starts to fly.
I'm so sappy, I cried on her first day of kindergarten,
I cried when she got her award at the YMCA tiny tot gymnastic
ceremony—but I never let anyone see.

I'm seeing my daughter, with fresher eyes—
I'm seeing the sentimental pop music she likes—
romantic, and the new beauty she is becoming,
as she flies around
and grows up in the cracks of the cement.

You have to be brave,
to Love, to Care, to Try, to Be
and not let the old house fill up with spiders

She dances nonstop. They play the Spice Girls.
The three really bold good figure dancing girls
make up these dances spontaneously —
putting on a really good show, like what
you see on TV in ice skating
they are quite dramatic—
then they skate fast, fast, and tough
and hard to see like vampires through the
night. (they will let no boy beat them in the speed skating
competition, this is their place and they excel)
Slowly she edges closer to them,
the self confident ones. She dares to do a bit of
a dance with them, then they skate off and leave her.
She doesn't want to try again, to bother them.
She talks to one girl by the snack bar.
Their mothers are in skating competitions. The more she learns,
the more they will like her. They like good skaters.

They wave goodbye to her when we leave.
I had to get her attention—"see, they are
waving", she waves back, the damn is broken,
there is a flood of waving.

I think I am getting closer,
to getting to be their friends,
perhaps one day,
She says.

Poem

My great grandmother was an authoritarian,
no need to yell when you can spank.
My grandmother ruled by guilt,
and made them do the right thing.
But I don't believe parents are always right
I don't believe I'm at the top
I don't believe in hierarchy.
Maybe you got to have a tribe in order
to be free equal people.
cuz between you and me
I yell a lot
I yell and go crazy
I yell cuz you drive me crazy.
but I don't believe you are wrong
and I am right
and you should do whatever I say.
I just don't believe that.
I do believe you are a person
I can't hit you, or control you—
Without a conscience like it's my god given right.
Parenting, and real problems, that's where it's at—
tell me how to get anarchy like that—
speak to me - practical common sense.
Maybe you need a tribe to grow a child that free
cuz we teach by modeling—monkey see, monkey do—
I wish my child could see more anarchy in the u.s.a

Good Enough Mothers

If you can work on it—try to be better or figure out the problem or make a change—do it. If you can't fix it—and you are doing your best—then you are doing the best you can in the present situation—and that is all you can do. Don't feel guilty. Forgive yourself, and forgive your child, for human error. Apologize, make a fresh start. Don't feel guilty for not being perfect, for caring about your own needs, and for being a little selfish sometimes. Taking care of yourself is what your child ultimately needs you to do, not total self-sacrifice. (Although motherhood does require some self-sacrifice and it's hard to know where to draw the line.) You can't control the whole world. You are doing an important task—a hard job with not much thanks. So we thank you! Keep up the good work. You kept your child alive for another day, hurray!

I know there is no end-of-shift beer in this job of motherhood—no fellow employees to commiserate with and no getting off after 5 p.m. No girl talk between tasks and no recognition of the quality of your work. But there should be—shouldn't there? So this is the zine for you!

Monique

I walked into a little party at 3 am and sat down. I looked across the room and saw a beautiful butterfly of a woman. She was very striking in that she was dressed in such bright colored clothing, platform heels, striped dreads, with a delicate crescent shaped bone in her nose and in her ears, and she was very very pregnant. She was sucking her thumb and waving at me. So I came over and engaged in conversation. Her name was Monique and she invited me to see the cocoons she made one day.

Four months later, my daughter and I finally got a chance to see her cocoons, and her and Per's baby: Star. Monique makes her own paper by taking natural substances such as reeds or cornhusks and boiling them in water for many hours. Then she steps on the fibers, to mash them with her feet. She uses her homemade paper to cover structures made out of branches - cocoons. She makes masks of her face with this paper and incorporates them into the structures or leaves them as masks with teeth and hair added. Her bed is within a giant cocoon. Her artwork is incredibly beautiful —her apartment feels like a forest with these organic primal tribal looking creations. She even made the cup she was drinking out of from pottery.

I was surprised to find out this light airy and mystical abode was described as Satanic by a nurse who did a home visit from the birthing center. The nurse, a devout Christian, had written a report on them, saying they had Satanic artwork and dressed in black, even their windows were covered in black, and their child should be taken from them. This is strange and untrue, Monique and Per favor bright colors. (The midwife dismissed the nurse's report.)

The more I talked to her, I saw how her family was being judged for superficial things and not by the loving caring way they were raising their child. She said as new parents sometimes they had their doubts and insecurities but instead of receiving support from her mother they were criticized. Her mother cared a lot about money and good credit; she thought now that Monique was a parent she should act and dress "normal" and pursue a good job. Her mother made "jokes" about taking their child away from them.

Another way that Monique, who seems to me strong and self confident, was being undermined as a strong and confident mother, was by the medical profession. Once when she took Star to the doctor for a cold, he probed ears in a rough way and made her scream, said she had an ear infection and gave her antibiotics. Monique felt something was wrong with this assessment and went to another doctor two days later, who said the baby's ears were not infected. Another time, a doctor was doing all kinds of things to Star and gave her a vaccination before Monique had a thought or choice. It was so out of her hands and she felt intimidated by the doctor. Doctors can tell her the wrong thing, even lie to her in fact ad she does not have the information to understand and make a good decision. She does not like going to the doctors when they bamboozle her like this. A mother deserves to make an informed choice without a doctor overwhelming her with his quick moves and air of authority.

We talked of what we don't like about the school system. She says that when kids say the Pledge of Allegiance in school it reminds her of Hitler Youth or something. Also she told me that a lot of the mean and violent ways of treating children are very American; it's better in Europe. She and Per are going back to Europe, to travel.

Per is from Norway and very interesting. He is a Lap and is interested in learning more about his heritage. Laps remind me a lot of American Indians because the government outlawed their language and songs, and took their children away to schools at one point in history, as they were trying to assimilate them and kill their culture. Their TV shows stereotype and makes fun of Laps. They live way up North, where there are reindeers.

I think Per and Monique plan on staying travelers for a while and showing their child the world. Monique says she will send me her diary of "traveling with baby" for the zine! I am looking forward to that.

Talking to her I saw the troubles people can put on you for being a free spirit or simply looking different or being artistic. And how vulnerable you can be as a parent, on top of that! The goal of this zine is to spread information and support within this loosely based tribe of ours. Monique and Per are really life positive people and one sweet family. I thank them for all their hard work as parents to give this world a beautiful new being and I wish them luck as they journey on in the changes that are taking place within them as they embark on this new part of their lives, parenthood.

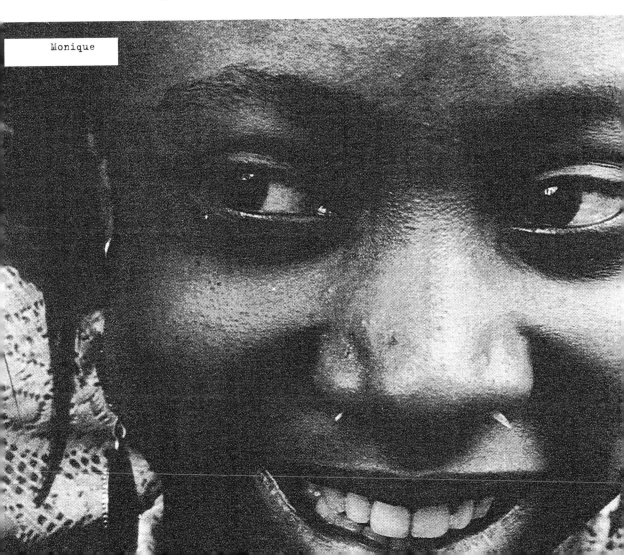

Monique

Fiction

I was reading in the introduction of a collection of African American Folk Tales, how the storytellers would make up their own tales, or take well known stories and alter them to fit their own experiences. I love that phrase. The word "alter" reminds me of sewing, thread and needle, taking in or letting it out a seam in a garment. Making it fit just right to your own measurements. Not factory produced, off the racks at K-mart, and not trying to get your unique form into a few standard sizes.

Our imagination as a country and our stories for our children are pretty mass-produced. Sold with a television jingle or a fast food kids toy. I like the idea of making up our own stories, handing down folk stories, and altering them, a lot better.

I mean, for instance, once I was part of a group of people who were painting a mural on the wall in a park festival in Minneapolis. A young boy asked me if I would paint a figure for him (a well-known action figure from the mass media) and I said I would. So as I painted, I asked him questions, on what does this character look like and how I should paint him. When I got to skin color and asked him what color is he, the boy replied, "White". But then he thought for a moment: "Could you paint him black?" Sure I said. Even in the simple act of having someone else paint a commercial character, I felt the boy had the power to interact with what was being made, to have choices, and to select the color of his own skin color. I believe that when we create something in fiction, it helps us to create something in fact. To realize you don't have to accept the script you are given, you can alter it to fit. You can paint your own truths into the picture.

When my daughter's friend complained there was no Cat Woman at the toy store; no female X-figure action figures either, she could only find the male action figures from the movies she watched, it gave me the idea to sew her a Cat Woman rag doll for her birthday. And she was very happy with my present! It feels so good to make something yourself and I realized the possibilities of what I could make with thread and needle were boundless! I could make a Sigourney Weaver (in *Aliens*) rag doll, I could sew any character from any cool fairy tale! Clover has picked up on this too and modifies her Barbie dolls. She turned one into Tank Girl. When she sees something she likes, 5 times out of 10 she will say: "Can we make that!" (Not buy it.)

As many people as there are is as many different ways there are to modify something with the imagination and materials you have on hand. I learned when I was teaching people how to sew in my rag doll workshop—that you just can't go wrong! Everybody thinks up something unique from each other and just the fact it is hand made makes each doll come out different than each other.

When I read stories with my daughter, sometimes we discuss them. What we think of the story and why we think that. I told Clover she could rewrite a story to come out the way she wished it would. She thought that Cinderella should rebel from doing all the work for her mean stepsisters and throw down her feather duster. So we collaborated on making own little story, taking turns with each page, one of us created the story line and the other the text. It was really fun! We did a whole series of "tuff" girl fairy tales. My mother always drew pictures with me and it comes naturally for me to draw pictures with my daughter. It's a pleasant way to pass the time and you don't have to be a great artist. Drawing is awesome!

Imagination is not meant to be a consumer product or just part of the Disney monopoly. Imagination is for everyone. Storytelling while amusing, is also a way to pass down timeless human dilemmas and messages. There is a lot of truth in make-believe, and a lot of make-believe in truth.

Me

Hope

and

Dream

"Nobody can stop you if you think you are unstoppable. No System, No man, No Government. No Nothing."

—Roseanne

Faith as a child in Baltimore

Clover

Clover

China

The Future Generation

the zine for subculture parents, kids, friends & others

·ALL THE ARMS WE NEED·

issue # 9

the 1996 Federal welfare reform law cut Federal support by $7 billion annually - an amount almost equal to the yearly **government subsidies** given to U.S. **weapons** manufacturers

cont. ▶

Welfare Mothers make better LOVERS

Inside; critique of consumer society, the educational system, welfare reform and talk about living more fully alive from the the cradle to the grave ... & more!

Dollarocracy

Corporations are holding us hostage to the tyranny of the bottom line. Corporations influence laws, nations, and wars. Corporations are not accountable to the communities they operate in. More and more of the earth's resources are being held in less and less people's hands. The rich are getting richer. The poor are getting poorer. The planet is getting wrecked. (Read *World Scientist's Warning to Humanity*.) The world can't continue this way! 70% of the people living in absolute poverty are women. U.S. corporations get welfare too, annual government subsidies of 85 billion dollars! Business as usual is destroying the world. Television might tell you to hate welfare moms—but welfare moms are telling you to shoot your TV. We need sustainable lifestyles, not more poverty!

Welfare Mothers Make Better Lovers

"The 1996 Federal Welfare Reform law cut Federal support by $7 billion annually — an amount almost equal to the yearly government subsidies given to U. S. weapons manufactures."

— *Hip Mama*

"America's role as arms supermarket to the world was the #1 under reported news story of 1997, according to the 22nd annual survey by the media watch program Project Censored. In These Times Aug. 11 story: "Guns "R" Us" reported that America's share of the global arms market has grown from 16% to 63% in the last 10 year. The Clinton administration thinks this is a boon to the U.S. economy. The last 5 times that U.S. troops were sent into conflict— the American forces have faced adversaries that previously received U.S. weapons, military technology, or training."

—*San Francisco Bay Guardian, 3/25/97*

When you look at how the Government spends our tax money, you see that there is never enough for children's needs and improving civil society, but always enough for stuff like wars, or corporate profit making ventures.

When I say, "Welfare mothers make better lovers" its just to have fun, to grab your attention. Welfare mothers have been so slandered in the press —so I'm just saying, I'm not ashamed that I am an economically-disadvantaged-single-parent-head-of-the-householder-as-a-group-using-One-Percent-of-the-tax-budget. (The lover on the cover is me—China Doll.) I used the 280 dollars to pay for my rent and bills and wind up 20 dollars short on that. Welfare usually just about pays your rent. In states where the cash assistance is higher, the food stamps are higher—so I got a nice 200 dollars in food stamps. (I received $80 dollars in food stamps in California where my cash grant was $500 and my rent for a bedroom, bathroom, and kitchen was $400.) This leaves you with no money for let's say, toilet paper, bus fare, a phone, entertainment, etc. Having no money for anything but almost and not quite covering rent and food is the biggest incentive for getting off welfare. However welfare was a safety net that would let you raise your own child and not be dependent on a bad situation without an alternative, as disagreeable that alternative seems to most people.

I'm not saying I deserve welfare. But I do feel I deserve a productive life and a part in society that cares about the health and safety of its members. We need cooperation to provide for the young and old members of society. As of now, the only legit way to raise children is with a husband supporting you; with you working while your child is in daycare; or with some partnership with your significant other, friends, or employer. What if you don't have some cool helping partnership in your life? What if you want to raise your own child, mother and nurse it and you don't have a husband? What if there are problems in the concept of the nuclear family? What if society is not very flexible in providing for the needs of mothers? Purely economically speaking—isn't investing in families as important to the outcome of society as investing in business? Purely speaking of facts and figures—money is a funny thing—why is the yearly cost of eliminating poverty estimated to be about 55 billion dollars and the Saving & Loans bail out is running anywhere from 160 to 500 billion dollars? Why are you not supposed to have children if you don't have enough money, yet the total financial wealth of the bottom 80% of U.S. citizens is 6% (*Labor Research Association/ Z Magazine*)! There is some pretty serious class inequalities here to say poor people don't have the right to have children. That poor people only have the right to be hired to look after the children with parents who have money.

Economically speaking, why do the poor have to shoulder the brunt of cut backs for the sake of the economy and tax payers when the top 10% of Americans own 80% of the federal government's debt? How can mothers and human needs that are not measured in dollars and cents compete to exist in a world where everything revolves around money? For mothering a child is hard

work, it is a human endeavor, is time consuming and is unpaid. For women, as a group, do not have anywhere near amount the money as men as a group. Not everything we do in a culture is about money. Just because mothers don't get paid doesn't mean they are not working. Like Lucinda Marshall so wittily put it in *Hip Mama* #15: "Moms are like CEO's whose job description includes: Chef, Transportation Director, Residential property manager, Chief financial officer, Triage Nurse, Sanitation Director, Activities Coordinator, Education Director, and Procurement Specialist. Mother's work involves regular over time and they are on call 24 hours a day, but they receive no salary!"

The truth is that many mothers, who are not poor, would be poor if their husbands left them. They call that male subsidized childcare. A little while back it was even more so, a woman would be scared to leave; more vulnerable to being under the control of her husband because of that reason. Now I know men would not like to be in that position, of many of them being poor single parents if they had no wife. Theoretically, welfare wants to return the financial obligation to the fathers, but in actual practice they are pulling assistance and putting the sole burden on the mothers wage-earning capacities with their children in daycare. (Actually, who knows who they want to return the financial obligation to since not all welfare mamas are going to be able to find jobs with the statistics of available employment.) Welfare reform idealizes the nuclear family and downplays the idea of community responsibility.

This is a subject about women—welfare reform. A lot of men don't realize how hard mothering a child is until they have to take over 24/7, you know. And I understand that because it's hard to know what life is like if you aren't walking in those shoes. But these men (politicians and commentators) are so obnoxious about their remarks on a life that they haven't lived! It is a woman issue. Why do we women always have to be so personally scrutinized about everything? I am just an individual living my life but because I was a woman and could conceive life, my life was more complicated and I'm still trying to figure that out —the meaning of life. Aren't we all? Living as a woman with a child, I see life is about cooperation. Everyone needs someone's help. Real help is a beneficial thing, it doesn't hurt one's pride in one's self. While we all need support and connection with other people, we all still need our own independence of spirit and to be respected.

Welfare reform paints already struggling mothers as leaches on the system and inferior parents. If the issue is only about money, I say come on! It's time to really talk about our economic system! Why is the ratio of an average corporate executive's salary to that of a blue-collar worker in 1980: 25 to 1? Why do we put up with so much corruption and why is money the most important factor in America?

We have to hold with worth, the dignity, liberty, and equality of each of our citizens if we are to be a democratic nation. Money has blinded us to the fact that the richness of each country is its people and its future is its children. We all do affect each other; no one is an island. We do not need more jails, more correction, and more protection from our neighbors but an increase in improving our civil society and our quality of life. Increased welfare checks isn't going to buy this for us. But slandering welfare mothers, cutting out welfare as punishment for those who "abused the system" isn't going to achieve this either. All it's going to do is further the desperation of some people, lessen the security of some children, and make some other people feel good that they can blow off steam giving just deserts and snubbing their nose at those lazy poor that are not as good as they are.

Clover at 9

Clover cut her hair for her 10th birthday

I'm scared to think of the results upon the lives of those effected by welfare reform. The women who will be pushed into a market flooded by people seeking to survive on minimum wage jobs; and the children who will go needy. Yes we all need to take care of each other independently from government assistance. But by creating and propagating horrendous justifications for welfare reform and slanderous myths about welfare recipients, we are not working towards that. It is basically starting a philosophy that for the poor single mom—daycare should be the norm; and the underlying message to us all is that mothering a child is not an important job, not a hard job, and not as valid as a job which is paid. But it is a terribly hard, overwhelming, demanding, and exhausting job that will suck the marrow right out of your bones at times, especially when you are alone and poor. It is an important job.

Welfare reform is forwarding a philosophy that blames the poorest of the poor, leaves them more vulnerable to predators, while it reinforces survival of the fittest and keeps the hard working blue collars blame off corporate America. All it has achieved is to take away the rent and food money from some isolated families that were struggling to survive in a state of crisis and instead used the money to make and give away weapons for the profit of weapon manufacturers. Nobody has saved any money here. No solutions have been found.

Everything Is Connected

I was reading critical thoughts on education and came across this quote by John Holt: "What I want for all people is a life worth living and work worth doing …not just, or not even, something called 'a better education.'"

I'm seeing a common thread running through my reading on how to increase the liberty of my child and myself, and that is to increase the liberty of everyone. After all, as I thought to myself when I was a young mom reading manuals on how to better raise a child: How can I raise a free child if I am not a free woman? And how can I be a free woman if I am not living in a free environment?

At the core of those who wanted to escape the jail of school, or the jail of being a '70s housewife—was not a desire just to escape outside of their own confinement into another larger prison, but the desire to change everything. Just like the Black Panthers, they didn't just want a piece of the pie. No they wanted to throw that whole corrupt pie out. Make a new pie.

Life is dependent on us all, young and old. Life is a woven tapestry, a balance between negative and positive forces. Life is a creative destructive ever-changing process. Yes, we have human flaws, we all have our bad sides; life has it trials and tribulations. But the corruption that is magnified by the few who hold too much power (gangsters, legit or not) over our lives is out of balance, it is too much! We humans are deserving of more Love, more Trust, more Respect, and more Self-determination than that! The paranoid negative controlling beliefs of those in authority really harms the masses.

When I read a book on Gandhi's civil change tactics, methods, and results, I really was impressed with what nonviolence was about and the change it made. You had to risk your life, it wasn't "sissy" stuff, it was deep and transforming. I'm not ready to risk my life for any revolution at this point. But I understood his beliefs in a flash, it was a lot like all the ways I have learned to act with my child. All about respecting the individuals reality and knowing you don't know it the best but completely acting on your principles by being non-compliant in things you think are wrong; trying to show and convince other people of your convictions without forcing them by violent threat to do it your way. All the world deserves the love and respect I have for my own child, the new ways I've found in psychology and techniques and politics and understand and dealing with this flesh and blood will of her own and my responsibility to raise.

This might not sound as cool as armed revolution, but I am a lover and I love this world. I will extend to others and to myself the patience and understanding like I do to my own child. I also understand my need to protect myself from all that will abuse me, even take advantage of me in the name of love. You need more than to be "nice" in this world. I will defend myself, and I will restrain myself to give those less powerful than me the respect that I myself would want.

It is a sign of strength to be gentle, to hold a dialogue with children and not to break their will to yours, to listen to them. People think being strong means getting your way, bossing around others to do what you want them to do out of fear, but I think that is detestable. Is it not better to convince someone that your way is better by reason? Is it not better to show by example that the strong do not have the right to control the weak because of their superior size? Is it not better to show kids how to treat people with respect and compassion, by treating them with respect and compassion? To teach them how to get along socially, not just be ordered around or order around others? To give self esteem by merely never taking it away?

Sexism exists everywhere

"

. . .

Everybody today is oppressed. Everybody is depressed and deformed by the capitalist society as a whole. I can't say that women are any nicer than the men. You still have the competition and the jealousy. Every attitude you have in capitalist society is found in some men as well as some women. I've seen so many macho women. "I'm not gonna be a weak woman. I'm gonna be different. I'm gonna be a man." It's like they're searching for what to be so they take on male characteristics. ohh...macho! I saw this alot in Berlin. There's this anti-kid stuff. There are certain women who say, "I'm not gonna be oppresses as a woman; therefore I'm not gonna have children." The main way I see women are oppressed is through children and childbirth. Especially during pregnancy. They're totally abandoned. Totally by themselves. No support at all. To me the women's issue above all other issues is child rearing,pregnancy, and childbirth. And women who want to liberate themselves by rejecting that part of their life is one thing but to reject that as a whole for all women is to reject women's struggles and to become a man and take on a man's life. "I'm not dealing with kids. I'm not dealing with reproduction. I'm not dealing with women with kids. I'm rejecting oppression and becoming a man in society and I'm refusing to deal with it." A woman who deals with women's issues and women's oppression deals with kids. If they don't want to have kids,fine. I'll never encourage anyone to have kids that doesn't want to. "

taken From; squatting in the lower east side transcribed from 'interview w/friend in NYC" IN an old zine (oh like 1988) called AFteRbiRth put out by Susan K.

(not to be confused w/the New Afterbirth by Faith same name is co-incidence)

(Susan- where are you?)

Children, even babies, have something to teach, so it's not hard for me to want to listen to them; to enjoy their fresh approach without wanting to mold them.

It starts here. Like *Yo Mama* says:

"Every visionary knows that child rearing is a high stakes field. You can raise people to question authority, or you can raise people who will be accustomed to oppression. The human spirit may be naturally rebellious, but as parents and educators, we have immense power to thwart self-confidence, reward 'stoicism', and bury that revolutionary spirit until it is all but irretrievable.

"Social change can not take place without familial change. If we envision a patriarchal society, we have to be sure that every woman has a patriarch of her own to keep her in line. If we envision freedom and justice in the world, we have to ensure freedom from abuse and democracy within families."

—*Hip Mama #15*, "The Parental is Political"

Good child raising doesn't mean a total focus on the child, although they need tons of your attention when young. You need to know when to stand back and let them live their lives. You have to stick up for your life! They will learn from watching the life you lead. You can't just stare at them, ask them what do they want all the time. You are a person, you've got your ways, you need to be respected too. Children aren't the only miracle, we all are. It's time we got to be living—a better life for all!

The Story Of The Day I Applied For Cash Assistance

I was at welfare for 3 hours, the smallest time I've ever been there. I'm all prepared to go through the machine, prepared to fill out a million forms. The place is deserted and the forms are smaller. Still I initial a lot of small print.

I remember last year when I went in, after welfare reform, and read some of that small print. It said I would agree to never get any money for any children I have in the future and that welfare officials would have the right to show up at my house, unannounced, any time they wanted to, to check if the information I gave was correct.

So I waited in line for three hours, as I was demanded to, without explanation, missing my anatomy and physiology class (which did affect my next lab test grade) to be told and *only* told this: "Get a Job—Welfare doesn't exist anymore."

It didn't matter that I was in school trying to get practical job training. I was told I could get assistance if I looked for 10 jobs a week. Since finals were coming up and being the practically straight A student that I was, I focused on studying and didn't look for work. Somehow I wound up still getting welfare until this point and not having to deal with it. A miracle. I've given up trying to understand the mysterious ways of welfare long ago.

I recently stopped getting my $80 check (it was reduced to that when I was working at my last job) and two hundred dollars in Food stamps. And since I am going to look for work anyway, I thought it would be good to reapply for assistance while I look. So, here I am, back at the welfare office, prepared to be patient and do whatever they ask.

First I saw a man to talk about looking for ten jobs a week. I was required to work 30 hours a week. He gave me the forms to fill out and send in, every week, with places, names, and numbers that they would call and check. He asked me to fill out a form stating I did not have a drug or alcohol problem. Then I saw a man about the whereabouts of my child's father; I stated I didn't know and filled out a form. He asked if anyone was abusing me. Nope. I saw two desk people. So far everything is going smoothly.

Then I get called to the third office. I give her all my paperwork. She tells me I will have to look for jobs for a month, 40 applications placed in all— *Then* they will give me cash assistance. I will have to come in every week and talk to someone about why I can't get a job, if I don't get one. I must take any job offered. (No problem, they won't know if that's true or not.) I'm getting hungry, now we get into problems. She searches her computer and says I'm still employed. I wind up raising my voice because she won't believe me and keeps saying, "Well the computer shows…" I explain to her how I sent in the form that says I wasn't employed, but my word wasn't good enough, so I got my ex boss, who I didn't want to see, to write a letter for me. Look, I have it right here, I tell her. It says I got terminated in December, it has his phone number, fax number, and signature. "Well", she says, "I can't accept that. It doesn't have the exact date on the letter. Bring him this form to fill out." Also the letter I got my roommate to write with all the right welfare jargon about how we don't prepare meals together and so on, is no good. She needs to fill out a form letter. And I need Clover's school to fill out a form; and a doctor to fill out a form about when was her last check-up. And when all the forms are filled out and I have a month worth of job hunting under my belt, then I can receive assistance. According to her computer I should still be receiving food stamps, although I'm not, but she can't help me with that. I will have to call my old social worker.

Now I am starting to feel discouraged. In the old days they would give you emergency food stamps in 3 days. After our tempers flair at each other, for some strange reason we calm down and just start to talk. She's a black lady with a picture of her older son on her computer. The people who work here aren't so bad really. I hear them talking to each other in warm sing-song voices. Except for one lady who keeps laughing about someone who applied who had four children. "Four Children!" she keeps shrieking in disparaging laughter that rises above the other medium-toned, neighborly even, office chatter. "And on her form she put 'slave driver' next to her boss's name. Can you believe that? How is she going to keep a job with an attitude like that?!" I was starting to get ready to go over there and tell her to shut up and have more respect for her clients.

Anyway, I start talking to my social worker and we start talking very openly, calmly, even though it is the lunch hour and we have both grown hungry after this morning's events. "So what you are saying, "I said, "is that there is no more welfare".

"Yes, yes, you are totally correct, there is no more welfare," she says like I have in fact hit the nail on the head for all of us. Before this she has simply told me that I will not get welfare unless I look for jobs; and that when I got a job I would no longer qualify for welfare. It's kind of a weird Dr. Seuss loop.

I tell her what college means to me, that it is my number one priority. That after a year, I'll have a graphic design degree and that is somewhere to start. I tell her about nursing school and how it didn't work out and how demanding it was. I tell her I am doing this only to get a job, only to be practical—that is the way I see myself getting

ahead. That I'm not qualified to do anything and would like something more than to work at Burger King. I tell her stuff quite candidly. She says, "Yes I see."

Earlier, when I told her I had strange hours (day, evening, and weekend classes; these were the only time slots they had when I enrolled at the last minute) but that I would be done with the semester in a month and a half—She told me that I must drop out immediately and get a job. Take evening classes. She looked at me, the same way the worker looked at me last year when I talked about college. It was like telling them I was on crack or something. "You can do that on your own time. You need to get a job now." They act like going to college is a luxury. Last year, when I was close to tears the worker said, "Look the way we see it, we all got through college on our own, why should you get special support? "She also said the same words the worker said now, "Some people have abused the system by going to college too long, they just stay in school so they can stay on welfare." It must be the official line. I replied that I had never met a person like that and why don't they just make a cut off date after four years of college. She nodded her head like that made sense. I tell her that I believe that welfare should support those trying to get a trade. "Look," I said, "I'm not really equipped to go into the workforce. I've been a stay-at-home mother and a welfare recipient for a really long time. Now I'm trying to get job training, a very practical, responsible, socially approved thing, and it's not supported."

The reason why I'm being candid is because I've given up on this meeting turning into a good thing for me. I just want to communicate with this lady on a personal level. The interview is over; we are just talking. "So," I say, "explain to me, who does get welfare, surely the mothers with babies do?"

"Mothers with children up to one year old get welfare. But if the mother has not received her high school diploma, she will only get it for 6 weeks."

"So as to encourage them to get their diplomas?" I ask

"No, they just only get welfare for 6 weeks." I know she must be wrong. The point must be to encourage them to get their high school diplomas or GEDs. And then she says to me, "But really I see no reason why a woman can not go back to work after 6 weeks. I did."

Now, I understand what I am up against. The pain she must have felt, or perhaps the disconnection, the pain she never felt. I don't want to hurt her and talk about it. I want to proceed in the terms of her own logic. So I ask, "But if a woman has a low income job, she is mostly just working to pay the babysitter".

"Yes, I remember, I felt like I was just working to pay the babysitter. That is how it was."

The things running through my mind! *"There is no reason why a mother can't return to work and leave her baby with a sitter after 6 weeks!"*

First of all, what about breastfeeding? I remember how Faith said the worker looked at her, like how my worker looked at me when I brought up college, when she said leaving her daughter to go to work would be a problem because she was solely breast fed. The worker said that was her personal choice. And then looked at her oddly. A personal choice, something that easily could be displaced for the better goal of employment, a frivolous thing to be discarded. But have you seen some of the statistics on breastfeeding?! They are amazing. Children who are nursed have decreased incidences of diarrhea, otitis media, allergies, urinary tract infection, bacterial meningitis, botulism, insulin-dependent diabetes mellitus, ulcerative colitis, Crohn's disease, the usually fatal necrotizing enterocolitis and/or sudden infant death syndrome (American Academy of Pediatrics). Certain immunity is passed from the mother to the child's immature immune system. Plus the fact that breast milk contains the perfect nutrition for babies—for free!

Breastfeeding also creates an emotional bond between mother and child and is related to the enhancement of cognitive development in infants. Swedish and English studies found that breastfed babies grew up to be 8 IQ points higher than formula babies. *The American Journal of Epidemiology* found that pre-menopausal women who had breast fed for at least 20 months during their lifetime had a 50% lower risk of breast cancer than woman who had at least one baby and not breast fed. I don't want to offend anyone but I believe babies to be titty-mongers and nursing is a big part of new motherhood. The AAP is con-

servative and late to change but it recommends one year of nursing and wants to promote more breastfed children in America by having pediatricians better educated about breastfeeding. Apparently they were giving bad advice. (Call LeLeche League, it's in the phone book, for good advice and help.) The World Health Organization recommends all babies be breastfed for at least two years. The worldwide average age for weaning is 4.2 years. One doctor said "Some Canadian women nurse to 4." I followed the "nurse on demand, wean when they want to" school of thought and, although I sometimes got sick of it or encouraged her to wean her sometimes, I nursed her to way old. I know a lot of people from when I lived on the West Coast that did, too. The philosophy is that giving a lot to them when they are young turns them into secure and confident independent kids and people. Not over mothering but giving them what they need, what they come to you for. They start off in your body, then you got to hold them on your body, and then they run away.

And what all about the Clintons and that big study that was all over the newspapers last year, about the first three years of life being so critical to human development!? All the scientific data they gathered.

Wasn't it on the cover of *Newsweek* and *Time* too? It was this big deal. Well, duh, of course the first three years of life are important and influence a lifetime. And in my experience, no one is as sensitive and giving to a baby as its mother. I'm not saying mothers don't need support and time away; that mothers are perfect and babies don't get on their nerves—just that when I see Faith with Malila I see how her maternal instincts are honed and mine are off, now that it's not my child. She changes with Malila's development, she notices dangerous small items on the floor, hears the first sounds of her cries, and is charmed by her more deeply. Strangers in daycare are apt to be less sensitive. And that leads me to daycare …

Of course all mothers want good daycare, where kids can play with one another, where mothers can achieve independence. But do they want daycare for 30 hours a week? Probably not. It is wrong to force a mother to let go of her child before she is ready. A good option would be a drop in community center, a few hours a day to start.

When mothers feel that their children are ready for daycare, they want a daycare they can trust and feel secure in, that it is a good place for their child. Hello! Reality Check! Welfare gives you one or two dollars an hour for daycare, saying you can find a relative to watch your child. Have you seen some of the daycare out there? I have. Twice in desperation I put Clover in a daycare. First, in San Francisco, I located a network where you could find local at home certified daycare providers in your neighborhood. It looked like a good thing, cheap, a community nice thing run by grandmothers and so forth.

The neighborhood woman I found was a loving authoritative lady that watched 8 children, 2 of them babies, in a two-room apartment with a small pen back yard. They never left the house, drank Kool-Aid and watched television, not so good for childhood development. Later in Baltimore, Clover went to another home daycare for a short while, one that had more educational toys and little desks and stuff. There were two babies here too, who were in the crib or playpen at all times. One was passive and unresponsive. The other was told it was bad when it cried and not taken out of the playpen. I am not lying. This is ordinary. You want cheap daycare well you can get it, by oppressed daycare workers who need to take in enough kids to make it pay, who are numb to, overwhelmed, or unaware of the requirements of infant care, that they would be too overwhelmed to provide with anyway. The best daycares, I think, are connected with colleges, that have studied children more and hire more people and so forth. All I am saying is I can imagine a daycare nightmare especially if all welfare mamas must find cheap daycare. The places I mentioned were not seedy places, I am sure there are worse.

And finally, Oh it's so great to work full-time, is it? (Everyone in the welfare offices tries to impress on you that you will be so better off making minimum wage then in receiving assistance.) Rebecca of *Velvet Grass* zine did the math and wound up with this conclusion: "The only difference between receiving welfare and not receiving welfare seems to be that someone else is raising her child while she goes off to work. She's still broke."

I believe welfare should exist at least up to Kindergarten age, at the least! It's a nightmare that it won't. I have family resources and that's why I don't deserve welfare. I just take the money because I can, because it makes things easier. I have always had family handouts on top of welfare to purchase the things we need because welfare is not enough to live on. Poverty is about running from one crisis to the next and it is no brilliant solution to reduce the numbers of those dependent on welfare by simply cutting them off and telling everyone to "get a job." All welfare offers now is a bunch of job listings, a telephone to make calls on and a computer to write up your resume on. Oh and two dollars an hour for daycare.

Luckily people with infants can still get assistance. There is no job counseling, training, or any kind of assistance besides this. If you have heard good things about welfare reform in the newspaper, then they are selling things that aren't true.

Well I rushed home from welfare to make dinner for my child before I leave her alone and go to school. (I go to classes 2 days and 2 nights a week, and on Saturday mornings.) She does have Faith right next door, we share a house. Clover was unhappy when I came home, school had been stressing her out. We talk. I am there as a sounding board, a caring presence. I try to find her someone to play with but the kids aren't home at Stella's, and so I buy her some candy like she wanted. She feels better by the time I head off to school. In class I become totally immersed in my project and with what I am learning, and return home late.

I need to be there for my child, and my studies at college absorb me—going to college and raising a child takes more than it sounds like it does. I think back to how the worker told me to work during the day and go to school at night and wonder how could I ever pull that off? Not be there for my kid. Be so hectic I would get less out of school.

When I come home, Clover and I both show each other the projects we created that evening. She reads me the story she wrote, and shows me how she painted her nails. I am siked from doing good work at school. We dance to the radio. I made some biscuits and we ate them with butter and my grandmother's peach jam. We laugh together and go to bed past bedtime.

I did not look for 10 jobs this week. Maybe I am in denial again because it feels overwhelming. They did their job in discouraging me. I had decided to do whatever they wanted me to do when I went in that day. Maybe I should fill out all those forms and fill out the job applications hastily at the Mall, it would be worth the $280. But I just can't bring myself to do it. I finally got the $1,000 loan I took out from school, it's the first time I've ever taken out a loan. My car needs $200 dollars of work, the cat needs his rabies shot, and my boots are falling apart but I'm not going to invest in shoes, that is frivolous stuff. But I know the rent and bills will be paid next month.

As we drive down the road, Clover sees an old fashioned car wash and gets excited. "When we have money," Clover asks, "can we go through a car wash one day?!" I say, "Maybe." It's lazy, it's wrong, but a long time ago Clover started being happy about things by asking me, "One day, when we get money, can we?" If I say yes, she is satisfied. Only occasionally she asks me, "When are we going to have money?" I mostly don't tell her what I think, I think in my head, we are never going to have money.

I did tell her about the loan, that we have some money, but it's like we don't because the money needs to be spent on certain things. She is more likely to ask about the food stamps. She really

Malila + Clover

misses them, and knew them more of a likelihood in her life. "Can you pack me a lunch for school when we get food stamps," she asks. "When are we getting food stamps," When she went to her grandmother's, I said, "Now you will have plenty of food." "But I'm worried about you, what will you eat mom?" she replied. I told her not to worry about me, that there are plenty of beans and rice and I am not picky like how she is.

I am kind of worried about her feeling deprived of food and that this is going to give her a food complex. We have stuff to eat, maybe there is not always a big selection. But I guess it is a worry, where is our next meal going to come from, sometimes. I have to keep that worry away from her. I miss food stamps because they were just for food and you never felt guilty spending them. When she comes back we should sit down and plan a menu together and stock our house with food for the week. Cooking good cheap things takes time, like baking cookies instead of buying them. I have time for that. I'm not going to look for a job right now, gonna let it slide until school gets out.

How I Feel Right Now
(uncensored, unedited, and authentic)

I feel I can't put out a zine because I am depressed and that's not the proper attitude to have. Most of the reason why I'm depressed is because I'm poor, a single mom, and society sucks. (That combination by the way, doesn't have to depress you and you can be depressed without that combination…but anyway.) I feel stretched thin—and that I have no time to make a zine.

How is it now you have a zine in your hands, you might ask? Answer, two years in between issues is not uncommon.

It's not that it is so hard to write, its that its hard not to dislike what you write, endlessly edit, and take notes for articles never completed. It's hard to make the prolonged effort that results in a final, zeroxed, and stapled product. And when you are done, it feels great, DIY from the heart. And when you get a couple of letters from people, even better. It encourages you, that yes, this zine should exist.

Back to the subject of feeling stretched thin. I'm going to school for graphic design, that is my hope for achieving a job I can somewhat put myself into and escape sub-poverty. So I have my

You do not win
by struggling to the top of a
caste system,

You win by

refusing

to be trapped
within one at all.

The woman wins by calling herself

beautiful –

and challenges

the world to change

to truly see her.

photo at Clover Vottainine Words by naomi Wolf

schoolwork. And my home making work: cookin', cleanin', washin', payin' bills, fixin' the car, puttin' out the trash, etc. Which seems like such a big gray beast that is never done—it's a big job holding down the fort. I take care of my child and deal with the emotions of living. I feel really alone in this and I don't like being a single mom any more. And I fight depression. (I think it's just in my nature to have that tendency.) I don't have a job so I live on sporadic handouts and denial, knowing I need to earn money but when and where?

Since I got fired at my last job I just don't feel confident to be a waitress anymore. I applied as a maid at the Holiday Inn and as an X-ray person at the Airport, which seemed like the most interesting things to do around here, but I didn't get called back. I don't know why anyone would hire me. God, looking for work is one of the most depressing things and I hate being interviewed and then turned down. I guess I'm a spoiled little welfare princess because I can't deal with the thought of working at the 7-11, Dennys, in a mall, or at a factory. Also it is the fear of the unknown. I can only imagine getting a job someplace if I know someone there. The restaurants I worked at before in the city were bohemian places where I could look how I pleased.

I don't know how other folks do it—parent, work, and go to school—because I don't feel strong enough to do it all. But I guess they don't either, but they have no choice. Something always suffers. And I feel so isolated. I try to be strong, positive, and struggle but my little light always seems to go out.

I decide sometimes to cut out my artistic creative self-made goals, my deepest most personal objectives, so I can devote myself to school or survival. I did that when I was in nursing school. It was the only way I could get through it and do well. (I thought it was my future occupation; that I could write again once I became a nurse. I was doing that mature self-sacrifice think-ahead-to-get-ahead thing.) I've put aside writing at times. And at other times I've put aside my erotic longings—turned them off actually—(It just didn't seem practical or self affirming to have them) so I could get through school and take care of my child. I only "go out" probably like four times a year. Hanging out in bars just seems less fun these days.

Nothing seems to work but I can't give up.

Depression hurts too much. I have to try to stay happy with what I have, that I am alive, and enjoy that.

When I put out a zine, I like to do collages and nice layout and include well researched political articles with lots of quotes and personal stories—to put a lot of effort into it to create what I imagine I want it to be. I can not put a lot of effort into a zine right now, what with a shortage of time, clear thinking abilities, and money.

But isn't that just it? Isn't the reason why I can't write a zine—exactly whey I started this zine? To express what's going on, stuff that has to be said. To find a voice, to share, to network, to communicate with others—for those of us who don't even have the freedom to read or write but have so many thoughts in our heads. That's why there should be a zine. To define what is wrong with the world and try to make a better world or at least make some better free zones within it. Saying this, I feel better. Expressing myself. Expressing my discontent. I don't like this society! I don't want to live like this! I'm not a nobody, a nothing! Nobody is asking me what I think, that I should write but I'm gonna tell you what I think and write this, anyway, in spite of it all.

Why It Hurts So Much To Be A Writer

It hurts to be ambitious. It hurts that I always have to get so serious about the things I do (photography, art, projects at school, etc.) and get consumed with a drive to create something how I imagine it, and not at all take it casually like a fun hobby I can put down. It hurts to take the time to write, to put all my energy and be consumed by writing for 2 days and know I'm putting the practical concerns of living on the back burner—and then to feel I'm on the tip of the iceberg. To know I really need to invest so much more of my time and energy if I'm going to create a well-crafted final result, and that I would willingly do, but I can not. I need to write through my pain, write through my bad writing until I find the shape I'm looking for. Buried in papers, knee deep, my life on paper, yet I can not edit and form it; make it so others can read it, be part of society with the thing that drives me to make it. To try so hard at something yet to not be able to complete it. It is just writing—not making a better world for my child, not feeding us, not doing anything. The time I write is considered being a bum by my family since I'm not paid for it and it is not graded or measured. Feeling weird because I'm compelled to write. Feeling weird because my desire to put the truth on paper has nothing to do with real life, could it be a dysfunctional bad habit like sucking my thumb?

Why is the calling to write such a monster thing? Why is it so hard just to make books to be read? I'm a woman, I'm a mother…I can't sacrifice everything all the time, just some of the time, to my writing. I want to burn down libraries because I know I will never get to have my books on their shelves. It makes me feel angry. I will never get anywhere. I will burn my heart and soul on this for years and years.

I believe the publishing industry is all about money and won't publish most writers. I sometimes view my escapist reading tendencies, as bad as watching television too much.

Sometimes I don't feel I'm ridiculous, sometimes I see the meaning of writing—When Georgia tells me that books are good, that with books we can travel from the here and now, we can dream. When I see the church billboard at Christmas time says "and the word became flesh". I think, yes, the word can effect reality. Reality that seems not affected by me.

It hurts most of all because what is my natural calling is not wanted or valued from the world. It hurts because, as a mother, writing seems to be a bad habit to detract from what is needed out of me; and mothering seems to limit my writing so I can never soar in any direction…just all my attempts blown like dust on the wind. It is my authentic expression, I don't want to be all stupid about it and call it the highest of my callings as a human, because it is not. I don't accept to be recognized for it. I want to find peace as a woman, as a writer, an unknown writer, and live a good life—not a life in hell with a fine book famous after my death. I want to be balanced about this. But sometimes it hurts, it hurts a lot, when the time runs out and I have one more day to write with papers laying everywhere that would take a months work to get a good minimal finished project. Then I think *What have I killed myself for?* For nothing, for nothing is completed. And I do not know when I will have this time to write again, a

few days of my own—not for another month and a half I suppose. And then I will have to start at scratch again. I am worried that I will be unable to pick up where I left off, that it will accumulate with the other undone projects. I worry that if I don't finish now, that it won't get finished. Maybe I'll get struck by depression again that will debilitate my free time, as that has happened to me a lot in the last half year. And when I wake up out of this focus on writing, I'll have to meet the obligations I've put off to write. At least I have a $1000 dollar school loan to pay next month's rent with and fix my car. My neighbor has to come up with $225 this week or be evicted with her 17-year-old daughter.

I would like to be guaranteed 5 hours a day to write and write things people could read. I want to work, I want to fine tune it. It is just a little thing, not the most important thing for society, but it is part of me, part of who I am. There is no one who backs me on this. When the world is full of books, why can not mine be among them? I do not know the way to get there. I put a lot of time, a lot of labor into something that I look like an amateur at. I want to do work that feeds people, that is practical too—I just want 5 hours a day behind the typewriter; a cash grant, a man behind me, something that would make it possible. I feel driven. I want to be the female Bukowski, the female Burroughs, but instead I'm just the female. The only one who needs me is my child and she needs me in a big way. I'm too old for this. I want to be valued by society. I am a big whiney brat, my worst fear, and this is some kind of journal writing, how detestable! I just want to write books. I have a big attention span and a desire to do it so it hurts that I can not, is all. I want to refine my writing, I want to get feedback, to get taken off death row because I'm declared a national treasure for creating such a novel. I want all of us to be able to get on in the practical world and be able to fulfil the things inside of us. Not for every dream to come true, but through hard work, some of the dreams we need to come true—to come true! I don't want to be the best writer, I don't want to be famous. I just want to be allowed to write and a chance to be read; a chance to work at being the best I can by the standards I set for myself.

Stoney Run Road

Stoney Run Road

Well, I've been living on Stoney Run Road for just about a year! It's a rolling dead end road going by farmhouses, looking like Virginia or something, full of lilac bushes galore, air smelling sweet, daffodils, crocus, wisteria in spring; turning into rose bushes, honeysuckle and raspberries as we near summer. And plenty of ticks and low flying airplanes, of course. We live by the BWI airport, with planes flying over our house. It's a farm ghost land, next to the encroaching suburbs, fifteen minutes away from Baltimore City.

Hanover is a little secret nook of country folks, rednecks, and "hippies" (rednecks in tye-dyes that smoke pot) and punk hillbillies who let the youngin's run naked. OK so that is just us as we are the only ones with the baby running naked in the 'hood. One day this land will all be parking lots, warehouses, and shopping malls. The airport has been slowly taking over, growing, encroaching ever more.

But for now this is a bustling little community centered around one family owned corner-store, Haneys. There are horse farms, old houses, lost graveyards, empty stretches where the houses were bought and torn down, and one trailer park. People are friendly. Our house has been inhabited by wild people for a while, kind of how Crazy House was in Minneapolis.

We live in a big house divided into three apartments with Faith, Gunar, Malila, and a changing assortment of people in the apartment on the side of the house. We have 3 acres of land and space on each side of our house. I have mostly lived in cities before this. We have seen a year in Malila's life! We've seen her learn how to crawl, walk, skip, talk, and become a little person—that is very cool! We are a household, yet separate when we want to be, and have gone through times of being the best of friends and times of being mad at each other. But we have always been good neighbors; watching each other's pet, helping each other out with problems, borrowing stuff from each other, and helping with each others kids a little.

Sometimes a lot of kids come over, like when Stella and her three kids lived here and Candace came over. And there have been empty spots when nobody much came over. There have been times we have hated living here, but right now I am appreciating it so much. I can visit my grandmother who is 5 minutes away. We've put down a bit of roots.

Well, the first big change when we moved here was no TV! Yay! Clover watched too much television when we lived with my grandmother. This is what you do when you don't have a television: you make art; you cook; you talk to each other; you read books; play with animals; and you laugh at each other. Between nature, a baby, kids, and adults there is a lot of amusement around here. We hang out in the backyard, we have the space to have a garden or a bonfire. We clean the house, listen to music, and make collages. The kids play dress up, make haunted houses, and sew Christmas stockings for their pets.

Stella and her three kids, Aimee, Matt, and Ryan (14, 12, and 10) moved in after a few months, and that was really cool, if a bit crowded. It was like a real family, Clover has a family. Having more kids around made it easier to be a single mom, it wasn't just me and Clover. I would take them all to the grocery store with me and stuff. I am very attached to them. They are enthusiastic and radical kids who don't like school but who are very sweet. Real punks!

When Clover first met Candice she seemed kind of bored and tuff. I made a list of possibilities they could do and they decided on a treasure hunt. She also loved my cooking, which is a big endearment for me. She was an adventurous eater of new foods. Candice thought life would be boring without school, since people would do nothing if not told to, without the entertainment of buying things that is. I think school gave her a constant place, somewhere to do good, since her home life was chaotic. But she changed, as we knew her more, and she let her silly side out.

All of the kids I've mentioned are not from typical suburban families so Clover could relate to them better. They had experienced more, were pretty independent and strong kids with responsibilities at home. Besides, everyone around here has enough problems of their own, so they don't judge each other so harshly.

If you read the last issue of my zine you will remember how I talked about Clover wanting to be a popular girl and life in the suburbs. Everybody in her school is mostly the same: white; middle-class, girls with blond pony tails or boys with baseball caps, wearing new clothes from the mall. It was a big change in second grade—moving from an African-American and Native American… ghetto, I guess you could say, in Minneapolis into my grandmothers house in a white middle class neighborhood. I think race and class issues affected her social interactions in a way that young children can not understand. In our Minneapolis neighborhood, the color of her skin made her unfavored. (It was never as bad in Baltimore as it was in Minneapolis. I think that is because Baltimore, while racially divided, has more minorities than in Minneapolis, which is such a white place. And we lived in one of the very poorest minority neighborhoods in that city, where she was a complete minority as a white girl on a street where only the black boys played outside. She tried to make friends; I marched to their doors and had a talk with them when they punched her in the belly the first time she went over to say hello—a first in her young life. They were all only Kindergarten age! But she never could get beyond being an outsider, even though she continued to try to join in and one day the boys told her they didn't like her because she was white. She had never thought about such a thing before, coming from Baltimore and used to playing in a diversity of ethnic groups.) Yet in the suburbs she didn't fit in either, in part, I am sure, due to us being poor and alternative. There is a lot of pressure among elementary kids, it's easy to stick out and get picked on. People pick on small differences the very worst in the middle class white suburbs.

It was easier for us when we moved to a poorer white neighborhood by the airport. It was relaxed. This past year, in the 4th grade, Clover did much better in school, suffered less. Because now she sees another punk rock mom (Faith) who is similar to me, and she can be free to be more like who we are, not living with my grandmother in polite society. I think Aimee was like a big sister sometimes. If Clover had trouble at school, Aimee and her friends are more secure with being different and they would council her. Ryan would tell Clover to "Fuck Em" cuz he was totally not afraid to be different and not intimidated by the kids at school. Ryan likes to be a freak, he let Clover dress him up in dresses and he wants to run down the street like that. He's funny and a fighter. Candice would advise Clover on the ways of popularity, well that's what she was interested in, clothes and boys, Candice is 12. They would spend the night and have dance contests, twirl flashlights around in the dark.

I think that between the three of these kids and living here, Clover's self esteem was boosted. It's just not me talking, we have a whole household of supportive people. She is not alone. If she acts bad or cranky we are not going to abandon her, she doesn't have to walk on eggs like how she does with her friends at school. There are people at home, a home life. Ryan was like a brother to her.

At first they were so pleased to find each other as playmates with an interest in animals and stuff. Then Clover felt crowded by him (we shared a room at that time and Stella and the kids were in the room across the hall) and started being rude to him. I had to send her to her room for being mean and throwing his juice box in the woods when they walked back from the school bus. We would talk about it, there were issues to be worked out, just like having a brother.

So Clover was having a little better of a time with her self-identity, but my whole-life-centered-on-getting-through-nursing-school-so-I-can-have-a-career thing was falling apart. I was accepted into nursing school and started my training in the hospital but real-life experiences were making me cry every week; I hated the reality of being a nurse as much as I had loved the book learning. And while I thought I could deal with western medicine, I couldn't. It was a stressful demanding boot camp like program, which I think I could have gotten through if nursing was the right profession for me.

Still I was determined to finish at least the semester. I was stressed out between my chaotic home-life (there are always soap operas when you live with other people) and my demanding school life. I was now taking care of patients, practicing what I was taught at a rapid rate. And I was fumbling, no matter how hard I tried, I was not good at the hands on practice and always lagging behind and grossed out. It was heavy-duty shit at the hospital. And I was afraid I was going to fuck up an order, just like you do time to time as a waitress, but this time it would be someone's life that was at stake, not their dinner

It was at this time that cooking became my one relaxing time of the day, and the kids would come into the kitchen and help. We would talk and eat together, it was this really nice thing. Kids became my favorite thing, since they were so cool and enjoyable company. When I came home from school and everyone was fighting it was a nightmare, but one-day I came home to see Ryan and Clover's fort in the front yard, with them eating their lunch inside it. I was so happy to see my child doing well. It made me feel refreshed to see these wonderful children. I took a picture of them. I loved the buddha, hubcap, fire, whale decorations that they did. I made a poster of them because these two kids are punk, are anarchists, and they come up with the most intense cool shit. They are both true wonders and have big hearts. One of the best things about moving here was to see my kid, act like a kid sometimes. Like tree forts, picnic lunches, laughing, and kid stuff. Kid stuff is rare these days. Fights, sadness, violence, and problems are not. Hearing a kid laugh a real belly laugh feels good.

These days, Stella and her kids moved to their own house down the street and I see them less. Candice moved to the Bronx. I dropped out of nursing school and returned to college two months later as a graphic arts student and feel that's more me. Clover now plays with Faith and Malila or the new girl up the horse farm, Mandy. A bit ago, Clover and her had three days of zooming down hills on a boxcar like wagon at break neck speeds. They had a lot of fun. And a while ago Clover went swimming with Ryan in a nearby stream under the dappled sunlight coming through the trees, with a white Crane like bird standing in the distance. I talked to a man as they splashed around, who said he grew up here and his parents, too, swam in this stream that deepens in places. They played on a tire swing that hangs outside the big tree behind Ryan's new house. This is a cool place to live.

ANARCHY

The Future Generation

issue #10

the zine for green haired pregnant tree climbing women

+ subculture parents,kids,friends,etc.

inside:

poetry/parenting/politics
thoughts/self-expression

"Home Sweet Home"

Issue # 10
November
1999

The Future Generation

Anarchist Family Edutainment

communicate

since 1989

Rosa + Clover (my daughter)

█████ 465
█████ PA
█████

* I use my mom's P.O.B. because it is permanent. I really live in Maryland.

Treana + Walt

About the coverbabe;
   Anne Ness arived back at
Home just in time. She went
into labor on the drive home
to MPLS from her E. Coast
Trip. (She was actually one
month further along than any
one knew!)She had a *Homebirth*.
Now Anne + Walt have a new
   little baby daughter. And
      Rosa (10, who is *Home -*
      schooled by the way)
      Treanna (6) have a
      new little sister!

Issue Ten

November 1999
Home Sweet Home

"...the little must precede the great...the local must be the basis of the general...there can be a free federation only when there are free communities to federate..."

—from Anarchism & American Traditions by Voltairine de Cleyre

Walt and Annie

This issue comes to you from Stoney Run Road, a country road smack dab next to the Baltimore-Washington International Airport.

The airport is taking over my neighborhood and is in the process of building a parking lot where there was once only forest and homes. The stream in our neighborhood is polluted by the airport de-frosting chemical run-off, the watershed in our state is endangered and animals as well as people are losing their habitat. The question I want to ask is—If I can't control what happens on my street, what can I control?

If I can't find a meaningful life for myself, if I hate my job, or am unemployed—what hope can I provide for my children? There was a time my house mate and I wanted to start a home-school collective for all the unhappily schooled children on this street, to give them power and help create a better way to truly educate them instead of to incarcerate and dominate them, one where their voices counted. To show them, life is what you put into it instead of criminalizing them for being rebels without a cause in their boring schools.

If we could have done that, we could have really done something. Start taking over the street and working together. Change - where does it start? In our schools and workplaces, when we feel helpless to the "system" and the "way things are", we are unsatisfied. When will we have the space and time to build our own lives and live our own dreams?

Living in this society teaches you to believe what you need to fix your problems and be happy, is money. And lord knows I need money. But there are things money can't buy, like community life and meaningful attachment to others. Studies show job satisfaction comes less from how much people earn than from the challenge of the job and how much control they are able to exert over it.

We are angry over those we see controlling our lives, but we don't have the autonomy/responsibility to work out and learn from our own problems instead of just blaming the "man" and feeling ourselves to be the blameless victims of creating this way of life.

We all feel too busy in our individual struggles to collectively care and work to protect the down home way of life. The truth is we have no models in which to act together, this way of life is all we have ever known. To do our own thing, and when they come and pick us off one by one, to go, angry and grumbling, but to move on as they wish us to. For corporations are strong, stronger than we are; I can't imagine any way we could have fought the airport and won.

How far we have come from the ideals of democracy that this country was in part, founded on. We had a revolution to overthrow kings, set up checks and balances to protect us from what we knew was the corruption of power. Yet how soon the people were sold out. What is democracy now (?) to the school child, but a boring set of facts to be memorized in order to be tested for a grade later.

This issue is all about home and identity. The focus is, as always, on self-expression and commu-nication on how we go about our life and raising children. Dedicated to the concerns and empower-ment of parents and to the positive influencing of society, which our children and we are so affected by—with the hope of encouraging non-parents in their social parenting skills. I'm motivated to write by the problems in my life and the isolation of motherhood. Mothers do not get proper respect.

I believe mothering is important work, and also that to want to be a "stay at home" mom doesn't mean we want to actually be all-alone at home with no support. Home sweet home can also be hell itself—ask any mother stuck inside with a toddler during bad weather for instance. Or like Neal Cassady's wife wrote in "Off the Road"—of what she, an intellectual artist mother, stuck at home with the kids, dealt with as the beatnik boys roamed care-free. We need homes, and jobs, social places, where our kids can come. Motherhood and Childhood has to stop being such a ghetto!

This issue is homemade! This issue is also to give a voice to the poetry and stories of the kids who live on this street—you rule! Keep the home fires burning, ya'll!

Me

Nothin' much happens on Stoney Run. Sitting + Watching the road is one fun activity we do. *Will someone drive by?* Here, Mandy and her cousin Timmy are wearing Eric's masks from down the basement - they will wave or goof for the entertainment of passer-byers.

Mandy has recently moved away from Stoney Run, 10 min. a way to Tim Buc Two. She says "I thought I would like it here, (because there's people everywhere) but I don't ! The kids drink ... but their not Stoney Runnish! I like to dress up stupid and walk down the street. (My personal favorite activity, along with dancing in the yard when I'm happy + throwing dishes out the door , when I'm mad).You can't do that here."

Clover is 11 now and quite the young lady!
I can't write lots about her anymore - for that will invade her privacy. But I still can write some about her and hope she won't mind. luv ya boo

Malila 2 1/2

Faith n Gunnar n Malila moved to Baltimore a year ago. I got new house-mates (Hi Debbie,Brooke,Shawna + Will) Now Faith+Gunnar and Malila are on the road. looking for a new home, in a better place, in another state.

Home Sweet Home

In my thirty-three years of living, I've had 24 homes in 7 states and 2 countries. My daughter is 11 and has lived in 10 homes. I grew up moving around a lot, not exactly an army brat but my dad worked for the government and it was similar. I have no hometown.

I continue the pattern with my daughter, moving when things get sour or fall through, moving for adventure when I was younger and then later, moving in search of a better place to raise my child (Colorado, California, Minneapolis). Each time, I wind up coming back to Maryland, to be in the proximity of my family...when I get broke, or have a messy break up, or my friends leave town. My friends tend to move a lot, also. I've never really found that better place, and never totally find the support I need to raise my child. There is nothing as permanent or supportive as my own family, even though when I was young we declared our friends to be family and found our own values and lifestyles, so different than our kin's. I've never really felt I had much of a choice in the matter of my transient lifestyle.

Maryland, My Maryland

I was born in Maryland and lived here until I was 4. Then again, from when I was 13-18, I lived in the suburbs outside of Washington DC. (Where I put down no roots whatsoever and had a pretty crappy time. I lost touch from my best friend from that time like 7 years ago.) I lived out of state for the next 6 years or so, except for the year I lived in DC. I returned to Maryland when I moved to Baltimore when I was, I think, 24, and lived there for about 4 years, in three different houses. I really connected with Baltimore, as my hometown, although I had never lived there before.

My grandmother has lived in Maryland all her life, although she is widely traveled. She moved to a house in Linthicum (outside Baltimore) when she was 8, and now lives in the house she had built after her divorce, on the property her mother gave her, right next to her childhood home. She has lived in 5 homes in 80 years.

If I have any roots, it is with my grandmother, who has lived in the same place my entire lifetime, when we came to visit throughout the years from distances as far as Texas and Germany.

Suburbia

When I was younger, besides the short period I lived on "the economy" in a small German Village, I lived "on base" in military housing or in planned suburban communities, everyone else as transient as myself. Appearing as rootless, historyless. Our landscapes were sterile and replaceable. No place that one returns to visit. All natural landscapes are being wiped out, anyway, for new roads, houses, and shopping centers.

Who Am I? And How Did I Get Here?

I've had so many homes. I've lived in cities and traveled to many places. But I want to talk of the here and now. I want to talk of my home, for really I am such a homebody! I value home and community, I like to build and collect; I'd love to own my own house.

Today is a beautiful Fall day, crisp but sunny enough to wear a T-shirt. I took a little stroll down my street to look at the leaves beginning to turn. Funny how the seasons are like a slow-moving firecracker show; plants come into their own en masse. Everything now is about ink berries drooping like grapes on stalks the color of rhubarb—and daisies. The woods and meadows are full of little wild daisy bushes with small pale butterflies above and crickets humming below. One thing about living in the country for a while (I've lived here going on three years) you start to recognize the rhythm of nature and see a clock in the seasons. There is a time for honeysuckle, a time for raspberries, a time for Queen Anne's Lace, and a time for ripe tomatoes. There are certain swells in time for the insects too: mosquitoes, fireflies, ticks, and fleas.

A week or two back was spider season; spiders were everywhere. An enormous one spun a 5-foot by 5-foot web on my porch. I say "live and let live" and put up a sign that said "Beware of Spider" so no one would walk face into it. It was nice to live around that web, even though it takes up half the entrance to my house. In the summer, my porch is full of wood bees. They've never bitten anyone. "Don't be scared," I say once in a while when they annoy someone, "they are my bees. Be good to them and they will be good to you." We have played with praying mantis and walking stick visitors too. Seen deer (they have a crosswalk next to my house), fox (and one was shot but not before it took down half of Mandy's chickens), hawks, turtles, rabbit (somehow they survive despite my cat's spring lust for devouring baby bunnies) and other critters. Nature is very rich on my street.

Human nature also runs a little wild here. There is space between houses and people respect your privacy, yet treat you friendly. This house before us belonged to drug dealers who grew pot in the back in the woods. They were busted and then we moved in. Ladybugs flock in mass, at certain times each year, remnants of the marijuana growers who ordered a box of them to eat the aphids off their crop. On the basement wall is hideous Day-Glo spray painted pot leaves. Walls and doors have holes in them, left by angry fists, but all and all this house has a good feeling to it. No ghosts.

Dana's house has a ghost. Her mother had experiences with it when she was pregnant. Their house was originally a chicken house, then turned into a bar, and now a home for the last 50 years.

Stoney Run Road, Hanover, Maryland

Oh, I should explain to you where I live! If you look on the map you would see a large gray area where the Baltimore-Washington International Airport is. I live within that area, on old farm property now turned half hillbilly, between the empty lots where the airport has bought out people and torn their house down, to keep the property for future expansions. Planes fly over my house. You have to pause in conversation when they do, for the noise drowns out voices. If you live here, you get used to it and don't notice it so much. Folks park on the bridge nearby, just to watch the plans take off and land. It's kind of exciting. And good for us, it makes the rent cheaper and we have so much property, woods behind us and empty lots on both sides.

My street, Stoney Run, is a dead end road, home to little more than a dozen houses. It is an old road, my old man neighbor remembers before it was paved, when it continued through before the airport was built—before it was cut off by newer roads and the many highways that loop around here. Where I live is like a secret world.

There are meadows, trails, and old empty farmhouses. In one direction I can drive to the suburbs and small town centers; in the other direction is beautiful winding rolling roads through country out to the old town of Elkridge. That is where my great-grandfathers family lived, in what is now Patapsco Park. Their home is now gone, and that spot the site of a parking lot. (Ironic, how parking lots are a recurring theme, but that I will explain later in due time.) Elkridge was established in the 1700s and once was a port town to rival Annapolis, back when the river ran deep there and not shallow like it does today. Slaves put tobacco on the boats. I read that information on a sign. I was shocked to think of slavery right here, I always think of that down south.

The area I live in is a surprise to people not living in it, for it is country—with no reason to drive through if it is not your destination—yet so nearby to everything urban and suburban. I found out about it because of my city-punk friend. She found out about it through her boyfriend who first came to this area, so many years ago to drink and play cards all night on Tuesday nights at the "Compound", a rambling assortment of houses at the curve in the road. Home to a rambling assortment of people: heavy drinkers, strippers, drug-dealers, and mechanics. Families who sit down to dinner prayers, alongside tales of an escaped boa constrictor and a bleach blond alcoholic grandmother who wears too much make-up, and stole everyone's rent money to go bet it on the horses.

Funny stories, I'm sure I could gather enough to write a book. The wild times people had, and the times they calmed down. This is a family street, not a dangerous street. Though some people do spend some time in jail for petty things. And I do know of a story of a murdered mob husband, in the name of self-defense. This is a good sign. This is a street where women survive, and have guns. But not everybody has guns, at all. It's a nice street, with respectable people too, where people appreciate nature and grow vegetables in their garden. There are older folks left from the days when this area was predominately a poor Polish community, which grew produce to sell in Baltimore, as well as to feed themselves. They call this "truck farming" for they took the produce to sell into the city on their trucks. There are horse farms. And down along the way, a trailer park, in the middle of the glorious woods and rolling hills. There is a junkyard, full of abstract sculptural metal towers of smashed vehicles, where the kids once set a car on fire for excitement.

Danah

We have had some great kid friends here. Watched Malila grow from a baby to almost three. Ate supper with Candice, and when she moved to the Bronx - god did that girl cry. She had always gone to school here, always been on the soccer team, always did well - and loved it here. When she came back for Clover's b-day, she yelled in the night air " I love Maryland." It took her almost a year to fit in to the Bronx, and stop being my daughter's pen- pal and never be heard from again. Other kids too, have loved living here, and been terribly heartbroken when their parents moved them and took them away from all they knew and close friends they had for years. Oh that's normal, they'll get over it right? But I know what it's like to always leave town and friends…I mean, god, what would it be like to keep your childhood friends all your life! Wouldn't it be fantastic, I think. I know some people who keep a lot of touch with those they grew up with, even though they change.

My grandmother is one. I talk to her and I see what its like to keep continuity. She goes to the same church since she was 8. My grandma was a school teacher, and such a beloved one, that she still gets letters from her 4th grade class, they all sent her wedding invitations and birth announcements. I've had a taste of what she has, so I can imagine … the kids I've known for a few years, cooked for, listened to, cared about, and did art with, talked the meaning of life with - What if I got to see them grow up? What if I got to live in a community where people knew me, I mean when I was old, that would really pay off, having adults respect me for remembering the stuff I did for them in their youth. That's something I don't have, nor expect to, but hold on in my own way, anyway. I put energy in people, and they go off in the world, never to be seen again. But I feel fine, thinking how we all live in each other, all the experiences we've had.

I know I heard Scott Haney talk once, while at the cash register of his family owned corner store, with this sense of continuity that my grandmother has. He grew up around here. A boy came to cash his check, (perhaps he worked there, Haneys gives the young jobs sometimes, and cashes checks and provides little friendly I-know-your-face-and-name services to the community) and he wanted it all in one dollar bills. Scott asked why, and found out the boy was bitter at owing his mother money and wanted to pay her in ones. "Oh no, you don't," he said, " I know your mom. Growing up here, I could tell you stories about everyone on this street, how they treated us kids. Stories about every bastard and bitch. But not your mom. She is the only one I have not one bad word to say against. Not one bad word! Don't you treat your mom like that." Scott is just a bit older than me, of the Rock and Roll generation. It's funny to think of us, taking over stuff. Haneys is a family owned store, with good ethics and spirit, not something like those corporate owned chains. And it's a neighborhood, a loose one, where people can know who each other are. Just because you are here, well then you are part of Hanover. A diverse crowd.

I want to go back to talking about nature. I love it here, the woods so wild, the roads so rolling, and the forests so beautiful. I roam the countryside when the sun is going down and illuminating the bright trees, yellow, red, and some just painted on one side. I sit on my porch and watch the tumble of one leaf to the ground, or have them all pour down on me like rain when the wind blows. I'm getting to know the plants around me; the peace you get by walking right out on your porch and seeing only trees, sky, and winding road - instead of cramped city living like I was. ("Happiness is…being able to piss off your own front porch," says Faith's mom.) And then I think about my grandmother. She loves her oak trees. She cried yesterday, because one of them got cut down yesterday. It was dead, hit by lightening, and on her neighbor's property (who she sold her mothers property to) - yet still she cried. "I grew up with that tree. My playhouse used to be next to it. I hope they make something good out of the wood. It's hard to get oak. Hope they don't just sell it for firewood." Yeah, my grandmother loves her oak trees. I look at them in the front yard. How old do you think they are? Three hundred years old, she says. They are mighty oaks, and oaks grow slow. I think about that. Three hundred years!

Me and Milo

Sign I painted to protest
"Tree's are better than parking lots"

I've researched how the town of Linthicum has grown up with her ...and its history, indeed all of the United States history, is less than that three hundred year old Oak tree, for sure. But what's a tree?

Like where I live. The bulldozers are coming. Half my street is going to be turned into a 60-acre parking lot, rental car facility, and a car wash. They started bulldozing a new two-lane road so people can come here. I always knew, moving here, that this was a temporary place to live. One day the airport was going to grow and build more stuff. And then I would move somewhere else. But I really am living at the end of an era; I'm seeing it all end. It's been going on since 1947, when they built the airport. The farmers had to get out and their land was claimed. Ever since then it's been slowly spreading.

History
Progress originally came by way of the railroad and the waterways. Towns were built around occupations such as charcoal making from the

aerial view of Harundale 1952

dense pine and oak trees, pulled by horse and wagons over dirt road to sell in Baltimore for use in iron smelting furnaces. Land was cleared and corn and wheat was planted. Waterways were a big deal. Trains were a big deal.

And then real estate development would prove more profitable than farming culture. Lawyers, these were the money men. In 1908, the Linthicum Heights Company was formed. In 1909, electricity was brought here by B.G. and E. Prior to 1916, there was only 50 residences in the Linthicum area. The progressive area was to begin!

A new 8-room brick schoolhouse was built. And then in 1926, my grandmother at 8-years-old moved here. Dirt and ash roads turned to gravel, were paved, and then were widened, and widened again. The Heins company turned from hauling ice and wood to delivering coal to delivering fuel oil.

In 1930, Glen Burnie became a true town, which originally, it was an intersection spot of railroads and site of Curtis Creek Mining, Furnace and Manufacturing Company in 1888. In 1949, Robinsons opened (there were only 2 traffic lights on route 2 then) - later my mother bought her lingerie for her honeymoon there. Planned Communities were built.

By 1957, the Expressway was built, making Baltimore just 18 minutes away by car! The

By the 1950s, Glen Burnie's downtown was a thriving business district and even then, traffic piled up on Baltimore-Annapolis Boulevard. But the 1950s also brought the first hints of things to come with parking problems and the opening of Harundale Mall began to have impact on the old business area.

Harundale Mall opened in 1958. It was the 1st enclosed mall ever built, East of the Mississippi. My mom's high school band played for the opening of it, and John Kennedy, at that time a senator, came and gave a speech.

In the 50s Glen Burnie boomed. In the '60s it took a nosedive. And then revitalization projects took place. There are tons of these cute tiny '50s houses all around Harundale Mall, like they were the first suburbs. The highways are full of pretty kitschy stuff too, now there are bigger highways, freeways and expressways. Traffic becomes a problem. We become a service society.

Glen Burnie is a town center with movies and stores and the courthouse. It's a few minutes away from, and kinda funkier than Linthicum, which has been described by some as snobby. Linthicum is a suburban community—which was described as "the best of both worlds. The proximity to metropolitan areas and industrial complexes, expressways, airport—jumped the population from 2,00 in 1940 to 15,000 in 1972. Linthicum has stability, quiet, old community with the advantages of being at the cross roads of Baltimore Beltway, Baltimore-Washington Parkway and Old Annapolis Boulevard" in a booklet at the local library.

In 1973 (I was 7) *The Sun* paper reported, "the housing explosion has produced mass identity crisis: most of us live one place, work another, and never really feel quite at home in either. What's missing, we are told, is a feeling of belonging. Linthicum, Baltimore's back bedroom, will try to recapture some of its misplaced community spirit when it's 1st and annual Linthicum Community week is launched. ...The teenagers are skeptical. They think people are apathetic and don't care. They're always saying 'nothing happens in Turkey town.'" (The nickname came from the abundance of turkeys running around, which is hard to imagine now.)

Land

My great-great grandfather came to America with the dream of owning his own land to farm. In Germany, it was too crowded to easily own land. He worked as an araber on the streets of Baltimore, and then in a German piano factory, until he saved enough money to move outside of Baltimore and buy land.

My grandmother tells me about her grandfather's farm. It was a 50-acre farm with a small apple orchard, a larger peach orchard, also pear trees, and a vineyard. He grew fields and fields of tomatoes to sell. Later his son told him the money was in raising chickens and they turned to that.

His house was as old to be standing in Civil War days, built in front of a dirt wagon road. In fact, once an old lady came, in my grandmother s youth - to knock on the door—and ask to see the house she grew up in, during the Civil War. My grandmother drew a blueprint of the house, trying to remember it all. She told me of the workroom, that it was magical to her, with rolls of wood shaving everywhere on the floor, cherry wood, and every other kind too. For her grandfather had been a cabinetmaker in Germany. He also had tools to fix shoes and stuff like that. There were great storage places to put away food and all the tools of self-sufficiency. She shares with me her childhood memories of playing in a bucket of rainwater among the mosquito larva, of watering tomatoes and of sweet cows—

Then she told me of the time, not that long ago, when she drove to see the place that had been her Grandfather's farm - but it was nothing but miles of factories and long low buildings. She was disoriented - yet she knew in this space had been the farm she spent her childhood summers visiting. It was all gone, all flattened, all an industrial park. She sat down by the train tracks and cried hysterically. Now, I can understand, but only in a the tiny amount, what she felt.

Conclusion

I think of all I've known and all those who have lived here before me. Construction has uncovered graveyards from colonial days, bones that no one knows who they are; arrowheads; and even mastodon bones.

I think of the transportation, the roads, and cars and planes, that are stamping out a way of life, again. I hear everyone hurry, hurry, hurry, and wonder who has time to watch the leaves fall, or to do all the jobs of the home, that make culture and life meaningful. To raise the young and visit the old. Television has truly taken over and some mistake commercials for meaningful fashion predictions. But I believe nature is a strong force. I see the vines cover the junk car in the back woods. I see how cement can be broken up. I believe nature will prevail in the end. I also believe man is a force of nature. But does the ordinary person have say in progress? And does progress benefit him or her as it takes away a community and the natural scenery and leaves nothing but roads and windowless rooms, restlessness, and boredom—living in our man made world?

The natural world is one of such adventure and lessons for children—without it, their play seems to be the destruction of the man-made one, as they try to make use of their surroundings, ones they are often told, not to touch. Without being literally, grounded in this world—we are more apt to believe only in the television images. I see the difference between my mother who grew up on a farm and me. Ecologically speaking, we know we can't go on, destroying the earth under our feet? Where will live? But no place is safe from development and the urge to make a profit for some. The rest of us, unorganized, and often unfaithful to our neighborhood - are no guardians of the places of this world. Isolated and alienated - the more we move the more rootless we become, the less powerful to organize. Other communities, around the world, which are stronger in culture and sense of home - who do fight to exist are met with guns and military force. The governments of this planet are more military back up for Corporations and Profit, than any organization of the locals. Yet most of us aren't informed but by the views of what the richest most powerful interests want us to know. We live in the shadow of the radar here, of Howard Gruman (which used to be Westinghouse; that is where my parents worked and first met). They develop war technology and we think that they are "We". That we are the U.S.A. Then when the soldiers come down with Gulf War Syndrome we see people who have faith in the government are used as replaceable fodder. When we go to the mall and buy things, do we realize our fashionable expensive clothes are made by others who are paid so little and whose cultures are destroyed - so as to support ours? When will we see we have more in common with all the people of the world - than those on top of the food chain who have no allegiance at all to their fellow country men and women?

I see how the ways of community life, mutual aid and independence—are dying. Even the basic knowledge of how to cook, sew, build, fix, grow, decorate and be a good neighbor are being lost. And found. For I'm not here to glamorize the past, (even though one does get sentimental about what one loses) that would be ridiculous. Change is constant and part of life, I am just making an argument against the trivial and damaging change of building Mega- Malls and Parking Lots, when what we need is something different indeed. The natural vibrant life of this community is being destroyed by outside interests. What government program or implement of progress can replace what is being lost here?

Eleven

My daughter is 11 years, 8 months old. She is growing up fast. I'm an extremely tall woman from an extremely tall family, so it's no surprise my daughter is tall—but wow—to have your kid be big is something. She wears the same shoe size as me, is almost 5 foot 9, and she looks like a 14-year-old. Her best friend, the girl up the street, is 14. So, I've had to deal with adolescent stuff, that really surprised me, stuff I didn't think would happen until, well at least until she turned 12 years old. Her internal clock reads the beginning of adolescence. The changes caught me off guard. Really, 10 was such an easy to live with age—her growing up was a pleasure—it didn't prepare me for 11.

I had no idea it would be like this. I actually believed it would be somewhat easy to have a teenager. That the parents who had problems with their teenagers were the ones who didn't set good groundwork in their younger years, and who didn't respect their children as individuals. Now I think this time is just inherently difficult. It takes almost as much work to parent a teenager as it did to parent a young child—but it's hard in totally different ways. I understand things that I always thought were cliches! And I'm becoming such an adult—Jesus Christ! Hey, you don't understand until it's your kid! I always got along well with other people's teenagers and didn't understand why their parents acted like such freaks. Now I'm afraid that I've been too permissive with my daughter; perhaps all my child-raising beliefs have been wrong and my kid will turn into some Jerry Springer ghetto kid. I'm afraid she doesn't have good boundaries, doesn't always make wise decisions, and that 11-year-olds are just stupid sometimes—they do life-endangering things on the spur of the moment. I know I did. And she has.

September 1999
"1st day of school"

I've always been moderate and relaxed—that's how I raised her—but now she's surprising me with some truly fucked up things and I have to change my standards in response.

I've always been so "cool", so open about everything I know, and I've tried to be so respectful of people of all ages. Now I'm going, God, I don't want to be the only adult who kids tell the truth to, this stuff is too much. And I don't like their language—the excessive ugly cussing wears on my ears—and I say so. And sometimes the kids treat me like crap! Is this the price for developing too friendly a relationship? Everything confuses me! I've always been pretty open about myself, and I've always tried to give information when it seems relevant to do so, with humor perhaps, on the subject of sex, drugs, and my values.

Sometimes I feel out of control of my home, sometimes I try to gain control with normal parental behavior like "you're restricted, grounded, and no TV—I have to be firm to teach you to think twice before you drink the beer I hid." But that didn't really help. I had to keep enforcing the punishment until I'm exhausted and Clover's climbing out the window and running down the street. Then I said, "You not being able to watch television isn't really getting a message through about not drinking, is it?" And she said "No, it just makes me angry at you." So I gave up typical discipline (which I rarely embark on anyway) and somehow we just get through things. But I can't give up, or think I'm going to be free of this worry, fighting and work. I have to be a participant in the drama of teenage years. I have to be "the mom". Then we get through the thing, and the behavior didn't happen again. But at the moment, I thought, *if this is 11, if this is the beginning… Oh I'm scared.*

I get shocked by things that happen, that seem out of character for her, and then I fear for the worst. There's been, like, four incidents this year that I'm thinking of. Each time she was with her best friend (the "bad influence" friend), let's call her "Jamie". Once, I restricted my daughter from seeing her, but she just would not listen, and she wouldn't get in the house. She looked in my face and said "No". That hadn't happened before. I realized my daughter was physically as strong as I was and it would be impossible for me to control her on that level. Even if I could get her back in the house, she could just walk out later. That's intense. I've found that in those kinds of situations, you have to keep working on the good principles, and on care and love, because that is still the only thing that is going to get you through the problems—when the situation calms down.

The one event that scarred me for life was when she took a mix of pills that her friend gave her—some combo of motion sickness pills and Ritalin, I'm still not sure—and she tripped for two days. At first I was calm and supportive, willing to work out the details when they came down. On the second day I was afraid Jamie's heart was racing too fast and called my friends and poison control because I was too scared to tell her mom or the hospital because they would return Jamie to this harsh juvenile jail if she got caught doing anything like that. I'm telling you this was bad, a big bad, that scared my daughter too. Didn't I ever tell her not to take pills? Especially pills that she didn't even know what they were; hadn't I included that on the list of bad drugs? I would have never thought she would have done such a thing. Before this event I had been like, *Well you can have a little glass of wine or smoke pot once since your curious.* But this whole experience scared me straight. I even quit smoking to be a good role model.

Sometimes I'm at a loss. Things aren't making sense like I thought they would about the self-regulated young. I don't want to be a negligent parent—I want to look out for her; I want to hold her back from things sometimes. I tell her she can't go to party—or anywhere with her 14-year-old friend for that matter. She tells me the things they do—running the streets, getting into fights, and going to parties with sex and drugs involved—and they aren't anything 11-year-olds should be doing. But at the same time, I have to trust in my daughter. I have to give her room to grow in. It's a balance and you go on gut instinct.

Things get so tricky. I've believed in slogans like "Trust in your Desires" for so long, yet now I'm a bit distrustful that my daughters self-regulated needs have been influenced by television, society, and others—and will blow up in her face. She's spent all these years getting retarded and abused in public schools; that doesn't prepare a child to deal with their desires. It's a lot to deal with. I talk to a lot of people to try to gain perspective. I get too wrapped up in the kids. I realize I have to stay calm and positive and not obsess over my fears, like, *Oh god, what if my kid overdoses one day, or gets in a car with drunks and crashes, or gets pregnant before she is ready or runs around with no sensible boundaries whatsoever and gets hurt?* I don't want to get consumed with thinking the worst just because the kid had a few scary experimentations, because what if my negative expectations made those things happen?

I still totally believe in the values I raised her with. There are some things I would have liked to change — to have tried harder to live my values and protect us from abuse. When she was little and told me the kids at school were calling her ugly and treating her bad all the time, I should have taken her out of that stupid suburban school. "But mom, it was my choice—every year you asked me if I wanted to go." True, but sometimes she wanted to home-school and I told her to hang in there because I was going to nursing school.

For the most part, I'm over parental guilt. Nobody's perfect, and guilt really doesn't help anything. Feeling guilty just rips you up inside and then sets you on a seesaw of unbalanced behavior where you try too hard to compensate for your mistakes, and then eventually blow up again when your efforts aren't appreciated or don't work out how you wanted. No, that's not for me.

Writing about all my worst fears for my daughter and events that shocked me—it's almost taboo. But I need to confront this stuff. If I have these feelings, others must, too. It's just this weird stuff about teenagers and parents; parents who used to be teenagers—and how different it is now being a parent than it is looking back at your own adolescence.

My theory has always been that people who are not so repressed and messed up are the ones who won't do compulsive, destructive things. I thought that if we weren't so polar in creating these distinctions between pure good and pure bad, we wouldn't create this attraction to the darkness and ignorance about what lays there. I thought that if a parent didn't have a drinking problem and you let kids have occasional sips of wine in family situations, they would be balanced about it. I've always been about expressing life—all of it—and creativity; taking chances for freedom, love and joy. The whole compulsion to be either subordinate to mainstream values and authority figures or to a reactionary slaving to trespass all the values of such is both a tedium and a malady that holds us back from self-actualization. Everything can become a destructive thing in the hands of a person who is lost. Everything is a stereotype. It's unsettling how many things people can do halfheartedly. And in this society—divided so often into Control vs. Chaos—so few have the skills or practice to take care of themselves and work with others in a non-oppressive atmosphere. I expected more out of my daughter and tried to raise her with healthier habits. I thought most teenagers could take care of themselves. Now I don't know what I think. I'm playing it by ear. I'm just like any typical parent.

So that's one new topic in my parenting life this year. And the other is sex. She buys a "hootchie mama" skirt and I hear her talk some of her bad rap lyric talk. I think she is exploring her sexuality—still growing up—talk and skirts are just that: talk and skirts. These are still the stages of maturity. *What am I afraid of?* That she will plunge into sex before she is ready? Everything in this culture is at once supersaturated with and totally ignorant about sex. I hope she learns about sexuality in slow steps—like blossoming—first kissing and touching. But all the kid-talk is about "doing it". Everything is about sex and not caring and at the same time a lot of rating, judging, and shame. Silence among the vulgarity, silence among the tastefulness. Who knows maybe sex is just a scary thing. Maybe I've read too much Wilhelm Reich and tales of aboriginal children playing sex in the woods and growing up free and well adjusted without violence.

Another thing that gets to me is how my daughter has low self-esteem. She feels really miserable and feels mistreated by others. Sometimes she's so sad. Adolescent girl emotions are draining!

I give up and let her feel sorry for herself and stay out of it. Well, for one reason—because she very strongly tells me too—over and over again. I've given her all the empowering, wise advice that I can think of. She doesn't want to hear another word. I talk too much. She is adamant about that. And I read too much and I write too much and she doesn't want to hear any of it.

At my stage of development, I've gotten a second chance to really work out and understand my own teenage years—I'm just full of advice. At her stage of development, parental advice is like the word "No" to a toddler: you better use it sparingly or you will make your child deaf to you. I've realized that I and many of my friends went through our own personality building Hell, who am I to deny her hers; to deny her the full range and depth of emotion, adolescent girl emotion, by trying to get her over it and be a woman? She's going to have to find it for herself, and I'm going to have to save my advice for people who ask it.

So I say stuff like, " I think I hear you crying, and you yelled at me last time I asked you if you were OK, so I'm going to leave you alone and go about my life. But I want you to know it's not because I don't care, so please come to me if you need me." Who knows if she is even listening.

I've stopped telling my daughter to clean her room. I wasted a lot of breath over the years on that one. Now it just doesn't concern me. It's her space, her consequence. If I need to think about cleaning, I can look at my own room, ya know? I bought her an alarm clock and I try not to watch the clock and yell that she is going to miss the bus. It's all about the little things, letting her be in charge of her own crap.

And I don't monitor her television use anymore. Sometimes she watches TV like a zombie. This dude I was seeing over the summer was like, "TV kills creativity and is horrible, you must know that—forbid your child from watching more than an hour of it. Other parents do it. Just tell her how it is." He thought I was totally lazy. But I didn't feel like being swayed in how I raised my child by the new dude in my life. I just told Clover what I thought about her television viewing habits and placed a book called *Four Reasons for the Elimination of Television* on top of the television set. If it gets to a point, maybe we will get rid of the TV. We lived without one for many years. But I pause over even stuff like television because of her rights to her own life. I know there are times I've been a TV zombie—and I don't like people telling me how to use my time.

I'm learning to let go. I once told her (to her annoyance, usually what ever I say is annoying) that she's responsible for her own life. "All that work I did of raising you. Well you know, look at Malila, look at all the things Faith does to care for her. That's just like what I did, that and more. From growing you in my body, giving birth to you, and changing your diapers every time you messed them, to the last 10 years of parenting you. It's a lot of work. But really, I realize all that is just the beginning. Its you that's going to make you. And what you become—its all going to be because of yourself. You have the work and the responsibility of your life and creating what you want to be."

I understand why she was annoyed (what teen wants to be reminded you changed their diapers?) but it was such a stark realization for me. At first a harsh one. That this child who has been raised with so much feminist and bla bla bla agenda— well, she might turn out anorexic and neurotic or she might wind up with an abusive boyfriend that she chose for herself and there would be nothing I could do about it. This child might fuck up or die in the process of growing up, because of some mistake that so many survive but some do not. Something might happen to her. But it's up to her to make her own life, to make her own mistakes, to get the credit for the good she does. It's out of my control, and it's all too much for me to deal with. I don't want to have the responsibility of her life plus my life. I had to transfer some power to her.

My daughter is looking towards the world now, the same now as always, in expanding circles of vision. I remember when I held her as an infant on my lap, sitting on the cliffs in front of the Pacific Ocean. Her focus was the blade of grass in our immediate proximity while I watched the hawk that flew over the sea. Both of us were equally enthralled. Point of view is everything. Who is one to discredit the other?

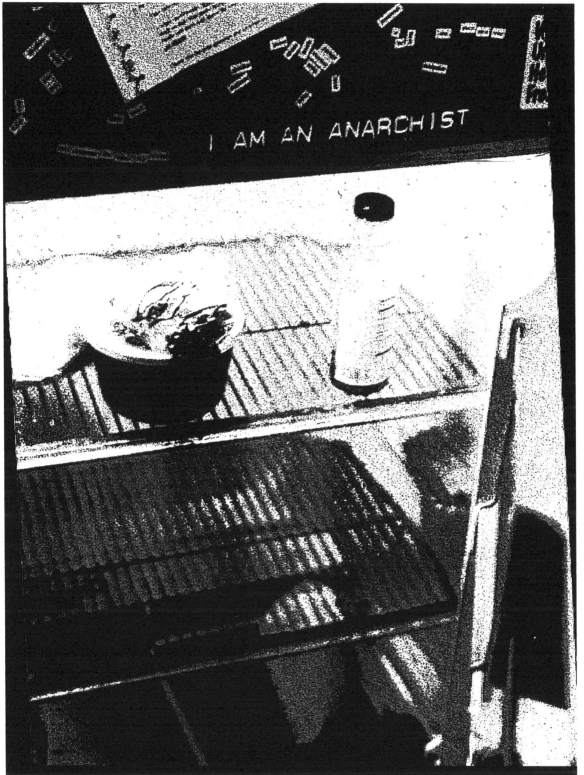

I AM AN ANARCHIST

My refridgerator is empty

Mandy likes to dress up in characters and come down and surprise people. She had us laughing + laughing the day she dressed up like an old drunk crazy lady. She put apples in her shirt for saggy boobs and spilled some beer on her to smell authentic. Then she realed around and spoke like a perfect dramatization of a drunk. Here she is on stoney run, to the R. of my house - with Clover.

"I remember the first time I ever smoked a cigarette. Everyone in my house, my mom, my uncles, was always running around saying I need a cigarette, I need a cigarette when they were stressed. One day I felt stressed and I thought I need a cigarette. Almost without thinking, I took a cigarette to my room and smoked it. It made me feel better. I felt weird for the rest of the day. I just laid on my bed and thought about it. I was just like them."

Aimee at 13 had already been smoking for 2 years. The image of her smoking was such a disturbing one that I wanted to photo-document it. Back then she seemed so old to me, out of the league of being in my daughter's age bracket (who was 9).

Thirteen seemed pretty grown to me. I knew how I felt at thirteen. Now that my daughter is getting older, bridging the distance to thirteen, I see that 13 is also young. I can't stand to see kids smoke anymore. Last time I heard, Aimee, at 15, had quit smoking. I really hope so. A lot of people grow up in smoking environments and to smoke means that you are respected as someone getting older now. 11, 12, 13, 14...this is the average age to begin smoking. It looks cool doesn't it? Be a rebel, Hollywood style. But look around you, at the people smoking on the street. A lot of them don't look cool, many of them just look yucky.

It's not worth it, to be addicted, to lose your sense of smell, to feel unhealthy, to rub off on other people so that they pick up the habit too, to see them hurt themselves. Smoking is a trend that should change. You need to be able to run from danger. You need to get the chance to grow old. (You don't care now, but believe me, you do.) You don't need to walk around all the time saying I need a cigarette. YOU DON'T NEED TO BE JUST LIKE THEM!

By Ryan

CHAPTER ONE :
Blood at the Old Man Harry's Mansion

Once upon a time there was a kid named Jesse and there was a mean old man at his mansion. One day, after school, Jessie was walking home from school and the Old Man Harry kidnapped Jessie and made him be his slave and he Did lots of things like feeding him, getting drinks for him, Doing everything around the mansion!

So one day, Jessie woke up on the pile of hay he slept on, and he told the Old Man Harry that he was tired of working every night aand day. So the Old Man Harry killed him and that is when Jessie's parents found Blood at Old Man Harry's mansion.

CHAPTER TWO:
The Pay Back

The next day Jessie came back to life and haunted Old Man Harry. When Old Man Harry woke up, he coud not move! Because if he did, he would of got his neck cut. So he took the knife off his bed and then moved. And then he looked around for a killer and went back to bed.

Then he woke up again and spray paint was on the wall. It said on it - It's Jessie and I am back from the Dead. BOO

Old Man Harry ran to the police department and brought them back , but it was gone so the police put him in an mental institution for half a year. And when he came back from the mental institution, the spray paint read, this time, How was the mental institution, Old Man Harry?

CHAPTER THREE:
The Bleeding

The next day, The Old Man Harry went Trick or Treating. Jessie ripped a big hole in his bag and all of his candy fell out and then the old man had no candy to snack on. And then he went home and J e s s i e haunted the Old Man.

The Old Man was tired from walking so he went to bed. And when h e woke up he had blood dripping from his arm a n d he did not have anything to wipe it with so h e went to the CVS to get a towel, but they would not let him in. Then he went to Taco Bell and got some napkins.

CHAPTER FOUR:
At the Church

When Old Man Harry was at church, he saw Jessie's parents. His mom's name is Kimberly Martens and his sister Clover was sittting crying because Clover and Kimberly missed Jessie and wished Jessie would come back. But they didn't know that Old Man Harry had kidnapped Jessie.

And Right in the middle of Church, Old Man Harry stood up and said that he was a Devil Worshipper and he hates God and then he said that every one hates him and he does not have any friends and that he wants to Die. Then he went home and had some- thing to eat, because he was very hungry, because he did not eat breakfast.

CHAPTER 5
The Second Kidnapping

The next day he tried to kidnap Clover, but a cat named Mustard saved the day and scratched Old Man Harry until he got out of the house. And so Old Man Harry went home and wiped all of the blood all off him and went to bed. Then he tried to kidnap Clover again, and this time Clover's mother kicked the Old Man Harry out of the house. And then he went back home and slept until 11:04 and tried to kidnap Clover again. When he got there, Clover was at school already so the Old Man Harry could not try to kidnap Clover again.

CHAPTER 6
The Graveyard

So Old Man Harry went to see his dead grandmother. Jessie's grave was right next to the Old Man Harry's grandmother's grave. Jessie's ghost locked Harry in the graveyard with Blood, Bones, Skeletons, coffins, graves, tombstones and Lots of other scary and nasty weird stuff. Old Man Harry was being buried by Jessie, when he fell asleep.

When Old Man Harry woke up, he could not open his eyes because if he did, he would get dirt in his eyes so he finaly dug his way out but he was a mess. So he went home, when they opened the fence, and changed out of his clothes and put on a clean pair of clothes. And Jessie followed him home.

CHAPTER 7
The Break In Continues

The telephone rang at Jessie's House. His mom picks the phone up and says Hello, what do you want? The Old Man says, I want you and Clover to come to my house. No! She hangs the phone up.

Harry apeared at her house. He tried to open the door. He can't. She forgot to lock the basement door. The Old Man Harry walks up the stairs and he goes to Clover's room.

She went down stairs because she forgot to lock the basement door and when she got there the door was open - so she ran up to Clover's room and she was not there. So Kimberly ran outside and ran to the Old Man Harry's house.

CHAPTER 8

And she snook in and looked all down-stairs and then she heard Clover scream and then she ran upstairs and Old Man Harry went to go and get some duct tape. Then Clover's mom ran back down stairs so she would not get caught in the house and the Old Man Harry went in the kitchen and got the tape and Clover's mom ran as fast as she could up the steps and got Clover and hid and Old Man Harry was looking everywhere for Clover and the Old Man Harry heard someone say "shhh Quiet" and he heard someone else was there.

And then they ran out the window and went back home.

CHAPTER 9
The Loser Dies

This final chapter was never written

It's Jessie, and I'm back from the dead.

BOO

The End

Ryan wrote this story for a class in his 5th grade. He got so into it, that he took it home and kept writing on it. He told me, "Now I know how you feel China, about writing - this is the 1st time I've felt like this" He was so excited. He never turned in the story for a grade since he "was too proud of it to have it messed up by the markings of the teachers red pen". He lost these stories, but found them again on moving day, and gave them to me.

China—

Hi, My name is Breen (like Green). I'm a 20-year-old woman who read your article in *Slug & Lettuce.* I loved what you wrote and I've seen friends have children and feel that they need to leave the punk scene behind. I wish our community had more resources to help take care of punks' children. I'd like to see punk-run day-cares and play groups, help with babysitting, workshops on raising children, maybe even plans to make home schooling possible, material and emotional support. I hope you are very proud of yourself. Does your zine still come out? If so tell me how much $ it is so I can get it. My boyfriend and I also put out a zine called *Disgusted Life.* There was a very small punk show and skateboarding competition in our town this past June and for the most part I was bored, only one band was worth hearing and I am not into skating. But it'll be one of my most memorable shows because of the family unity. A brother and sister set it up. A skater brought his girlfriend, their baby, and his mom and step dad. One band had a husband and wife in it, they brought their two kids, mother, sister and nephew. My boyfriend's aunt, uncle and cousin came. A drummer took his dad. A bass player brought his little sister. There were brothers and cousins everywhere, it was beautiful. I wish it was always that way. Please write and let me know if you still do your zine. I'm looking forward to your next column in S + L —

Breen/Uniontown PA

China—

I got this address from *Slug & Lettuce.* I've been reading yr column I think since it started, and I just wanted to say good job and thanks for the inspiration.

See, I've never been very good with kids—I try to mug it up and all but they always cower in fear of me. So I never thought much about kids—until I started reading your column. Then it kind of all clicked, how we all have amazing abilities and needs when we are kids and how those needs and abilities are ignored by adults, how psychology traces a lot of insecurities and problems to childhood, and how fucked up our society is... I started to think a lot more about children and how I should treat them.

A few weeks ago I went to live on a farm with some adult friends who had their grandson up for the summer. When I met this kid (his name was C-) he kinda scared me. He was nine but he acted like he was four—he was bent on destruction and derived pleasure from killing slugs and spiders — and he sometimes talked about how he wanted to kill himself. His dad had been in the army and took him hunting and fishing. His step dad was an alcoholic, and maybe abusive. Also C- had ADD and was hyperactive. So I was kinda nervous when he, for some reason, decided to attach himself to me. But I realized—thanks a great deal to yer column—that I could only treat him with love and respect, encouraging his "good" side but recognizing that, as an equal in his and my eyes, I had no right to punish his "bad" side (although I never hesitated to tell him what I felt when he tore a slug in half or blamed me for a mistake he made). The result? In two weeks C- seemed a lot happier, showed more respect for things, and basically stopped acting on (or having?) violent impulses. And despite the age difference, we became really close friends—we would spend hours talking about stuff, and now we write each other.

As a result of that experience, I've been learning even more about kids and how they grow. I am going to college next summer for a class on alternative education, and I hope to one day help, teach, or even start a free school. All of this learning and joy and hope I attribute to you and your column. So, thanks. Just wanted to let you know you made a difference.
Stay strong!
P-/Maine

China,

I got *Future Generation* a few months back, I decided to pick it up and read it again — I was totally overcome by utter pain and it totally sucked. (not your zine) I'm kind of reaching out to you, hoping that you might have a word of advice. My ex-boyfriend, (I totally think he is amazing), tells me I'm passive. I don't feel like I don't have will power, but apparently, in relation to the rest of the girls in the punk rock scene, I am. He constantly tells me this and it rips me apart 'cause his opinion means a lot to me for some reason. I don't know what I'm asking you for at all, it's just that I feel so weak and stupid. I want to do so much for women today, but I don't know what to do, or where to begin. I don't want to be considered passive, but I don't know what else to do with a situation but walk away. When should I tolerate things? Why does his opinion matter anyway? I know you may not have the answers to my questions, maybe I really have no questions, or maybe I'm so frustrated that I can't get my point across and you have no idea what I'm talking about…I don't know. I just know I don't want to be passive, what can I do, how can I be stronger? I know it's silly but I know that I am better than this somewhere.

Thanks for listening, S- / from Ohio

Dear S-,

Hi! Well, I can't give advice but I can tell you my thoughts and experiences on this subject because I've had a lot of similar (perhaps) experiences. I feel pretty comfortable with myself now, and I've worked out for myself how I feel. But I am 32 and I bet you are a lot younger.

I remember when I lived in San Francisco when I was 19 and I would look at this group of girls that were skate punks and squatters — they would look kinda down on me and I would look down on myself. Because I was so timid and girly and wore make-up, wasn't athletic, and never got in fights. They seemed so tough, so strong, slam-danced, and so on. But they had the support of each other and I was new in town.

There were other experiences, with other women that I felt lacking in comparison: they were so bold, so hardcore, so cool. This happened to me often.

It's good to reflect on yourself and your femaleness. I went through a stage I didn't wear make up and shaved off all my hair because I thought that having to be pretty is oppressive. There are male qualities I have nurtured in myself—like letting people judge me on my personality and skills and not so much what I looked like; and being more assertive and confident in my needs.

But being confident means realizing the point is to be myself — cultivate my own style — if sometimes taking things from other people's personalities that I admire. When I was a waitress, I was trained by someone I looked up to as the goddess of waitresses—she could handle any situation, she was funny and brazen, people loved her. But I realized I had to be me, had to be real, and found my own kind of waitressing style. Why should we be intimidated to be tougher and rougher? Aren't we then, like boys? I think it's important to stand up for yourself as a woman and identify, express yourself. We are all different, right? The so-called "tomboy" had it hard in the past, you weren't supposed to act like that. Now we all are. What the fuck about what we are "supozed" to be! Everyone woman is different, with similarities and often criticized. So I think celebrate the diversity, appreciate other people's good qualities and strengths as you appreciate your own individual way of expressing strength. Fuck any way that you "ought" to act!

I look for strong woman characters in children's books to read to my daughter. Or just characters period. Not every girl animal in a child's book should have long eyelashes and a bow—she should just be a character, a person, and a female. Now we have Zena and Buffy, and a lot of other female characters—cool. I didn't have that when I was a kid. A plain old character was male. Female was other, defined by sex, or Cinderella ya know. I am more than my sexuality, I am a person, and I am also my sexuality. I am going to talk from my point of view!

I view myself as strong and gentle. I think most people are best with these two qualities; some softness, some hardness, some yielding, some hard-headedness.

Now I have noticed, in all our looking for the female role model, the strong woman, we have looked to the Calamity Janes, the female Pirates, the bad girls, females who went against the grain of society and did the so-called "male" defined things which were really human things. But we never look back and celebrate males who went against society and did so defined "female" things, which are really human things. I mean, we don't celebrate any male in Victorian times that was like, "I want to stay home and raise the children, Damn it!"

This to me is like, nobody respects women, not even women. I like the so-called "female" and "passive" part of human potential as much as the so called "male" and "aggressive" part. I mean, we need all different qualities to be well rounded! And maybe some people's natural temperament is slanted to certain qualities more than others, so as a group we balance each other out.

We need people to listen, to think, not everyone to be bold all the time. It is for you to figure out how you feel. Yes examine yourself, have you internalized oppressive patterns of sex roles from your society and your parents? Explore. Read books, talk to other women, think about what you admire and what you want to be. You will become what your thoughts turn to and you can change. When I was younger my shyness was killing me. I felt locked inside myself, too afraid to express myself, locked into a fantasy of what I wanted but unable to get on stage, to dance, or speak up. It was horrible. I lit some candles on an altar and concentrated on the qualities I wanted to have. I didn't want to be embarrassed of myself, always double thinking myself. And I thought of the qualities I was thankful for. Witchcraft. It took a while but I am definitely not shy one bit anymore.

My friend Georgia just stopped by and I told her about your letter. She said "Oh fuck, I hate guys that try to make you feel bad about how you are, what bullshit, and compare you to this idea of women they probably don't even know so well." She said weakness means you're open to things, you listen, you might see all kinds of things that an assertive person wouldn't. She said, be proud of all you have to express, express yourself, and be as weak as you can. Try to be weaker. Find strength in your weakness.

I like Georgia. When I first met her she told me that she thinks cowards are braver than daredevils because they live longer so over the course of their life the little acts of bravery add up to be bigger.

I think of myself as pretty strong. I think my strength is often mental, in my thoughts, in my will, and inside myself. I don't fight, I can come off as easy going but I know myself. My bravery is that I take chances opening up, by trying, traveling, exploring, and by staying true to myself. By doing what I think is right even when the consequences are dicey and people may disagree with me.

These are my strengths. Other people may be physically stronger or able to build things or whatever. There are all different kinds of strengths.

Well, I think we all have our feeling of self-doubt. You're thinking about yourself, you're growing. Sometimes it hurts to grow. Don't be too hard on yourself. No one is perfect. Please don't feel stupid. I don't think you sound stupid at all. Yeah, of course you care about others opinions and he is your ex so ouch. But even if he is totally amazing, no guy can know everything about you—it's good to get support from girls and people outside of your relationship with a guy.

Well, I hope something in this letter was useful to you and just ignore anything you didn't find useful. I thought it was kind of cool that you would ask me for advice, like something in my zine communicated with you.
Take care,
China

P.S. What's wrong with being sensitive, gentle, flexible, giving, receptive, caring, patient, thoughtful, and excepting…? Nothing! Stand up for your right to have feelings.

Me

"The way I see it, if you want the Rainbow, you gotta put up with the rain."   - Dolly Parton

"Something worth doing, never comes easily"

"If your not rejected 3 times a week, your not really trying"   - yiddish saying

Freedom without stealing"   Responsibility is -Redneck Heaven

If only the forest   best birds in the would sing - the forest would be an awful quiet place

"To light a candle is to cast a shadow" -Ursula LeGuin

Matt and Clover, playing that timeless game; "Lets fight over a stick"

Funky the hermit crab

"Women in Black"- Mandy + China against the aliens

Malila

Gunnar + Earl, (w/ his hair cut) dressed for court

the future generation

ISSUE #11/MAY 2002/ 2$ a zine for subculture parents, kids, friends & others

Issue Eleven

May 2002
Self-expression

Greetings from Baltimore

Dear Ethel,
Did you know that pregnant ladies in Baltimore like to don hot pink bikini's with tu-tu's and do syncronized swimming numbers in the public pools in the summer? Yeesh, things sure are different than down on the farm. Well, actually not that different. How is Huey? I'll be returning soon.
love,
Dottie

Hi! This is a zine for subculture parents, kids, friends, and others. This is a zine so I have an outlet for self-expression and communication with others. This is a zine I am siked to be doing.

Last week, I went to get a cup of coffee at the Common Ground. I like that place and I needed to get out of the house. I had invited my friend to come too but her kid was having a temper tantrum so she didn't come. Perhaps it wasn't the right time to deal with being in public for them. My friend is having a hard time, especially based around the circumstances of being pregnant. When I got there, I saw a mom smiling to her small child with a baby in the sling. I tried to say hi to her, but couldn't do it without going out of my way and looking like a dork. In my head I was thinking, congratulations, you are the 2 out of 5 moms that have actually made it to the café, that tried today.

I am telling this story to say if, if I had a zine, I would have been the dork saying, "hey, do you want a copy of my zine?" and I would have had something to share with her. I want to have a zine so I can lay it around town. A zine to give to my friends; to send to people I think are interesting; and finally, so I have a reason to go bother people and talk to them about what they are doing in their lives and if they have something they would like to contribute.

I do have a zine. I just haven't done an issue for three years!

I have received some great letters, zines, and submissions from being a zinester. But I was never a reliable network or zine. I put out the zines, whenever, and they changed over time with my changing interests and daughter's growth—Plus the big fact that they were too huge to be economical or numerous, I would only make like 50 to 100 copies of each issue. I stopped doing them for a while when life was too ruff and instead wrote angry struggling mom manifestos that never saw the light of day. I also stopped doing them for these last 3 years when I lost an interest in motherhood as a topic, since my daughter is so old and I am gaining independence as a woman on my own.

Hip Mama did it better anyway. *Hip Mama* Chat (on line) was the perfect answer to what I wanted to make, a network for sharing practical, philosophical, political answers, for emotional support, for Everything! The web was instantaneous in a way zines can never be, and it was deep as crap in a way that sometimes you have to be anonymous to ask the questions that are most troubling, and it was real. With so many funny witty women participating. I see what a true cobweb of mama power that exists out there. I don't know if I can explain it to anyone who hasn't been on it. I have seen the manifestation of what I felt we radical mamas most needed.

The "grand experiment" is over now and they have shut it down. It was too big and I think they were tired of people arguing who is hipper than who or people coming to the site and insulting each other (for example: those who dis people for having kids, or post racist, classist things). Perhaps they were burned out. My other friend said Hip mama is definitely not cool enough. Great, I say, we will stay in our own subculture ghetto, with a membership of 4 or 5, and we all talk shit behind each others back too. I believe

the grand experiment was a grand success and a profoundly useful massive network within our community. However, things do change, and the energy behind that project is still alive, just going in different ways.

With the fall of *Hip Mama* chat—although my addiction to that stopped over a year ago when my modem broke—I even more realized the inspiration I feel for putting out my zine. It like dawned on me, as I checked the boards, everyone rushing to exchange addresses, to make there own local groups, web sites and zines—it dawned on me that Small can be very Beautiful. It was something Bee Lavender wrote about growth.

Lately, I realized that the point is not to always grow, to always get a name for yourself. (Not to say that is the goal of other people, but it is something I can get envious of those who do.) People misunderstand you, misrepresent you, make fun of you, and criticize you—even with small fame comes some small bullshit to deal with, you know. There is bad that comes along with every good thing too. The point, I really feel this deep in my heart, for me, is to have a zine. And if this touches 5 people, it is all worth it. I have a few friends I want to share this with. If I get the joy to make this, and if I get the joy to see other peoples art and self-expression—I have like put lots of goodness in my life. After 12 years of having a zine, of never really getting it streamlined, timely, together, or widely known—I feel like a total freakin success still. And I still love zines. DIY. It is fun. It isn't about getting famous cuz that is an illusion. My life, just how it is, with its ups and down, the falling rain, the sunshine, the cloud watching, the rainbows falling from the star crystal my grandmother gave me, in my window as I write and the lilies of the valleys I picked, and all this… This is very real and the most a human can ask for. A single life—truly lived. I am free, very free to make this zine however I want and to move it along to a few folks and to do my part, like many others, to add to some creativity in our scene.

The Pregnant Synchronized Swimmers of Cirque de L'Amour

Frenchie the circus clown is in despair over being knocked up and then abandoned by her lover. She even tries to drown herself but a sweet bumbling clown boy pulls her out. She is still in despair until to her surprise and salvation…she is welcomed into the sisterhood of pregnant woman as represented by a synchronized swimming number.

This was part of the storyline of a play I saw in the Patterson Park pool last summer. Well, a French-silent-movie inspired, only-in-Baltimore synchronized swimming extravaganza. My favorite part was definitely when the six pregnant ladies in hot pink bikinis and little tutus did their synchronized swimming number with their bellies floating out of the pool; then came out and did the Pony to frisky Go-Go music, dancing to the front of the pool where they each in turn bumped bellies to the center where Frenchie stood, now smiling.

Do you know how beautiful six really pregnant ladies, one a week overdue, in hot pink bikinis are? Dang! I read about them in *The Baltimore Sun* paper article entitled: SWIMMING IN SYNC AND PREGNANT—EAT YOUR HEART OUT ESTHER WILLIAMS, before I saw the play. I laughed at the description of their "vacuous, overly enthusiastic smiles" and "theatrical hand waving" where the reporter saw them practicing for their play. "I must be hallucinating," he wrote and also "they hit the water like they were tied to a refrigerator." When I read about their attire and that half of them had tattoos and one a nose ring — I said to myself, "What is this swimming production put on by FLUID MOVEMENT? I must be there!"

And so I went to see this show entitled Cirque de L'Amour (Circus of Love) which the mamas' performance was just a small part of. Sure it was tongue in cheek but I was impressed by their actual exuberant smiles, their lively bouncyness, sometimes they looked like children to me in their pigtails. How fun. They did a good job. And how happy to think how one woman of this very creative dance troupe (their next show is going to be the story of the Loch Ness Monster on roller-skates) got pregnant and then she wrote this part into the play and found all the other pregnant ladies. Will they remain friends after they have children? What a find! Yay sexy wild pregnant ladies, good luck to you all.

Taking a Walk in Woodberry

Every day Sara takes a walk with her daughter Lucy and her two dogs, Buda and Cayda. They live in Northwest Baltimore City.

They walk out her back door and through an alley. Then down a street and turn by the warehouses and old mill stuff. Duck under a gate and into Druid Hill Park.

Into the cool shade of the forest they go. Suddenly you are in another world, of peace and solitude.

They always stop to look at the ostrich. She is enormous, prehistoric, a strange surprise to find in the woods. This is the edge of the zoo, a pen to just hold extra ostriches I suppose, that no one knows about.

    At the end of the road, they slip into a small
path that winds through a tunnel of trees with dancing
sunlight playing on the leaves.

    This path leads to Brick Hill, one of the oldest
neighborhoods with houses over 150 years old, built out
of thick chunks of river rock, to house workers from
back in the Mill days.

Sara and Lucy look up in wonder at an enormous hairy
spider in an old decaying tree.

Taking a Walk in Woodberry: a photo-essay

As they walk back towards TV Hill and the landfill, towards the new playground, they walk by one of the prettiest yards in front of a big stone house, where Sara tells the elderly lady how beautiful her border garden is. Today poppies are blooming as the daffodil season is over. Next week will bring a succession of other flowers. It is well tended and thought out, very *Home and Gardens* elegant in the best kind of way.

Sara says hello to many people and dogs on their walk. When they get to the playground she lets Lucy down. They walk over to the meadow in front of the land fill/endangered wood and see how the tadpoles are doing in a large mud puddle. A troupe of 6 playground kids follow to look with her. The dogs splash in the puddle. Sara worries about what will happen if the puddle dries up, "I will bring water out here myself if it does," she says, "how precarious the fate of these tadpoles."

Then back to the playground. It's newly renovated. The floor is bouncy black stuff. We can rest from our walk here, as Lucy plays. I watch 12-year-old boys do daredevil stunts off the swing set and take stop motion pictures of them.

I think about this neighborhood, how diverse it is in many ways: racially, economically, and socially. We have walked by the houses of many families and even a crack house or two. It's a very old neighborhood, it's not as *hip* to move here as neighboring Hampden, but this place is a treasure. Indeed its been nominated to be declared a historic neighborhood. The green spaces here in Northwest Baltimore are pretty unique. The ex-landfill wild wood area forms a green corridor by connecting the park to the arboretum, which is ecologically important and animals can migrate this way.

The neighborhood is fighting the development of this area by Loyola College. They want to build 71-acre sports complex with two 6000-seat stadiums and parking lots for 770 cars. This is hard to imagine. These worlds are simply two blocks away from Sara, Steve, and Lucy's house, where their street dead ends.

Sara went to two community meetings to oppose the building. The first one she sat for two hours and still the community was not called to talk yet. Lucy was talking baby talk and Sara felt annoying looks shoot her way and she couldn't stay until midnight so she left.

She went to the second public hearing that was in the nearby police station in March. She was heartened to see everyone turn out, her whole neighborhood! The spirits were high. Then the Loyola people talked, and the officials talked, and the neighborhood waited for their chance to speak for one hour, two hours, three than four hours. By 11pm everyone started filtering out without yet the chance to speak out. "This is all a front," someone said, "it doesn't matter what we say, they have decided." Did they purposely do this to tire the community out and take away their steam?

Sara had to take Lucy home. She had wanted to speak out. She is shy but she had rehearsed her speech in her mind. She wanted to go up there, holding her daughter, and simply tell them that she walked in those woods everyday with her daughter and her dogs—how much it meant to them, that this is why they love living here. She wanted to add her voice to the opposition. I have taken this photo-essay, in the hopes of sharing that message with you.

"Mothers are the last riddle, the worst horror, the only consolation."
—Kiana Davenport, SHARK DIALOGUES

The Angst of Being The Parent of a Young Teen
Everyone remembers how hard it was being a teen and recommends all kind of sympathy and kindness to the teen. The parent after all, says non-parents, can be almost perfect. Raise 'em right. Do this. Don't do that. Give love and acceptance, be patient, understanding…Hmm. I have found advice from a parent of 8, on the topic of how to raise teenagers, very helpful—"Get a thick skin." Got to be tuff to protect yourself from your own offspring.

"When are we going to the grocery store?" asks my daughter.

"I don't know, sometime today, tomorrow… definitely this weekend."

"When?!" she yells

"I don't know. Right now I just want to go to the park." She's been invited but of course she doesn't want to do anything with me most of the time. I am fully OK with that and always ask her anyway.

I asked her earlier if she wanted to eat some of Matt's 'creation'—sometimes we get creative with leftovers—and she said "No, his "creation" makes me want to Vomit." I have accepted her strong objections to much about me—at least for now.

"What kind of Mother are You?!" she yells at me.

Not to long ago—I used to be very guilt tripped. What kind of mother was I to be so poor and an artist and depriving my child? But not these days. Not after I graduated from college and got steady employment. "No," I said, "I don't buy that at all. I work, bought a house, provide for you and now I am going to the park."

Get a thick skin. Tell it like it is. Keep your point of view and keep it simple. There is no need for guilt on either side. Be open to them and their point of view and be flexible… don't die under their pressure. Every once in a while, when you had enough, fend off their insults. Every once in a while, miraculously—have a heart to heart and feel pretty good about your relationship. Usually they don't want to talk to you. Just to yell at you.

No matter what you do, you are wrong.

Want to know something? It scares the shit out of me to have a young teen. Even more than having a baby. Or perhaps the same amount, but different. My ideals are kind of over. It's not an idealistic life—it's just another human and me, getting by, no better than the rest.

I have to cut her off a little from me, just to survive. I am a woman, I tell myself, just me—besides being a mom. This mom thing might not work out. I mean I get afraid—afraid of her existence in this world, her choices, her safety, her viewpoints, her mental health.

It's OK. She can hate me. She pushes me away as well—mom isn't "everything" any more. The child's over abundant love gives way to the teens plentiful disgust in mom. But I'm the same old me.

I'm just a lost loser in a way; confused; I'm not secure in my beliefs—so my child has just inherited my outsider status. I'm as scared as any childfree person—"hey, I can barely take care of myself, let alone a child." But I don't regret my decision have a child. If you are going to Live, well then you have to Live. To plunge in, make choices,

take responsibilities, see where it all goes. Things may be in your face, when you're a parent—but to me it is a magnification of issues we all have to deal with.

The angst of being a parent of a teen aged person is that you know all the terrors of growing up but your child doesn't want any of your advice of what helped you, nor think of any of your "improvements" over how your parents raised you are much of a big deal. They know everything they don't have and blame you for it.

The angst is—you see them go through this big muddle of growing up and entering the world and it's almost more terrifying than when you did it yourself. To watch somebody else do it and not know if they are going to walk or fall—and not be able to really help them or prevent tragedy, the big kind of tragedy in Life. You hope for the best…

I've gotten kind of cynical. Like, oh I did that idealistic child-raising thing for so many years. But guess what? It's true—we are all just a bunch of fucked up humans. Frail is Life. Everyone is someone's kid and every mother is a baby too. It can all hurt. Look at us all. Look at the mental adjustments we have to make—just to Live here—just to cope!

But I guess that is OK—it's the reality of Life—the tender and the sweet. Neither heaven nor hell, just a balance of the two—in our striving, dreaming, failing, succeeding, scheming, and Being here! How very human. Don't think that organic food and non-violent child-raising along with all your remorse over personal short comings in raising the brand new being—(who could be Better… who could have it Better—who could be—not like us—not like me) is going to save you from teenage angst. Click your heels three times because there is no place like home so you better love yourself. Humans are flawed, make the best of it. There is some angst in being the parent of a teenager. Like your child didn't grow up to be the super duper product of your super duper schemes, like your anarchist bookstore didn't pan out and your revolutionary plots didn't overthrow the corruption you thought it would. And you still have to deal with this crap, from within the ranks! Like beautiful nature still had fleas and ticks and violence and the best laid plans…well, well, well. It's just the little tragedy of Life.

You see, I never thought I would have a teenager. I'd thought I'd have a perfectly adjusted, independent happy young person—who was free of all the crap that we all had to suffer. She would just step over it—like history. But there is a saying: No matter how tall your grandmother, you still have to do your own growing.

It can be very terrifying to be the parent of a teenager. But it can be very terrifying to be a thinker! Sometimes I feel a deep down Arg. What's important to me is that I keep on, keepin' on—trying to live my heart and brain and spirit and flesh. Sometimes I feel so tough. I'll get through anything. Then I put on my blinders to block it out and pray for the best. Please don't let life send any trials my daughter's way that she can't make it out of—don't let the rainy days drown all the sunny ones.

Tonight I feel a deep weary pessimism and fear of life—fatalism—and oh well, I'll do my best and take my fun where I can. Feeling kind of old, I suppose. Still wanting to try. Fearing ecstasy, that happiness too extreme is a delusion, but depression is a killer.

Mom of Teen: not blown away by life and visions of the possibilities—been in the trenches so long, she has a different attitude. Used to it though. I'm used to it. Supporting another person who is your own weight or bigger. Feeding them. Twice the expenses. Trying to know when to give and when to take care of yourself—when to step in and when to step back.

You never know how it really is — until you walk in someone else's shoes; growing older we are walking in our parents shoes in a way. Even if we don't have children, we are the older generation that the children inherit the world from— what have we done with it?

Yeah, and like every job or position I have ever occupied in this life—Damn—it is a lot different when you walk in those shoes, then when you criticize from the outside.

Baby Birds

The picture of the naked kid covered in mud running down the highway (in Alaska!) on the back cover of this issue is Malila. That was a while ago. Now Malila is 5. We saw her yesterday at her little league game in Roosevelt Park. She takes off her baseball cap and she has green hair!

My daughter sat with me on the bleachers and watched the little kids play ball. Feeling sentimental she said, "I've known Malila forever, even when she was in her mother's belly. Why, her afterbirth was in my freezer."

So I am sitting there with my daughter, at age 14, and she is this pleasant and enjoyable person. We are just easy, talking to each other. I realized she is someone I can count on in a crisis. (I thought I was going to go see my grandmother in the hospital and in that case Clover would have taken over watching Malila for me; then gone home alone to finish her Science Fair project.) And then I thought back to the essay that I just wrote *Angst of Parent of Teenager*. It seemed mean.

There are good things about having a teen-aged child too. Clover offered to teach Malila how to bake cookies this Saturday after she heard how Malila looked up to her, that she thought Clover could do anything: even bake by herself. That made her laugh. You don't realize how big you are until someone looks up to you.

So, its late May, the honeysuckle is all over Hampden, and teenage baby birds are falling out of nests right and left. There are roses in vases at the 7-11, along with the manager's grandchild's schoolwork taped up to the coffee maker. Faith, Malila, and me are going to get a snowcone on the Avenue. We walk by Fraziers and Malila says, "Abby makes the best mixed drinks." That was funny. Bye!

the future generation
P.O.B 4803 Baltimore
MD 21211

the future generation

ISSUE #12 "The Ocean" a zine for subculture parents, kids, friends & others

Inside: All Mom Punk Rock Band - The LACTATORS inter-view; The Maryland Tradition of going to the Ocean - The Waves/camping with teenagers by Michele, Taking Lucy to the Beach/new mom initiation story by Sara, Down by the Boardwalk/"I know what I did when I was your age" by China; Photo-essay: 90 years of changing bathingsuit styles as seen in my family album;Water Birth story by Faith Void

Issue Twelve

April 2003
The Ocean

"Miss Ocean City '67" is the caption my mother wrote under the picture of baby me—that you see on the front cover.

I recently found a bunch of ripped out and yellowed scrapbook pages with square color photos of me from the 60s. Wow! My mother really had style back then. The pictures are incredibly cool in a retro way. All the scrapbook pictures have hand-written captions. Of special interest to this zine's topic is the ocean pictures: *"lunch on dunes"* features my great grandmother, my grandmother, my Aunt Susan and me. *"Look at what I found!"* shows me running after a boy on the beach. *"Bye Bye"*, yep you guessed it, is me waving. *"An early mornings walk with Mommy while family slept"* was pretty sweet. There's a picture with my mom and Aunt Pat looking like laughing girls with me running toward them and a wave in motion titled *"Caught wave in face while running down to Mommy."*

We get a look at all the seasons and holidays of my beginning years. (And a lot of "firsts.") The scrapbook starts in 1966 with *"New Father holding his 1st born."* Then goes onto *"1st drink from glass," "1st flowers of spring,"* and *"1st Christmas at Mum Mum Dee's."* Let's not forget *"My 1st home." "Real cute!"* (A little trailer in Brodskey's Trailer Park.) And *"1st trike."*

New Year's shows me *"Dancing for everyone and wearing Chris's collection of beads"* in front of the basement bar of my NYC grandparents. Jack (my step-grandfather, always just called "Jack") is the only one looking at me, and not at the camera, with a smile on his face. He was such a genuine nice guy. My best (and only) card trick, I learned from him.

An Easter picture (of me), at Mum Mum Elsie's, caption reads *"Our rosy-cheek Easter Bunny"* and (of my father) *"Handsome Daddy."* More picture captions: *"Under the flowering cherry tree supplier of much preserves and cherry pies!!!,"* and *"Jelly beans among the tulips."*

June shows me at *"Patty's College Graduation"*— my mother's youngest sister. It's kinda neat to see how we did all the traditional things. There's a picture of me at my christening, smiling being held by Pastor Zumbrum with a flowery cross and stained glass windows behind me. I find it all quaint. After all I've had a lifetime of very little proper ritual since. No high school graduation let alone prom. (I wouldn't be caught dead at such a thing.) No marriage let alone baby shower. I've never been to church very much in my life, since those first few years, and don't have an institution to bring either my vows or casket to. I've long ago rebelled from everything in society. Nowadays I more balance the old with the new as I try to rebuild some simple rituals to celebrate the special occasions in life. Its not easy, sometimes I am at a loss.

The more things change the more they stay the same—they say. I see my friends keep some kind of journal or album of their children's first years. They do things differently than my childhood—yet their children will no doubt look back in similar fancy. You know, we might as well subtitle this the "time is slipping and China is tripping" issue. Just a little bit. But mostly I am just being a bit retrospective, you know?

Hi! This was supposed to be the Music issue. The Lactators sent me their interview by "dead-line" the end of August—as I was preparing to go to the beach. Everyone I talked to was getting ready to take a family trip down the seashore *or* had just come back from one. As we talked, there was a certain group realization of what a Maryland tradition this is and a feeling of nostalgia.

Greetings from Ocean City

Dear Ethel,
It is so sweltering unbearably hot here in the city! We are going to the Beach this weekend to get away from it all. I will buy some Salt Water Taffee for you! But none for Huey - not unless he writes. ha ha. love,
Dottie

As zine making was slowed down by heat and humidity, and my other musical leads panned out—a new theme for this issue was born: The Ocean. And so Lactators, my sincerest apologies. I have been holding your interview like a pearl within the oyster shell of many months—that I will now present with a theme that is salty. Broken waters, water birth, rolling waves, and an all-mom punk rock band: I think it goes together.

Going To The Beach

(a thinly disguised story) by China

It's a hot August day, and we are going to the beach! But first we are going to the suburbs to pick up my daughter's friend from Elementary School days—before we moved into the city. The girls are 14 now and are going to be freshman in High School when September rolls around.

We pick up Tracy, throw her stuff in the trunk, exchange greetings, and eyeball each other for how we have changed. They have and I haven't. When we stop to fill up the car at the gas station Tracy sticks out her tongue at us with a gleam in her eye. "Its pierced!" my daughter and I shout out in unison.

"I just got it done. You're not supposed to kiss right after, but I have been," she says

"I was supposed to get mine pierced on my thirteenth birthday, but then my mom changed her mind," replies my daughter Sam.

I thought we got an early start by leaving at 2pm this Friday, but everyone else was thinking the same thing so we wind up in a traffic jam creeping towards the Bay Bridge without a breeze. I've nothing to do but listen to the girls talk in the back seat.

Sam pulls out her notebook and pen and designs a dress for Tracy. Tracy looks at the drawing for a while and says, "I don't like the tie on the shoulder, my shoulders are too big."

"Well, the beauty of this is that I can custom fit this dress to fit you just right. If I sew this dress I'm going to copyright the design by mailing it to myself."

We are hungry and I didn't pack snacks nor did we eat breakfast. I'm following my parent's car and I just assumed they would stop somewhere when lunchtime came around—but they are rushing to meet my sister-in-law. She is driving down from Philadelphia with my two little nieces. My brother will come later. My parents have rented a beach house for us all to stay in for the entire week. We will celebrate my dad's recent retirement.

"I didn't eat supper last night. I'm fat. I don't like my body," says Tracy.

This is a repetitive subject I have been hearing since the girls were eight. I'm weary of giving my spiel—especially to medium built girls who look pretty much like the media projected ideal—but this time I don't have to. My daughter takes over. "I think you're fine, your body is great, you're pretty, and you got it all," says Sam with feeling.

"Thank you, Sam. That's why I like you as a friend, I should hang out with you more. You're good for my self-esteem."

"You see," says Sam, taking up the slack with the self-empowerment speeches I've given for so long, "it's not what you wear, it's how you Rock it. It's how you walk, talk, and express yourself."

"Am I Rockin' this outfit, Sammy?"

"Yeah, you're rockin' it."

"Everyone is different and everyone looks good in their own way," adds my daughter.

"I'm hungry!" I say

"I got to get my grub on!" says my daughter

"I'm not hungry. I'm losing weight by eating nothing but junk food," says Tracy returning to her common theme which we, of course, debate.

Later That Night

The girls get ready to go to the Boardwalk. No one else wants to go. My parents suggest they take the trolley and go by themselves. "Wait a minute. I am the Mom here and I don't feel comfortable with that. We might work our way up to that," I say firmly.

I go to the Boardwalk with them and tell them that they can walk around by themselves and meet me in two hours. (I know what I did when I was their age.) "I would hang out with you Miss Donna…" says Tracy.

"I know. It's OK."

"You're sure you will be alright by yourself, mom?" says my daughter

"Sure. I'll go around to the stores and go to the photo booth," I say.

"And tomorrow I'll hang out with you. And we will get our picture taken together," she says.

The Rehobeth Boardwalk is crowded with lots of families; some teenagers wandering around on their own. It looks like a fine environment and not as racy as Ocean City. I like it for that. Once I pass by the girls and see them chasing after some boys.

Later when I meet up with them, Sam is glum. "How did you do?" I asked

"Sam did all that talk in the car but she got rejected by the first ugly boy *(He wasn't ugly! He was my dream.)* she sees and then she has no self-confidence for the rest of the night," answers Tracy. And then she says to Sam, "I gave a boy our number."

"Because he thought it was your number," says Sam.

"He liked you!"

"No, he liked you, Tracy!"

"That boy was cross-eyed from trying to look at us both."

"Don't tell *my mother* this!"

"Sorry."

"This dress is too slutty," says Sam. She has blisters from her platform shoes and is limping, going home sad. But when we get back to the house they stay up to 2:30 in the morning, playing Monopoly and giggling.

Day Two

"Last time Tracy and I came to the ocean (they camped with my mom two years ago) this boy played us" said my daughter. "He told me that he liked me and told her that he liked her. I was mad when they went off alone. This time, we have rules. No boys unless there are two, one for each of us. And we have to stay together, no going off alone. If we get lost we will meet at the Candy Store. Well, I made up these rules."

"They sound like good rules," I say.

After coaching them about where we live; what to look for; what to do—I let them go to the boardwalk on their own and come home on the trolley. "Be home by midnight."

My mother and I take my three-year-old niece Pearl to the boardwalk to ride the Merry-go-round; listen to the Fairfax Town Band; put 50 cents into a mechanical fortune-teller; eat soft ice cream; and people watch. On the way home I strike up conversation with a woman sitting next to me on the trolley. She says she also has a 14-year-old. "Would you let your daughter and her friend walk the boardwalk and come home by themselves?" I ask.

"Noo!" she replies. "Maybe next year. They are just not that good for me to trust them."

"Neither are my girls," I say and suddenly get trembly. What have I done? My mother is fine with it, but she is a little naïve. And wild. She used to put me on real horses when I was little (like 5 years old)—I would be scared, fall off or get knocked off. She was going to put Pearl on a painted horse to ride the merry-go-round by herself but she is a timid child like I was, so I was protective and got on with her.

Maybe I acted prematurely. Tracy acts like she does this all the time; like midnight was an early curfew to her.

And like I said earlier, I remember what I did when I was their age. I remember the first time I went to the boardwalk in Ocean City, back in 1979, when I was 13. We shopped in the T-shirt stores and got black tank tops with sparkly iron-ons. One said I *Get High with a Little Help from My Friends* with a pot leaf on it and another said *A Touch of Clas*s with a rose. We bought ourselves a pipe and a little bottle of Rush. My parents didn't notice a thing. Cruised for boys. One asked us if we wanted to "party". We went down on the beach, in the dark, sat on the sand, near the crashing waves and passed the bowl around until a policeman's flashlight interrupted us. We took off running, got lost in the crowd, and caught up with my parents who were none the wiser. Oh those heady nights, under the full moon.

Most of the time, I, too, would feel sad. Collecting cat calls but none from the right boys. A meat market, everyone looking for someone. I too, was best friends with a girl that always got the boys. It was never me. One memory I have is when I was 15 and was allowed to go by myself. My best friend and I went to some older guy's trailer. We were drinking together and they offered us cocaine. I wanted to try it but my best friend wouldn't let me. They drove us back home, when we wanted to go, without even a kiss exchanged although they were surly about that. I just think back and think—*how stupid!* You can be so stupid when you are young. It worries me that my daughter can be as stupid as I was, or maybe even stupider!

When I got home I expressed my fears. My brother said, "But you're the progressive parent, you have to let her go out on her own although the other parent wouldn't." My sister-in-law is from a small town in Germany, and likewise dismissed my fears of letting them go — "Oh, I was staying out all night, drinking at bars, when I was 14 although the legal age was 16, we would sneak in. I would walk home in the morning hours with my friend and get a treat from the bakery for break-fast. It was fun."

We debated the difference between American vs. European culture. I said I hitchhiked in Europe when I was 18 but I wouldn't do that in this country. That America is different. We have our natural instincts more repressed in this country which creates a society that is more destructive and violent.

I think I freaked her out. She said she was raised in a small town with independence and she was more prepared to be independent. That there was less drugs around her when she was real young, than the stories I told her of my youth.

I want to prepare my daughter, also, to be independent. But it is also up to me to keep her safe. As a poor person, as an American, as some-one who knows there are dangers—I don't want to be too lax. My daughter has given me reason to worry. But perhaps all I do is useless and only luck matters. Still, I must try to keep her safe.

Then the girls come home at 11 p.m.—happy and tired. They had walked all the way home on the beach. The trolley's route was interrupted because of the band playing out-door so they couldn't catch the trolley where I told them too. "We saw so many lovers walking hand in hand on the beach so we ran in the surf singing *Love Lifts Us Up Where We Belong!*"

"Tracy fell down in the sand. We asked some-one where our street was and we found it."

I felt relieved and OK about my decision to let them go. They are good. It was fine. Little steps of letting go, sometimes big steps.

Day Three

They model their shiny new bathing suits, belly rings, mermaid things, dresses—young sum-mer demi-goddesses. Tracy is feeling the power in her body. Sam fears her bikini makes her look too fat by societies measurements but still says *I must adorn myself* in gold with a glimmer flash of red in a Vintage style that is unusual and exotic. The females in our family understand the power of adornment. Gawky growing girls (like how I was) heads above the crowd at size 3 or sticking out in the larger sizes—we need fashion to make us feel better about ourselves. It is a surface level thing but as you grow older and learn to be more free, the facade of confidence sinks deeper until you feel good to be in your own skin. I always smile at my daughter's pride and bravery in her fashion sense.

This girl, who at the age of one, would run straight into the Pacific Ocean—over her head. I finally got tired of pulling her out before disaster struck and let her learn a lesson of the ocean's power by letting it knock her down once. And so it did and filled her nose and eyes with salt water—wiped out by a wave. She cried, recov-ered…and once again ran gleefully into the ocean without restraint. My water baby. My Pisces (it's a sensitive sign). I hope to see her again one day as brave, free, and uninhibited as she was when she was a toddler. To manifest her maturity, self-esteem won back, earned the hard way this time, not given as in birth. I see it in her sometimes. It's not that I want to keep her from reaching or climb-ing. It's not that I want to keep her from experienc-ing intoxicating experiences of love, freedom, and discovery. I want her to grow at her own level. It's just that I don't want her to get hurt. But I realize that sometimes it is by getting hurt that you grow to the next level. Still I am her mom. You know. And in this big world, you only got one mom, looking out for you.

I think they stole their precious loot. Well, how could Sam get a bathing suit for six dollars; Tracy get all that for 14 dollars? (My daughter does not shoplift, as far as I know, she is too scared. But she told me her friend is a regular kleptomaniac.) How can I question them? I am lax. I stole as a teen, quite compulsively. But now I think it is dan-gerous and in most situations, wrong. I know the thrill of taking all the fancy things paraded before you in shopping malls and drug stores—to take all you want. All you could never have, for yourself. To hold your breath, scared, as you walk out the door. Then to laugh delighted when uncaught, out and free.

"Our bathing suits express who we are," says Tracy. "Mine is girly but tuff. Pink and plaid."

"Mine," says Sam, "is very unique."

I don't feel like dealing with this. I can be so negligent—get an eyeful or a sense of something, and then let it go. I used to want to know less, like how my own mother knew nothing of my secret life when I was a teenager. But now I'm getting used to living with the terrible knowledge of my daughter who doesn't feel as pressured to hide as much from me.

Day Four

I swim out to where the girls are and float with them. Tracy says, "It feels like we are in outer space—floating—like in another world." It does. It feels psychedelic, sound and motion, floating in the salty brine, pulsing under the forever sky. That night when they go out, besides my usual little speech of what to do and not to do, I say, "Look, I have this feeling. Listen to me. Don't steal anything, Ok?"

They come home that night, bored. No money left and nothing to do. No success at love. I remember those kinds of nights—looking for a romance I could not find. Back at home, they laugh like children, pool hop at the nearby hotels, eat pizza, and play more Monopoly. I'm happy that they are contained at home like children and not on the town.

I know Tracy is a bit of trouble. Her mother told me that if she gets into any trouble to call her grandfather to come get her. But she has nice qualities to her as well as some at risk kind of qualities. I know my daughter is a bit of trouble. She is not usually a shoplifter though. (She tells me later that her friend stole her bathing suit for her. Which could, or could not, be the truth.)

When it is time to go home, Sam finds that most of the items she bought at the ocean are missing. The red shirt she loved so much and the rhinestone Playboy bunny necklace. She looks everywhere for her stuff. (Later she comes to the conclusion that her friend has stolen all her purchases, even the fake belly button ring that Tracy stole for her in the first place.) My mother buys another Playboy bunny necklace to replace the one that is missing, knowing how sad my daughter was to "lose" it. My mother is very nice and thoughtful. She isn't uptight about girls wearing things like that, and neither am I.

It's time to go home now. The girls never got into any fights until the last leg of the drive home. We drop off Tracy; and her mother and sister come running out of the house; yell her name and hug her. They all look the same size, like three sisters. There is such genuine love displayed. I remember how she had to call home every night when we were at the ocean. Now they pick up her bags and go into the house together without looking back. And then we drive home, back towards the city.

The Lactators Interview!

When I contacted The Lactators to inquire about doing an interview with them, we decided it would be cozier to find someone local to interview them. That person turned out to be one of the band member's daughters: Elcy Reclosado, age 10 and a half. She interviewed Paula Sutor (La) and her mother, Rachael Huang (Reverend Yellow) of The Lactators in Paula's kitchen in Pacifica, California on July 29, 2002.

Elcy: *How many kids do each of you have?*

Paula and Rachael: Soulmine, our regular drummer, has a 3-year-old boy and just had a baby boy in July. Karen, our fill-in-drummer and soon-to-be lead guitarist, has a 7-year-old stepson. La, our bassist, has a 2-year-old son, and Reverend Yellow, our lead vocalist and guitar player, has 2 daughters, ages 8 and 10.

Why did you decide to start a mom punk band instead of just an all-girl punk band?

P: I didn't start it! (laughter)

R: Well actually I never thought about having a girl punk band, I just wanted to have a mom punk band. So many of the experiences we have as moms are fodder for punk songs. We have had some people in the band who were not moms and they just didn't work out, mostly because they didn't relate to the parenting experience or they didn't relate to our scheduling problems.

Do your kids do anything in the band?

R: My kids sometimes sing backup. Even though the kids aren't necessarily in the band, they learn something about moms doing their own thing by seeing us do it.

Okay. Do you wear ear protection?

P: You should always wear protection, no matter what you're doing!

Which is scarier—having a baby or being on stage?

P: Well being on stage is very scary for me, but having a baby was a lot scarier.

R: Hmm, I would agree. Being on stage is pretty darn scary. But, when you have a baby, you aren't so aware that people are looking at you, but it's scarier because of what's going on inside you.

Do you write your own songs or do you sing other people's songs?

R: Well we started out by doing other people's songs and then very quickly…we started doing our own songs. Now we do mostly our own songs.

P: I've always written songs from the time I was 13 so…

Is it fun?

R: The band or writing songs?

Both I guess.

R: I think its fun to write songs. I don't always think it is fun to share them with other people. (laughs) That's scary, the first time you share it with someone else and it's not all polished and put together.

P: I like writing songs and I like being in the band and I'm not afraid to share my stuff with other people before I should (laughs). I'm afraid to talk to people. But I'm totally cool with playing a song that's half finished and doesn't sound so great.

Okay. What are your songs about?

R: My songs are about the things I experience. They really are personal rather than being more broadly political, although I tend to make them kind of funny and kind of trite sometimes.

P: I'll go with that, most of my stuff is about personal experience. Lately, I've been going through this series of songs about the alienation I've been feeling as a mother. And that's definitely based on personal experience, but I'm trying to give it a broader appeal — if that's possible! (laughs)

What do you like doing best in the band?

R: I like imagining being rich and famous (laughs). I like having lengthy discussions about what we're going to do when we're rich and famous.
P: (laughing) I also enjoy the fantasy world that comes with being in a band.

What's the hardest thing about being in a band?

P: Finding time to write music and practice.

R: Yeah, and figuring out how to publicize ourselves. Unfamiliarity with the industry is really hard for me.

P: And being on stage is hard for me.

How do people react when you play?

P: They bow before us! (laughter)

R: They come forward with tons of money and throw it at our feet. They scream our name for five hours after we're done. (more laughter) How do people react? They like us. We're sort of surprised.

P: Yeah, I'm still waiting for the one bad crowd to turn us off to the whole idea.

Okay. Do you have a CD?

P: I have many CDs. For instance, *The Best of Glen Campbell.* It's on loan right now, though.

I'm serious! Come on...

R: We're working on a tape. We have an mp3 and some video footage on our website. (now defunct)

Is there anything you don't like about the band?

R: It's more external. I feel like, either my kids have to hang around here at Paula's house while we're doing band practice, or I have this large struggle to get somebody to watch them, and I feel like that's sort of—I think it's just unfair. There's not a lot of support externally. In the band, yeah, it's great, but...

P: I have a lot of guilt wrapped up in the amount of time spent practicing and not being with my son. We did a gig last Saturday, and the amount of time I was away from him made me feel somewhat uncomfortable and questioning—how important is this, the band versus spending time with my son? But, you know, on the other side of it, it's important to me!

R: It comes from this feeling of "God, do I really deserve to...?" It's just so ironic, because our whole message is about self-empowerment!

P: Right!

Thank you for answering my questions!

P and R: Thank-you!

Mcdonalds

When she was young I taught her to stay away from the scary clown; the cow killing, environment wrecking, bad for you food.

Everyday my daughter wants things. I buy her things that I don't use, like razors to shave with. "Don't shave," I first recommended, but eventually bought her what she wanted anyway. She eyes the fancy vials of body products in the grocery store and the clothing in magazines. I bought her an outfit for the party she went to last weekend, which was a rare treat. She never has everything she wants and just almost everything she needs.

Everyday my daughter wants things. She is mad and embarrassed with me for not having as much money as some others; annoyed that I don't care for big TV sets or new cars. She says that when she grows up she is going to drive a new sports car. "What, just to work and back everyday - where you work to pay off your car bills?" I respond. So after years of young material lust and anger at me, my daughter's refrain changed to—I want a job. I want to get what I want for myself.

She is not unfamiliar with work. When she was 8 she used to help bus tables at the café where I worked during Sunday brunch. (It was cute to share that with her, sometimes people would tip her. She liked to wash the cups behind the bar and use the soda sprayer. Once she served some local boys: they whispered when seeing her on the street "That is the girl that works at Gypsy's Cafe,"- in awe that a peer had so much power. The elegantly beautiful bartender, who was usually not fond of children, was quite nice to my daughter and shared gawky coming-of-age stories with her. Sometimes, we would go eat Sushi afterwards as our treat. We both loved the cheeto-orange colored roe that popped under our teeth.) When she was 11 she cleaned her great-grandmother's windows in order to earn herself a summer wardrobe. She also worked a few hours a week as an apprentice, as part of her school day in the 7th and 8th grade. It was one of the cool programs at the GreenMount School—it got kids out into the community and experiencing life. When she was 12, she volunteered at the Family Learning Center, where she helped little children after school with their homework. The next year, I knew she was ready for something more mature. She was interested at that time, in perhaps running a café. She has many schemes like that, interests that come and go. What could be better than working at our local café? I asked the owner and he said "Yes" to me with barely an explanation on my part. (I look up to him for that, and for the gift tree he put in at Christmas to collect gifts for teenagers who were, you know poor and would probably get no gifts. Not many people think of that age group at Christmas time.)

Well she worked like a dog there, mopping floors, cleaning dishes in the basement and once cleaning out a disgusting refrigerator. But she was also learned how to cook potato leek soup (and made it at home for us!), helped prep food, was given delicious smoothies to eat and mentored by caring folk. We would argue about her walking home on the avenue at night by herself, I wanted to come pick her up. Sometimes I did anyway, although I was not supposed to and, for the most part, did respect her wishes, nervously waiting at home or looking down the street for her.

My daughter wants to grow up, feel capable and unafraid of it. I am still here for her, forever, when she needs me and accept any babyishness from her also. She wanted to work, her freshman year, and not a lot of places will hire 14-year-olds. (It is ironic that while I well resisted having my daughter sucked in by "happy meals" in her impressionable youth, I didn't escape the second round with McDonalds as the biggest employer of our youngest teens.) She got this job on her own.

So when she works at McDonald's, I don't see an unpolitically correct behavior I should be ashamed of, I see my daughter being proud, happy and self-sufficient. She's out of the house, busy and a part of something. Before this she watched too much TV at home, alone. Every time I pick her up, I see her looking alive, comfortable, waving goodbye to everyone and then she tells me funny anecdotes. About a man who is always a picky eater, asks for three tomatoes, fat ones, one in the top layer, one in the middle and the lower layer, extra mayo, extra, etc. Naming each thing when he could have said, Extra everything. She tells me of an old man that comes in for a "senior coffee" and gives her the other 50 cents from the coffee as her tip. Of the people who work there, "Pops" and her nice manager and the funny things people say. Of when the frosty machine blew up, a man wanted

to buy a Big Mac for a penny, or families that come in and eat only off the dollar menu.

Sometimes she is tired and says "I been a mama all day. The customers are babies: hungry, whiny, and messy. We have to clean up after them all day. My manager says they don't think we are humans and they don't. We are humans!"

She is learning something about life working in a McDonalds in this small town section of Baltimore City - and seeing a cross walk of human life. When I see this person through the window, transformed by a uniform…it is weird to see my daughter like that, from afar. But she could never learn this work ethic or responsibility at home where she will always be a slob and I am the typical nagging mother.

I mostly see her be grumpy at home and harsh on me, because she is a teenager. But it is not hard for me to look outside, and see how wonderful a person my daughter is. I don't wish she was more like me, or less conservative or mainstream in some of her ideas. I have gotten used to this person with growing independence and identity so separate from mine—and I have come to appreciate her own brand of strength and beauty. I respect and love her. I listen with interest of her tales of high school: an all-girls school (where they can see boys at lunchtime and at dances) with lots of school spirit. She loves chorus the best of all, loves her voice blending with others. At Christmas time they went to many places to sing and she told me poignant stories of the experiences. She is also an amazing artist, always has been. She draws these design fashions that just keep advancing; when schoolmates see them they express interest in wearing her creations. She is seen as a creative person, like for the collages she always makes on her notebook covers, cut out of Essence magazine. She definitely has an eye, and a way with design. She signed up for a group therapy class at school, where people can just go and talk about what stresses them out in a support group and are not allowed to say what others reveal in confidence. She never does. She tells me that she can't tell me. But says that it feels good to know she is not alone. That other girls get stressed and take it out on their moms too. She is very self-aware. And crazy funny. She has soul and joy for living.

Through my daughter I have grown so much and I think family makes you closer to people outside of your own little cliques. Maybe at some point I would have made fun of people who work at McDonalds—but no longer. I don't like the Corporation but I respect the individual people. Everywhere you go and everyone you see—that person is someone's sweet babe and has a story of why they are where they are—we should not be so quick to judge and stereotype other people.

Photo Booth Musings

My daughter is humoring me by squeezing into the photo booth to get our picture taken. By the last picture she is ready to go and annoyed. I am giving a goofy smile. These pictures did not turn out as good as I would like.

I look in shock in this picture, like a deer caught in the headlights. I didn't know if the picture was going to turn out since I had tried it twice before and the machine kept messing up. I would get a carnival employee's attention who would return my money and fiddle with the developing bath, and then I would try it again. I guess I was looking for answers: who am I?

The pictures on that strip remind me of my first baby picture. My head is big and oval. What an ugly baby I was, I would tell my mother. "No, you weren't. The photographer came around to the trailer and just set up his stuff and took your picture. He wasn't a professional; they weren't good pictures. You were cute." When I shaved my head, or when all my hair is pulled back, I have this long face like in that first baby picture.

It makes me think of when Kim showed me this newborn picture of her son, Lucas, and said that she could see him all through his life, in that picture. When he was an old man, on his deathbed, he will look the same. I could see what she was saying, how this one picture had captured him at his purest essence.

There is something you can recognize in people that is timeless.

I remember when I was a little girl, laying on my bed with my socked feet up on the wall, pawing at the wall, aimlessly, just thinking about stuff. And I remember walking down a certain stretch of road in the suburbs of DC that I walked down on a daily basis, when I was 14. And it happens too, as I write this. First I think about this thought. Then I experience déjà vu. It's easy to summon. I just think back

to that day when I was laying on my bed, when I was probably like 6 or 7. Then I feel my life recede into a dream that I am waking from, as if it wasn't my life at all, and I am waking up to what is real, right now, right this second. I am emerging from the waters into the island that is always the same. I am here, in that same lucid moment when I was 6, when I was 14. It feels like the time I learned to hyperventilate in my friend's basement, with her hand's on my throat and it actually worked—I just didn't pretend it was working—and when I came to my body felt fuzzy and my arms and legs were walking in place as I had been hallucinating that I had been walking down the street out front of the house. And whenever you think this feeling is going to come on you, then it really comes on in the next second, in a big wave.

Does this make any sense to you? Do you do this? Does all your life ever feel like one big dream you are waking from? It's definitely kind of creepy. When it happened, when I was walking down the street in the suburbs as a teenager, I didn't call on it. It just happened. That was the same stretch of road I dreamed I was walking on when I had my first lucid dream, when I realized I was dreaming. I realized then that dreams were not that different than life— before I lost track of the lucidity and turned into a pelican flying over the ocean. Have you ever had a lucid dream? Or learned how to control your dreams? To draw forth a window to climb out of the darkness of a nightmare? That is a good task. According to the *Egyptian Book of the Dead*, it's not so different than being between lifetimes and picking out a body to enter.

People say I look young for my age. And that I act young too. Its weirds me out because I don't want to be immature. When my boyfriend first met me, he said I was Bjork like, ageless, young and old. What a nice compliment. But he found out I can be a bitch— very unlike a Bjork-persona. How does Bjork handle it? Does her teenage son ever stress her out and she yells like a fishwife? I am not just a sweet girl. I love snowball fights but watching the Michael Jackson interview made me see how retarded you can look if you act too much like a child when you are old. I have no problem retaining a youthful spirit but I also want to be a mature woman. Do people have wrong expectations of what a 36-year-old is supposed to act like? Am I immature? Or is it just in my genes to look young for my age?

The waves swell up and crash down, breaking into a great froth, like beer poured roughly—releasing ions into the air. Where the sea meets the land and the horizon is open - that's where you'll find me.

On my beach blanket, under my umbrella with a cheap paper back and a picnic basket full of snacks - toes digging in the sand. I've got nothing to do all day but lay on the beach - with the masses. The spectrum of humanity: toddlers, young families, teens, old people; The spectrum of flesh: hairy backs, baby butts, bodies straining against bikinis. All the generations and shapes and sizes.

Sand Castles and wave riding. Dolphins, sea gulls and sand crabs for company. Sun above drys us off after we swim. The air smells good.

At night, I'll go down the Board Walk. Fun house rides, people watching, and boardwalk fries (with vinegar). Games and knickknack buying. Seashore business range from the nostalgic to the tacky with all the latest fads in between. Get your picture taken. Boys look for girls and girls look for boys. Take a moonlit walk on the beach.

Welcome to the Summer Seashore of Ocean City, Maryland or Rehobeth Beach, Delaware. It's been a Maryland tradition since the last turn of the century - to beat the hot humid cities/towns and have a get-a-way.

Its the simplest thing in the world: going to the beach in the summertime. Yet when we stop to think of it we realize our grandparents and great-grandparents have done the same thing before us. And that rocket ride we have a picture of our child on, is the same rocket ride we got our picture taken on when we were a child. We realize something special in this ordinary tradition. Something special in our ordinary beaches…

For when we travel elsewhere - we find that no other seashore is quite like ours. Up North, the coast is rocky with cliffs - they don't have our long sloping beaches and sand dunes. Down South, the sea is warmer and bluer - not so moody and without our big waves. The West Coast is also colder and lined with cliffs.

Nothings like our own Ocean. Its not glamorous - designed for foreign tourists - its just our own local populated east coast destination. We go to the beach to celebrate. For graduation, or a honeymoon - or for a simple summer vacation. We go to the beach for solace and healing. After a divorce or an injury. Rock me in your arms, Great Atlantic mother. Let me sleep as I hear your waves break: soothed by your sounds, healed by your salt water, all senses engaged by the elemental. ∎

My Family Photo Album
A seaside photo-essay of 5 generations

My Great Grandmother, Elsie Doretta Hueg 1917

My great-grandmother worked as an upstairs maid for the Mayor of Baltimore—Mayor Preston. (German maids were as in vogue for upstairs maids as the French were for downstairs maids. She calmed the little Preston daughter down when she had belly aches, arranged red roses in a silver Stieff basket on the piano, and admired the fancy clothes of the important visitors, like the Vanderbilts, who came to dine.) Then she was employed by the Abell Family—relatives of the Abells who founded and owned Baltimore's Sun Newspaper for three generations. When Walter Abell took his family to their summer house in Bayhead, New Jersey—Elsie was brought with them.

One of her tasks entailed canoeing across the Bay, every morning, to get the mail. She was very fond of her employer's child, Lydia, and would often help take care of her. When she helped the maid who hung Lydia's diapers—Bill Farinholt, the Abell's chauffeur/mechanic (He, as well as the car, had actually been given to Walter Abell as a present from the elder Abell) would come and flirt with her.

Bill was well liked by all. He was a man prone to do funny things, sing silly songs, tell jokes at times—yet remain quiet at other times. Polite with a long face and reddish hair. The cook would always save a little piece of cake for him, a uniquely friendly act that none of the other employees ever experienced with her.

This picture of my great-grandmother was taken by Bill. They had only known each other for a few months. They were married a year and a few months later—after he served a year in the Navy. He proposed on leave. I wonder at the time of this picture, if she knew he was her husband to be? She was 19 years old in 1917.

Elsie and Bill Farinholt had two children, a girl and boy. Their favorite summer activity was to go to the Beach. This is how my grandmother tells me the story:

"Mother didn't always want to—for it was she that had to do all the work: fry the chicken, etc. So Daddy would be charming and make her laugh and promise that he and the kids would pack and do everything.

They loaded everything—including her cook stove—in the Model Ford or sometimes a truck, and drove around the Bay (there was no Bay Bridge back then) for it cost less than to take the ferry across the Bay.

Then they would set up their tent in the sand dunes near what is now 33rd street. (Back then, there was nothing there, no hotels.) Daddy would go down to the local dump and bring back wooden boxes and crates to construct into a makeshift table, chairs and cupboards. They might have a cooking tent.

The picture at the top is Daddy (holding eels) with Mr. Larson and his son. The Larsons were family friends—a great big (8-10 kids) Swedish family that lived down by the Ocean year round. It was so much fun to visit them. The dinner table was full: 10 blueberry pies (we would pick the blueberries, Uncle Bill would help too, endearing him to Mrs.Larson), piles of fried fish (the males would go fishing) and lima beans out of the garden. They slept on mattresses filled with straw."

The bottom picture—(back row) Aunt Annie, Mother/Elsie, Aunt Bessie, Uncle Howard and Uncle Bill.(front row) cousin Helen, Kenneth (the boy) and Doretta (the girl).

Camping at Ocean City, 1930

My Grandmother,
Doretta Law,
Ocean City, 1940

This is a picture of my grandmother on her Honey Moon. (Her wedding just cost 27 dollars and 50 cents. Her mother sewed her dress and baked the cake in her typical can-make-anything-with-finesse way.) My grandfather, Fred Law, took the picture. They were married for 17 years, had three girls, and ran a farm together. Fred started a hardware business with his brother, called Law Brothers, which you can still find in Ferndale, Maryland. This might not be the best place to add, with this young picture of new beginnings, but it is notable that my grandmother also went to Ocean City after her divorce. She was very melancholy and her mother said, "Come on, let's rent a little house and take the girls, and just get away from it all." Her mother took care of her and it was very healing.

As unusual as it was to get a divorce in those days, and as traumatic as it was (my grandmother would have never divorced her husband, he left her for another woman in a mid-life crisis) she certainly did come out on top of the situation. She became a schoolteacher, working as she raised the girls, going to college at night and in the summertime. The principal at the school she taught at allowed her to teach even though she was still pursuing her degree. (It took 15 years to get her bachelors degree by age 53) Her experiences as a Girl Scout leader are what led her into teaching.

My grandmother is a world traveler and an influence on many: with her "Come Day, Go Day" sunny temperament inherited from her father and creative streak from her mother. Much loved by her daughters, gentle and giving, I can't say I have ever seen any event get my grandmother down. Her divorce, perhaps, set her free.

My Mother, Lynda Law, Ocean City, 1963

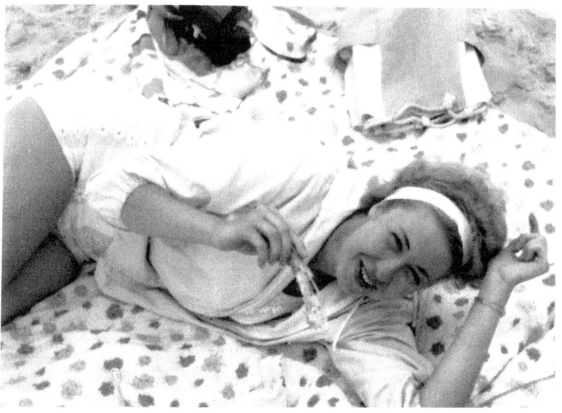

Here my mother is 19-years-old. The pictures are taken by her youngest sister, Pat. They stayed for five days at the Surf and Sand Hotel—and felt like big shots.

The chicken she was eating in the picture, was no doubt made by her Grandmother Elsie. And as for her tan, it was memorable—when peeling leaving behind a freckled back that lasts to this day.

She treated her sister to this trip as a high school graduation present to her. She had earned the money for the trip from her job at Westinghouse where she worked as part of the technical publications typing pool. It was her first job. And it would have never been if it hadn't been for Grandmother Elsie's encouragement, who told my mother to apply to this one last job even though she was tired, and sat in the car and waited while she did. "Don't be intimidated," Mum Mum said, " they pull their pants down to sit on the toilet, just like anyone else."

Fortunately for me, my mother did get that job—where she was to meet her future husband, my father, a technical writer from Brooklyn, New York.

Here I am in the surf with my great-grandmother. And with my little brother. The picture of my daughter in front of the sandcastle is from when she was much younger than she is now. That picture was taken in Rehobeth as now my family goes to Rehobeth Beach as Ocean City is much too built up.

Last summer, I saw my daughter wearing a hand-made beach jacket sewn from a towel so I examined it more and found a tag inside that said: Made By Doretta. It had once belonged to my mom. We tend to keep things forever in this family, and if you pick up something and notice it—well, there is always a story attached.

We drag out our old beach umbrellas and blankets and try to get together each summer and go down the Ocean—if not every year than most years.

I was lucky to know my great-grandmother until she died at 88 when I was 18. Listening to her stories from the olden days has given me a taste for "herstory"! I was babysat by her as a child and inherited that same streak of creativity—which I, in turn, handed down to my daughter: Nadja Atalanta Tathata, AKA Clover, born in 1988, a girl, of course, as my maternal lineage is first born girls to first born girls.

My daughter is now almost 15 and still has the privilege of knowing her own great-grandmother at age 83.

Myself/ My Daughter

Letter Writing

I was talking on the phone the other day with my Grandmother. She said she had gotten a letter from the *Italian girl.* She was working in another big fashion house—not Valentino's any more—and was getting ready for a show, putting in long hours. She had moved in with her boyfriend, and was in her 30s now. But it was a sad letter really, my grandmother said, for she wrote that her parents were both in very bad health.

My grandmother was happy to receive the letter from the Italian girl. It had been a long time since she had written and she had just sent a letter to her, saying to write back, just enough so she knew she wasn't dead or something.

I know my grandmother has a young Italian pen pal, as well as a young Japanese pen pal. They are somehow inter-linked with each other. A few years back my family stayed with the Italian girl's family in Rome. And a while before that, my grandmother went to visit the girl in Japan. These are things that I know, but I never questioned how this was. I am used to my grandmother's traveling and having correspondences. She keeps up with her old neighbors from "down when we lived on the farm" who have been living in England for longer than I have been alive. She writes her cousin in California, who moved away when they were still children. She is a real letter writer. The type who has a desk with special writing paper and who carries out correspondences over a life time. She wrote to "Puddles", her dear friend from Girl Scout days, who moved down south, until she passed away.

My grandmother is a retired school teacher (whose old second grade students sometimes write her with prom pictures, wedding pictures and baby pictures enclosed) who owns her own house, built on her mother's property. She has lived in the same state all her life. She is a world traveler, not because she is rich, but because that is one of her priorities. Her first big trip was after her divorce. She loaded the girls up and they drove to California and back. Saw the Grand Canyon. Even went to Mexico. She had always wanted to do that.

Now my great-grandmother—she was a truly great letter writer. I remember her sitting at "her chair" with the big arm that you could place a letter on, writing to her correspondences in the evening time. She would often enclose magazine or newspaper clippings in her letters—and detailed what she was cooking, how the garden was, and what the market prices were. Once she wrote her friend, "Come on now, you didn't tell me what you have been eating for supper! Write me a real letter, give me the details." She would always sprinkle her letters with at least one *ha ha* at the end of the sentence, so you got her joke.

My grandmother, less practical, more the extravagant one, would pepper all her letters with wonderful illustrations so you could see what she was talking about. Drawings of people, places, and the things that she was working on. She was very crafty: always working on things to sell at craft sales, collecting things for my doll house, sewing little felt mice or pressing dried flowers.

I still have all the letters they wrote me, as a child when I lived in Germany. They stayed in touch with me, very closely, although I was overseas for 4 years. (Between the ages of 8-12. I was a kind of "army brat".)

It's just something I take for granted. You know how you take your family's ways for granted. I go, "uh huh…yeah…yeah" on the phone while my grandmother talks about her pen pal. Then it occurs to me to ask, "Mum Mum Dee, how did you get to know this Italian girl?"

"Well she was in an international summer camp for girl scouts in Maine, that your Aunt Pat attended. Pat told some of the girls there, 'When you are done for the summer here, you must come back to my house with me, and then I will take you to meet my mother.' So, they came and stayed at my house for a week. I drove them to Washington DC. They were very happy to see the Capital and visit the Smithsonian. I took them to the Inner Harbor in Baltimore. I would also drop them off at the train station so they could explore by themselves. We had a good time together. Summer camp had been hard on them. Pat wanted them to have a better time seeing America."

Stuff like that is just ordinary with my Grandmother. Suddenly, I realized again, what a special lady she is. As we continued our conversation, I said to her, "You and Mum Mum Elsie have always been big with the letter writing."

"Oh yes, Mum Mum Elsie certainly was. I remember she used to write her cousins in

Germany. We have lost touch with that part of the family now. She used to write Uncle Krystal—I don't know why we called him Krystal- His name was Krystoff? Maybe it is German for Chris. She was very fond of him. He had been very nice to her, when she was a child and lived with him—after her mother died when she was 7 or 8—before they came to America. Anyway, when Uncle Krystal was an old man, after his wife (her father's sister) passed away, after WWII, after his own son died in a camp in Siberia—Elsie would send him cake in the mail. Pound Cake. Fruit Cake at Christmas time. With Coffee. And at that time, after the war, they had a shortage of coffee and such. He would so look forward to her packages. He would write her back letters of how happy it made him, how he would invite all the 'boys' over to his apartment—it was a one room place, very poor, all he had was a hot plate to cook on—and they would have coffee and cake together. Then he died. We later found out, that Uncle Krystal had been very sad, he walked down to a fast rushing stream, walked into it and drowned. That is, well, he killed himself. His daughter in law, Lena, then kept up the correspondence with mother. We visited her when we went to Germany. You were there."

"Yes," I say, foggily remembering, "…she was the grandmother, right? There was a mother, and a child."

"You went to the playground with her," said my grandmother.

I remembered what a dull time we had had. And then I say, "They had currants growing in their backyard!" *Yes, that is right*, granny says. And I feel triumphant, remembering this vivid detail—that ties me to this family; this story that I never knew; that my grandmother tells of now. I remember how we had tea and cake with them, and later a simple German supper of bread and meat on boards. I was only 7 or 8 at the time. I think it was when my grandmother took me to Germany, before I moved there. But it is the shiny red currants that stick out in my mind, the strongest. If I was writing you a letter, this is where I would draw a little picture to illustrate, the small shiny berries, that I had never seen growing in America.

A good deal of my nature to make zines is in fact an inherited tendency for correspondence. The act of letter writing has been lost in the modern world. I hope this zine brings you a little bit of the joy of a pound cake send in a parcel, or of a message from a far: of what another person is eating, how others are doing, and with clippings (articles and features) of interest. Make a cup of tea and share this with a friend.

the future generation
P.O.B. 4803 Baltimore, Md 21211

Great Aunt Annie, she's on the left, in the 20s.

the future generation

ISSUE # 13/ SEPT 2003   a zine for subculture parents, kids, friends & others

HAPPY FATHERSDAY♥

Issue Thirteen

September 2003
Happy Father's Day

Ⓔ☮♥ China

Dear Ethel,
I don't miss Mum Mums pies anymore, not since I have found out
about the Dangerously Delicious
Pie Shop. You go ahead and tell
Letta, I'm a city girl now and I
get my strawberry rhubarb pies
baked by a great big Rock Star!
ha ha

love, Dottie

Dad (Rodney); Mom (Heidi); Baby (Waylon); and friends outside the shop.

Dangerously Delicious: A family business

Rodney Henry, singer/guitarist for the country-blues-punk-rock band: The Rock Bottom Stylings of Honky Slim and frontman of the legendary (defunct) Glenmont Popes, is not just a fixture on the local music scene (and touring band as written about in *TED NUGENT CONDOMINIUM/* Apathy Press 2001). He's a new dad, business owner, and bakes pies that taste like my great-grandmothers did.

China: *How did you get started baking?*

Rodney: With my grandmother in Indiana (outside of Indianapolis). Every June, after school got out—we would go out and stay with her for a few weeks. I would get so bored, that I would bake with her. I was a good helper—it was Fun. She would make some seriously nasty rich stuff, real sweet.

C: *How old were you then?*

R: Like from when I was seven, until I was 14 (when she died).

C: *When did you start baking pies as an adult, for money?*

R: I got into pies more seriously, like when I was 30. I thought: maybe I can start baking to supplement my income. I baked for fun. For parties. I didn't have any money—but you can always afford some flour—not look like a punk, have something, to bring to a party.

When it came time to earn a living, then I thought—maybe I can do this as a job. I've always been handy in the kitchen—worked in kitchens between tours and stuff. And when I was on tour—I sold more pies than CDs.

C: *Where did you bake?*

R: At people's houses. You can meet a lot of friends through baking. Meet other people who bake. Bring a pie to a party or a barbecue.

We are having a show tonight.

C: *Live music?*

R: Yeah. The Night Lifers. They play honky tonk. A stand up bass and two guitars. We have live music play in the shop, every Saturday at 4:00.

As we talk, the music in the background changes from Honky Slim to Dean Martin (a locals choice) to Reverend Horton Heat and then to Peggy Lee. Some men come in, with big beards and long hair. They look over the wares. "Would you like some pie - we have Key Lime . . ." Up on the menu I see listed; Pecan, Chocolate Pecan, Derby, Sweet Potato, Pumpkin, Shoe Fly pie, Apple, Rhubarb, Straw-berry, Blackberry, Raspberry, Blueberry, Cherry and Peach. Everyone loves pie. It's cute to see these gruff mens attention completely absorbed by the homemade wonders in front of them. The next customer is a middle class looking woman and child. Then an elderly local. Another woman asks for the big cookies Heidi bakes.

C: *You get all kinds of people in here, don't you?*

R: Yes, all walks of life. I really like that. This is a place for everyone.

So, now that I'm a family man—its good to have a business. It gives us the chance to be together, work at our own business, and not to put our son in daycare. [Both parents express how good they feel about this] Waylon is a happy baby. He loves music.

We talk of his son. I say that Faith has told me I have to get a photo of him holding Waylon, over his shoulder, where I can get a shot of his new tattoo: a pie with Harley Davidson type wings on it and the words Dangerous Pie inscribed

underneath! Rodney says, "That's it! I'm waking Waylon up." He was sleeping in the back room. Heidi goes and gets him. They humor me and pose all over the place for me to take pictures.

C: *How about touring?*

R: I haven't been touring for the last few years - I'm kinda burnt out on it. Some guys in the band would like to. But, it's probably more fun here for me. [Heidi and Rodney smile at each other. "Probably," she asks?] No, it's definitely more fun for me here, he adds with a grin.

Eventually I'll take them out on the road like the Partridge Family.

cute!
Waylon with Pie (the pix that was up on the wall) & Waylon (upper L.) on May, 2003

The picture on the back cover is of Chris Calabrese and Lucy. He is not fond of this picture but I like it a lot. Chris is really tall, just like my brother Chris. That makes me feel familiar to him. The funny thing about Chris is that I have known him for so long: I mean, not really well, but he was one of the young punk kids that would run around with Justin and the Chesapeake Action Network, when we lived on E.Baltimore street. Then later, I saw him. When my daughter went to kindergarten at Grace and Saint Peters, I would walk by The Baltimore School for the Arts, and see Chris hanging out in the doorway and say "Hi." Now my daughter goes to High School. Isn't that weird? That I met him, when he was the age, or younger than my daughter. Another thing I think is really nice about Chris is that he helped me out, when I asked him to paint rocks ← pet with all the kids at the GreenMount school, when my daughter went there in 8th grade. He is no dad, but he is a good friend, I guess you would even say an Uncle, and lives with Sara, Steve + Lucy. And he is in the Honky Slim band. So that's the story of why he is on the back cover. The picture is by Sara. Isn't she the most awesome photographer?!

← like 10 yrs. ago

She gave me a picture of Clover and I, from a long time ago. That is really neat, that she had this picture of us. I was intriguing to her, as this person who had a kid. And now I know someone, who told me how she (Sara) was so inspiring to them, that they could be who they are, + be a mom, and it all be good.

Isn't time a funny thing? And how the cycle goes on.

↳ Neumayer
And by the way, Justin, well now he has two kids now and he lives in Europe with his wife. I am hot and tired and this is not well written, but this is the end.

(these are old pictures, Lucy is almost 3 now)

Goodbye!

the future generation
P.O.B. 4803 Baltimore, Md 21211

the future generation

Photo by Victoria Law

March / 2005 / 3$ a zine for subculture parents, kids, friends & others

Issue Fourteen

March 2005
Work

Victoria Law took the picture on the front cover. Here is part of an email she sent me from the trip this photograph was taken on: "I visited my mama friend Jessica at her house. It took over an hour to take the bus from North Seattle to South Seattle. By the time I got there, she had gone out to buy dog food. Her twelve-year-old daughter answered the door. "Hi, I'm Zahra," she said, holding her hand out to me. I remember Zahra as a five-year-old whom I used to watch. I remember two and a half years ago, Zahra dragging me around her neighborhood in Seattle showing me her world—the cafe where her mom worked on certain days, the pet store that she worked in other days.

"She remembered none of that. She showed me the chicken coop and the two baby chickens that she recently bought. She walks barefoot in the yard and crawled under the chicken house to catch them, handed me one, held onto the other. The whole time, she is wearing a spiked leather collar around her neck. Other than that, she could be a country girl. Their two dogs started barking, signaling more visitors. Two tattooed women come in. One introduces herself as Arianna. 'Jessica was really excited that you were here,' she told me, making me glad that I spent the hour and a half on the bus to come and see her. And making me sad that I could only see her for such a brief time. 'Do you live here?' I asked. No, she lives in Bellingham, about an hour north. She was just visiting. When Jessica and her baby daughter came back, we spread out a blanket in the yard and she and Arianna looked through a box of fabrics that someone had given her. Baby Nico cooed at my cameras, smiled when she saw one aimed at her, played with the bells attached to a piece of fabric. Arianna and I drank tea; Jessica tried to share her mango drink with Nico (who didn't want any). And I thought that this is the kind of household that I would like. One in which friends feel free to come and go, to stop in for tea or to look through a box of things together and catch up on old times, talk about future plans, share histories. The kind that seemed to emerge when I visit you—of hanging out in the backyard with Siu Loong and the girls or of sitting on the porch talking till the wee hours with Lauren or of the Clovers playing with Siu Loong."

Victoria Law is this issue's "featured photographer". She also took the next photo (of Lauren—a mama zinester by the way, the editor of *Are We There Yet?*—in her workplace at Atomic Books when she was in town visiting me. Other photographs in here are from China where she is photo-documenting a fishing village and from New York City where she resides in the Lower East Side. Her and her three year old daughter's photographs have been recently published in the "Mamaphonic" book. The title of their photo-essay is "Two Ways of Seeing" and it captures the protests against the War with her camera at an adult level and with a disposable box camera at a toddlers level: very interesting to see what captured their eye!

As well as a photographer and rad mama, Vikki is an activist and writer. She is the editor of *Mama Sez No War*; *Tenacious*; *Dear Cookie*; and a little known and littler distributed zine: *Fragments of Friendship* which is a zine we (Two mama writers on the move!) make for each other of our correspondences.

I love my pen pal! She's a mama, community builder, documentor, and interested traveler of life. She brings home the tofu by working in a non-profit office (bringing her daughter to work with her on some days and other days not as she is a single mama but shareparents with Siu Loong's father who watches her half of the week) and cooks it up after a house meeting in a House that used to be a Squat but is being turned into a co-op; and develops her photographs in the ABC No Rio darkroom where she participates in its running as a collective member.

All Sales are Final. Think Hard!

Photo by Victoria Law

Dear Ethel,
I got a job now on the Avenue - selling Ladies hats, purses. zines and other fine assesories: Now I am a shop girl! ha ha

Please tell Huey that it was wonderful seeing him but next time he comes visit please leave the chickens at home. That was embarrassing!

love,
Dottie

Introduction/Editorial

Hello! This is the "Work" issue—So think hard! Hard work and no return! Yeah, but we also have stories in here on working together, working for yourself, and the work of being a mother (which I still think is the hardest job I have ever had).

Actually this issue has little of parenting and a lot of being an individual in the so-called "work world". As a single parent and a mom of a teenager—and as a previous "stay at home" welfare mama for many years - making a living is one of my major concerns. I had a child fairly young and didn't have much work experience before that. Nor did I want it, I must admit.

My late teens and most of my twenties were about living in and creating radical community. It's the last 9 years of my life that I've gone through a slew of more typical jobs. I started this mission (after I bottomed out one cold winter) with going back to college when I was 29 with a mind to get a trade and rise out of poverty. However—I still don't have it together and I'm still poor. As my daughter approaches college age, I'm very concerned with how I will be able to financially help her and offer guidance as I can't even figure out what to do for myself

It gets economically harder as your child gets older. I really don't think young children require much money and laugh at all those statistics that say they do: it's all such unnecessary crap! But a preteen often rejects their parent's values: that might mean rejecting the thrift store for the mall! There's the "big kid" thing (eating as much as you, needing clothes more than you, thinking you suck) which is hard but then there is the stark reality of capitalism as your baby bird gets closer to be launched on her own.

I can't help thinking there is a special pain involved for the working poor parent—to see their child enter a system they can't win in. As many often focus on the war abroad and their hatred of the president, I am not surprised and non-too concerned to tell you the truth, dealing with the war at home. It is war: this class system, this division of wealth, ideology, housing, food, economy, media. It is part of the same war as the one we wage around the world; and it keeps on coming no matter whom you vote for.

I'm not saying that I don't cry sometimes seeing a picture of the wounded or dead that "my" country is responsible for and my actions contribute to or that I don't get infuriated at the lies in politics and manipulations in the media. Just that I am busy wondering if I am going to make it sometimes, too busy to wonder about if the whole world is gonna make it. It's the same old story: the rich get richer, the poor get poorer, there's always money for war but never for children; and the victims are most frequently: the young, the old, mothers, immigrants and minority groups.

I am aware of the indoctrination of exploitation, still I often feel stupid for being poor. I feel stupid when I have a demeaning job that doesn't pay me enough and I am dead tired and looking like a dork and I see some hipster looking freaky cool with more free time making art—they figured out a better way. Don't have to struggle in the rat race like the ordinary sheep. Why can't I figure out a better way?

Truly, I want to figure out that better way. I want a little everyday Brer Rabbit revolution. I know the way is within working together, yet you also need to take personal responsibility.

I know I can't dream all the time but I also know without my dreams I am like dead. I blame myself yet I see other single mothers whose phones get turned off and their teen kids are mad at them for being poor—AND they (unlike me) work full time and went to college right away in their early twenties. (Like the mom who interviewed me for the Mamaphiles review who shared with me her own story of coming from the similar DC political punk scene that I had once been in. She said she felt excluded after she got pregnant—everyone was so conscious of everyone else's oppression except unfortunately for that new mom in their midst. So she left that scene and found her own independent way. Now she works full time in a progressive clinic to provide healthcare for the gay community and she teaches about HIV prevention in jails.)

It's easy for a mama to fall through the cobweb of support of the counterculture; to struggle with a double work load and double standards in mainstream society BUT it's society that makes it hard and we need to Battle Creatively—even if sometimes we take conventional means because we must be responsible providers, conventional means alone are not the answer.

Greetings

Hi, how are you all doing this evening?

(they hung on my legs today, begging me to stay)

My name is Jackie, and I'll be your server tonight.

(I wonder if they miss me as much as I miss them?)

Our soup tonight is cream of spinach and mushroom.

(I hope I can quit soon, and fill my days with them again)

Can I get you anything to drink while you look over the menu?

(We haven't eaten dinner as a family in five days)

I'll give you some time and be right back with your drinks

(please let him get a job soon, please, please)

Any questions?

- Jackie Regales

me (China) when I worked at Gypsie's Cafe
in 1997 - picture taken by my daughter

❧ **waitress** ❧

The Employment Diaries

I went back to school for graphic design the semester after I dropped out of nursing school; and the month after I got my certificate from the community college - I got the first job I applied to. A neighbor told me they could use help formatting books at her work ("the Institute") and she took a copy of my resume into the office. I wasn't sure what it was all about: but let me tell you getting my first office job (Desktop publisher assistant) was a pretty large leap from where I had been sitting in my torn blue jeans on my hillbilly porch near the BWI airport. The first thing I did was take out my nose-ring (which was the second or third continuously worn ring since I got it pierced outside an anarchist gathering in 1987) and I never did put it back in. Just forgot about it I suppose.

And from there I proceeded to be able to support my daughter and myself, even give her an allowance and buy some clothes, and keep a savings account for a year (my goal was always to save money so I could periodically take time off to work on my writing).

I worked at the Institute for over a year building my portfolio. You see I thought I was working on a career back then. It was so obvious to me and to everyone around me that I—this old zinester—should be a graphic designer and not a nurse! I love making books and working with images and text. And I found I even enjoyed the so-called dull aspects of it. I think formatting scientific text can be an art—not that anyone will notice and especially not if you are doing a good job of it. I mean, one doesn't notice the formatting of a book when one is reading unless something is wrong with it, you know?

The office I worked in was very old fashioned so I introduced new software like Photoshop and Illustrator and created an improved template in Pagemaker for producing one of our journals. I knew how to use the scanner properly—no more reducing figures on the zerox machine and laying it out in Wordperfect for us! These innovations took time and I would have to give presentations in order to convince the technophobes.

It felt good to support myself; I gained a lot of self-esteem from my financial independence. For instance, when my daughter had school problems I showed up in my office clothes with an attitude

❧ **Desktop Publisher Assistant** ❧

❧ **Street-side Tailor** ❧

(Ladder Street, Hong Kong, 1997)

used to going to meetings and talking with bosses: I was confident and not intimidated for the first time. I said to the school authorities "Yes we have a problem, what are we going to do about it? How are we all going to work together to benefit my child?" and would not permit my daughter to be put in a jail school. (She was expelled for punching another girl in the nose and had been in three fights that year—suddenly inappropriately sticking up for herself after years of feeling picked on.)

After my daughter was expelled from her first year of middle school, I worked part-time at the Institute so I could keep a better eye out for her. I had a good reputation at work and they accepted me as a flexible worker, like the students. I did as much or more work as my boss (who had worked in a supermarket before this and had no graphic training) but was down sized from my own office into a small cubicle that I shared with many a new employee before they moved onto their own space. The cubicle was so small that our two chairs would touch: creating necessary co-ordination and surprising camaraderie. I would get my new office mates into drinking tea with me at noon and we would help each other with our work. I met a young poet from Honduras; a young female scientist from Puerto Rico; a depressed divorced mother of twins, etc. in this manner.

A lot of crazy things happened at the Institute and I don't know if I worked for good or bad - to tell you the truth. It was very hard to decipher the words but I did try to read what I worked on. We printed up the results of independent peer review upon projects that were up for mostly government funding. Now you know me, I trust not anything like that. But I somehow got pulled into it and swore to never work for anything shady again; this was just a really great first job to get me going somewhere. The Institute itself came off as formal and impressive -yet in fact was a crazy small business run by a small German scientist who liked to drink, laugh, and tell everyone that they knew nothing; and an equally small (but mighty!) old African American lady from a well educated Southern family. She taught me everything I know about being part of an editorial department. They were characters and given to grand speech making and colorful arguments they seemed to enjoy.

At a certain point I was ready to go. After creating holiday cards (I was known as the "creative one") logos, brochures, books, and pamphlets-and reaching the limits of what I can do; plus being tired of working where I could never learn anything new from anyone else and would always have to work within old fashioned and chaotic settings—I was ready to progress to a more creative job. Did I first find another job? No I quit first, assured I would find something, ready to fly, and had a great goodbye party.

I have done an informational interview with Eisner—excited to find we have an award winning design agency in Baltimore—and gone on many interviews with the *City Paper* and gotten turned down. The art director of Eisner had heard of me because of this zine, wrote an article on zines for *AIGA*, and was super duper friendly to me. He liked my thought processes but said my stuff wasn't really up to par: gave me the advice to create a zine portfolio to send to prospective employers. The art director on the other hand at CP scoffed at my zines and said to not include them: they were meaningless and didn't show what I could do. He equally put up his nose at all the scientific books as something that yes "we all have done that" but it's nothing creative to show in one's portfolio. The weird thing is I think I am creative and am proud of all that tech stuff I did. To me it shows craftsmanship and an amazing ability to do shit for a long time: like patience and that I can also be boring and hardworking!

So I kind of found out I wasn't all that. (Even though I just like "making stuff" you know?) And not only are designers a snotty bunch, there are a ton of them out there looking for work in a bad market.

Somewhere along the line I learned that it would be good just to have a job, any job. Because it was starting to look like any job at all might be out of my reach. I did finally get work at a Bakery, making Granola. Now this, I thought, is healthy and straightforward! Wholesome and Real! Can't hurt anybody just making granola for a living, you know. It's close enough to maybe even bike to work I thought (though I hate bikes to tell you the truth).

The funny thing was I had even joked about making this very local brand of granola: after purchasing it from the grocery store and eating it at the office with a co-worker; sighing in discontent I remarked "maybe I will just instead make

granola for a living." I remembered this statement the day I applied and mistaken for someone else, got the job when I was really applying for the bread cutter position.

Baker

Sheila taught me how to make granola. She was very hands on—and showed me how to "feel" when the granola was right. It was a very textural thing. Oats, almonds, sesame seeds, sunflowers, honey, oil, and vanilla were the ingredients. You needed to smooth it just so in the pans and bake it just right—a few minutes or uneven layer could make all the difference. You can't be afraid to get your hands dirty to be a good baker.

Sometimes she would play Belle & Sebastian at work and since I never heard them before I related that to granola making. Jamie and her explained to me how it would be cool if there was a video of them spinning in the granola bowl. I completely dug it and wanted to make the video. The giant mixing bowl was mesmerizing how it spun and when you cleaned it and then looked up—the room would spin.

Again, I had many adventures and wrote much coffee-fueled poetry late hours in the bakery on the back of oat bags. But in the end I found I am really bad at physical labor and being tall isn't good for working in a bakery. While the elfish art-school girls would balance a bucket of honey on their knee to get the right physics to pour it on the scale - I would wind up dripping it and spilling it with my gangly elongated frame. My boss said I made too many unnecessary movements. And I guess it's true. But I was pretty good at making granola, just maybe not fast enough. I made 300

pounds of the stuff a night. It made me tired. And I couldn't economically exist on a student's salary. Maybe if I was more suited to the bakery I could have gotten into bread baking.

So I went back to my previous employer, where I thought I would never return in a million years, with a new appreciation of being able to be paid to sit on your ass. And the day I walked in to talk about employment was the day the chief copy editor (who had been telling people he was General Lee incarnate; cursing a co-worker with grave dirt and voodoo for ratting him out for how a word in the cover of a book back from the printer was misspelled; and sitting on the floor of his office ripping up stuff and placing it in a circle around him) was finally asked to leave; and to leave at once before lunch; although everyone but the bosses had known he had been going crazy for the last half a year. So, I was told the only position open was the editor one and assured that I could handle it; I would receive training and could rely on their assistance.

That was an interesting experience. I picked up the project from the editor who went crazy, finished it, got it to printers and felt quite proud. This is the time when I tried to start an art gallery in the back of the office. It had been an idea I had been playing with for some time and after I left the idea lived on and a new employee heard of it and always wanted to do it. The office was so large, you see, and a portion in the back was under used and rarely visited. We would call it the "Office Worker's Art Gallery". The other graphic-design-er-wanna-be and me created flyers for our gallery. At one point I even gave some to employees from other workplaces in the building when I saw them in the bathroom and created interest. They would ask me: When will you have it open? We worried perhaps we had gone too far. It never did open though (as far as I know). I lost it and left screaming "NO" packed all my stuff and left one day after being in between my bosses fighting with each other for a few weeks with work each day being destroyed and started anew.

I always knew the copy editor had the most stressful job in that place but I hadn't known I couldn't detach myself from it now that I was more savvy to the ways of the work world. At this point I had additional stress on me since I had broken up with my boyfriend and taken in the homeless troubled teenager who was my daughter's best friend and the daughter of the ex-accountant where I worked (my neighbor who originally got me the job). She had been working on an

where are you going?

Do you work so you can pay your car payments so you can drive to work? Do you make yourself feel better by "treating" yourself with some new office clothes—bought in shiny megaliths; made in sweatshops by mistreated women and children that you will never meet?

Do you drink soymilk to not hurt animals; meanwhile a bus with your name on it is running back and forth yearly to the moon with the amount of gasoline it takes to transport your Ecuadorian grapes to you in the mist of winter?

Where are you going? Do you know? Is there somewhere or something that can save you? NO. There is not. Misery is a state of living. No matter where you are, you will want to be somewhere else. The only hope is to stop grasping at therapy, religion, revolution, and spirituality to fix yourself. Embrace the pain.

And while you are there—stop by the **office workers art gallery**. Always take time to smell the roses on your way back and forth in this endless commute of survival. ∎

~The office workers art gallery~ coming soon to an empty back office cubicle near you; in a Bauhaus installation incorporating storage articles. **Now accepting artwork!**

enormous drug problem as she was ripping off our employers for the last year without anyone noticing (just congratulating her on her weight loss).

It was just really hard never being home enough to take care of all the things that really mattered to me: my home life. Instead being in this crazy office commuter world where you never know where the wind was blowing day to day as you tried to keep your head down.

Then I entered a long period of unemployment. Many people told me that you should never quit a job before you get a new one. Here is an email from my dad just before I got a job with a temp agency that was supposed to be temp-to-permanent:

Dear China,

A life time ago I had a piece of paper from a tech school that said I had completed two years and had graduated with all the benefits and honors thereto. I had found a job with Westinghouse working as a tech writer - whatever that was. (It turned out that it was producing so many pages of text a day, every day, of technical information regarding how a piece of equipment worked and how to keep it working). Also, I was a casual night student at Johns Hopkins in the engineering program. After two years at Westinghouse, I got layed off - fired because the business was not doing well. Oh heck, after the shock, I decided that I would go back home to New York, file for unemployment insurance, and take a half year off. So home I went. I filed and darn it, the unemployment office found me a job for more money that I had been making the first day I applied. After about nine months, Mom and I got married and back to Md I came. Jobs had picked up and I returned to Westinghouse, and went back to nite school. Everytime I found another tech writing job that paid a few bucks more, off I went. After a few years, I was making enough to buy a house and I was getting closer to a BSEE. But I noticed a curious thing. Every time I went to school to register for more engineering classes, the lines of students waiting to register got smaller and smaller. Engineering was declining again. In fact, by the time I graduated, engineering in Baltimore was in a slump and unemployment for engineers hovered around 20%. I was still working as a tech writer but opportunities were limited. Also, I found that engineers with advanced degrees were applying to the place were I worked in droves. For the few jobs my company had they were offering these guys less money than I was making and I still had yet to complete the undergraduate work. Hum - seems like there is a message here. Get a degree, work hard, and if you are caught by a down business cycle when you are past 50, forget it. You are retired, like it or not. Or at the best, you may get a junior job competing with kids just out of (or still in) school. Did not seem like something that I should set myself up for. However, I am finding out that many people here do set themselves up for the same experience that I was fortunate enough to escape. John H.'s father had a similar experience as you described and refused to continue, he got fired at the age of 60. No pension, nothing. He can't find another job and he cannot draw social security for another two years. He is scrambling looking for odd jobs and part time work. John is mid to late thirties and has a job at a book publishing place where he has been doing the same thing for over 15 years. Packing books in boxes on an assembly line. He works four days on and four days off, 10 hours a day. After 4 days his shoulders and knees hurt him and he is worried about his ability to continue. Our next door neighbor, Allan W., drives from here to Virginia everyday (four hours round trip) to make $16 an hour. No benefits, no retirement, and when business is slow he is layed off. He is in his early to mid forties with some physical problems and no future in the work he has been doing for all of his life. Getting depressing isn't it. My way out of the cycle was to join the Government. I am only now really understanding how good a decision that was. I get a guaranteed retirement with health benefits indexed to the cost of living so long as we have a viable government and country. Eleanor R., my cousin, also has a guaranteed retirement with benefits from the state of Md (Dept of Motor Vehicles). So what is my message to you. Two things. 1. Find something that you can do for your entire life. Something that will be in demand for your entire life - like editing, teaching. Make it a priority to look for opportunities to grow in that work or derivative. Never stop looking for opportunities even if you are working in that field. As you have already found out, things you want and want to do will always cost more than you have.

The lack of money limits your choices to do things to the extent you don't have it. 2. Find a place to do that work that will reward you for good work, that will be in business for as long as you live, and that makes it a priority to promote and keep older workers. The older you get the more this will be important. You should not want to be on the street looking for anything you can get when you are 50 or 60 years old. My advice to you is to do as I did. Find a government job in your area doing anything it takes to get in. Secretary, clerk, editor, graphic artist. Make it priority to find out how and where to apply. Once you are in, you can stay in and grow. The government has many training and upward mobility programs where you can move into different types of work and can move to different parts of the country or world. The jobs may not always be stimulating or exactly what you like but you have choices and many guarantees and benefits with the government. Federal is much better that state or city because the size gives you more options and pays better. Make this a part time job that you work every week. Develop a plan of action that you follow and update to accomplish. You won't be sorry because the alternative is to continue working week to week with diminishing opportunities. One last thought. I found working with the government gave me the security I wanted for my working life and retirement years (hopefully). It may be you can get the same thing from a large bank or some other institution. You probably can. Regardless, you should still stick to the two principles I listed above. Make yourself desirable in some skill area that employers want; find a desirable and durable employer that you feel will provide you a good working and retirement income. To the extent that you do not, you will always be a victim. Stay well, Love Dad

Dear Dad,

That was a very interesting story of your work experience and those of other people. I am working for Provident Bank Downtown. A big building—I'm on the second floor. My whole floor does Loans. It is open kind of cubicles near each other, with some real offices around the perimeter.

I am doing Lending Tree. The two girls that do Lending Tree now are moving up and one of them trains me as I was hired to take her position. I don't do Boats (one person handles all loans for Boats)

so I am already a step up. The Boat girl couldn't handle Lending tree - it was too confusing for her. She has a bachelors in African History. The woman who is training me is in Nursing school.

I look around and I see there is definitely a procession. If you master your job and do well—you move up. There are all different steps to the Loan Process. We are always busy. It's a whole world of its own.

I have really lucked out - because the two girls moving up (who certainly look incredibly good at their jobs) both told me how they Love our supervisor and couldn't ask for a better one. Lots of people here have families, all except the two young girls who work with me.

My first day was very demanding and they taught me new things ALL day long. I was completely surprised that this "data entry" was so complicated. Faxes, searches for zip codes, taxes, formulas, forms. Not my favorite kind of thing. But yet I did it and survived. My second day—I feel so much progress. This is very comfortable to me. My work with computers and formatting taught me to look for efficient patterns in my work.

I have learned so far: A) Learning stuff is always good. Everything I learn seems to go over into the next field even if it's not directly related. B) Friendships and human beings and talking to people is a very important resource! I talked to my next door neighbor about looking for a job—and he gave me the information of the Temp Agency I work for, as he works for them too. C) At a certain point, I have to listen to my heart. I use my brain too. And I try to be sensible, I really do. I value good sense. But sometimes, I go somewhere, on this strange path of life—and the things I do that are true to my heart, make me who I am, and I like that.

I REALLY didn't ever want to be in a position where I was unemployed looking for a job. I learned my lesson the first time. I didn't plan to do it again. I was upset with myself for winding up that way again. I really do believe—in my defense—that where I worked was an emotionally difficult place. Out of the last 6 copy-editors I saw in my time at the Institute—3 gave their notice and left for another job; 2 walked out and quit on the spot; and 1 literally went crazy and was asked to leave.

I feel fortunate to get this position, because while every job will make you upset at times, there does look like ways to advance and it does look like the work is clearly defined and people can notice when you do well. At the Institute—no one ever advanced. Many people left to find a higher salary and it was known, there was no advancement. Raises were very rare and by very small increments. The bosses preferred to hire unskilled or under skilled people so they could pay them less. But it was worth it for me, because I learned so much there. I have a lot in my portfolio. And truthfully, I have even learned about how to get along with difficult personalities and authority figures.

So, those are just some things about me and how I feel. I think after I get used to my job and have time to think, at some point, I will access the situation and my career direction. But for right now, I am very happy to work in Baltimore, I am going to take the light rail to work. It's nice too, at lunch time, I am near the Inner Harbor and there are lots of nice things, all kinds of options of where to eat, and there is hustle and bustle, it's kind of exciting. Not shabby at all. A different part of Baltimore from what I knew.

I like it that I leave work at 5 pm! I am not sure what time I get home, but I know I am not so tired out that I can't make supper, as I was when I worked at the Institute—commuted—and got home at 7 pm.

So, right now, things are good. And I think I am developing skills as I go — that are transferable. And it is kinda exciting that this Bank is so big and busy and people advance. So we will see how it goes. How I feel about it in time. I don't think I have to think about that until I put some time into it. But I want a steady job — much as I did when I went back to the Institute — just mind my own business, go to work, and work on my writing career on the side. Today, when I got to the parking lot at work (I drove in just to be in time because I am new and was running late since I took the cat to be spayed) I sat for ten minutes in the parking garage and wrote down the ideas that were in my head along the commute. So that makes me happy. Just to write whenever I can, and then flesh out ideas, and to have a steady routine in my life.

Well, right now, I feel in a positive mood. It's good to be employed.

Thank you for everything, China

Down Town Hustle Bustle Lunch Time

Tall buildings like Tall people so much Taller than myself, lunch today in a beautiful garden in a courtyard of an old church; and coming back there was an old woman that was lost on the corner; looking for The Department of Aging, oh so frail. She had white hair. Bobby pin. Ill-matching clothes. Stiff gait. Lost look (Like how I get in the new job sometimes, totally lost, clouded over and the employees used to it all, take me by the mental elbow and guide me on). I had a conversation with another passerby:

"That's so sad," she said.

"Somebody should have gone with her," I said.

"Didn't they?" (Some people had given her directions—*a block away and across the street*. Big Blocks and Streets with courtyards and plazas, full of office workers all walking quickly: to eat, to smoke, to go somewhere and people from the Jury from the nearby Court, out to order coffee.)

"No," I look back. "They are walking away from her." The group that was concerned with her a minute ago. "I would have, but it's a new job and I'm due to come back from lunch," I said.

"I should have," she said

We walked on our separate ways, hurrying back to work from lunch. But. We should have helped. Walking too fast we are almost like drivers, seeing the hitchhiker in the rear view window, moving too fast to stop and help. Always busy always busy.

❦ **Bartender** ❧

My daughter used to come with me for Sunday brunches when I worked at Gypsy's Café. Sometimes she would bus tables and get tips or hang out with Rachel behind the bar.

Solar Flares

Ten of six o clock (6 am). Ten minutes before the alarm is set to go off. Maybe I can write for a little bit.

I woke up this morning thinking about CO—OPERATION in my half—asleep state.

I have a new job, you see! In a Bank Downtown. In an old building, and I go through big Gold Doors and get a nametag and up in an elevator. My whole floor is like a maze, hustle and bustle. And the streets at lunchtime—are a Baltimore I have never seen before. Barely any panhandlers or old people or children. People look kinda nice, kinda slightly well off—but urban (not like where I worked in the suburbs). Everyone runs around at lunch — to pursue coffee or cigarettes or to eat at the numerous places or sit in the numerous little nooks or little parks.

And so I was thinking, in my half—awake state, about my old job and my new job. And the various personalities. People who contain such grit. People who are like a universe to themselves. The woman who is training me—23 years old and is married with a husband and a two year old child—works full time and is going to school to be a nurse at night. I think of how well, with grace and firm strength—she handled someone who upset her in the upper department. She wouldn't take being talked to rudely. She never yelled, she kept her temper. She lodged a complaint. He emailed an apology. She said it was so fake.

These cubicles are smaller. I sit with her, petite and warmly dark skinned with her braided head, in her cubicle and she sings to "The Peoples Choice" this radio station I am familiar with because my daughter likes it too. The radio down low, the nice DJs and her singing to the radio, create a bubble. This cubicle among a floor of open cubicles. The mood is nice. The supervisor sits almost an elbow away—a giants arm length. She has pictures up everywhere of her 6 grandchildren.

Office Work is really all about co-operation. Really everything is. Music. Interaction. Collectives or Hierarchies—still there is a way of cooperation about the affair. Passive and Aggressive, Subliminal and forthright.

My old office was a CUCKOO CLOCK. People run and bump into each other. One person sets out to do something and it gets pulled by the back person, almost put in the right place—The boss yells,

it falls out the window and someone starts the whole project again from scratch. People smile, think they can do it. Things are nice. They feel confident they can bring order. A hurricane comes and chases them out. New people come and pick up the pieces. Some of the workers bring lubricant to the job and some have old wood spokes that are worn down. Some create a waxy exterior and some burrow down like wood bees. But some how—SOMEHOW — the cogs all move and set off reactions…and the clock works! Cuck Coo! The bird comes out(!) and everyone celebrates.

My new job works a little different than that. It's a Bank in a big building with many floors and another branch calling in. Dealing with money and numbers and counties and Zip codes—it's a little less obscure and personality based than the place I was before. We work very fast and pretty efficiently around here. This is a newer clock.

But still all the nuclear power contained within the SUNSHINE of one smile in one cubicle! Isn't there a way to harness this power better? The power of America, with its mothers and fathers and people working oh so hard?

I lay in bed and think about the power of co—operation. The mental health of a group united. How we affect each other. That really, so little of this is even about what we think it's about. There is a deeper issue. It's not about getting Trash A to Receptacle B: it's about the synchronicity of our actions and how we work together and what that creates. I can't quite explain it.

But its something I understood immediately. A new thought dawned on me. If we could only be together—for one moment.

I remember the Great Earthquake in Santa Cruz CA, many years ago. How fantastic it was to be as one. The ground shook under all our legs and we all felt it at once, together. We met neighbors we never saw before. Unlike heartbreak, natural calamity is something we share together. It really struck everyone as amazing and positive— how the town came together.

I think of stories of 9-11. I think someone wrote about the sound of a mass collective sigh—of everyone sucking their breath in together "AH" of watching what's going on. Eerie. Sometimes calamity does bring us together and we celebrate the good parts of coming together and helping each other.

MAYBE this is why we have Holidays. Just so we experience something good together.

I think of Christmas, which I haven't really liked since I was a child and then it was magical. Christmas—which is always so awkward. Christmas—which brings out so many peoples depressions, of not having money, of it not living up to expectation. Of how one is not close enough to ones family. I think it is supposed to be about: Everybody Give Something. Love. Joy. Children. Light in the Darkness. Birth in the Winter. Return of the Sun. Presents. Lots of Presents, Decorations, Food.

Siu Loong at mama's work

But even this, we can not unite on. What does it mean? Corporate Crap. Santa Claus is a lie. I certainly never taught my daughter about his existence. I usually gave her art supplies. We rarely ever have a tree (three times in 15 years) or decorate.

We do enjoy driving around and looking at the lights. She likes the music. My family awkwardly tries to sing. My grandmother enjoys singing and sings so shrill, high and off key. Everyone else holds something back.

JUST for one holiday. If we could come together and all love each other for one day. And just be a day to say—YAY.

But we have a bunch of different beliefs and different religions and different ways—and that's not a bad thing. No, far from it.

I just think that maybe we need some simple activity to learn how to work together. It's awfully powerful, and we are all so divided. Yet in the chaos and in the order and in the fascism—there is a melody. I hear it. It's life. Life finds its own way, you know.

My Third Day Working For The Bank

So I run off to work, walking down to ride the light rail for the first time. A bit used to dealing with the tensions between home problems and needing to be at work on time.

I run by a Halloween tree. It's in the middle of nowhere with orange and purple lights, and, for some reason, a ton of colorful plastic toys beneath it. I have always noticed this odd tree. I run by a little garden with beautiful roses hanging over—so beautiful and so abundant—I dare to pick two. My day still contains hope.

The light rail takes so long to come. The machine is broken that gives tickets. But so many people are everywhere, the train must come soon. I sit by a witchy poo. A small female in a pointed webbed and glittered hat. Pulled down to her eyebrows. A white and silver Feather Boa encircles her neck, and her legs are pink and black striped stockings. Bored, the witchy poo waits, talking to her friend with the Anne Rice book.

The light rail comes and I board. No room to sit down. I stare over people's shoulders. One is reading a book about ancient religions, in the chapter on flagellation I see a line about "christian idealism shines a light on the enigma." Elsewhere I see two people studying nursing texts. Newspapers. *The Wall Street Journal* has an interesting article on genes and color but I can't read it because the man placed his thumb on that section once I took notice, behind his shoulder as I was.

Oh, this is taking too long. What was I thinking, leaving the house so late? I had planned on giving myself an hour, since its a new job, a new route, that I am not sure how much I will need to walk once I get to the right stop.

And then the light rail stops. A message starts. "I apologize, I know we have a lot of impatient angry commuters here," it cuts off. Silence. We wait. Something is wrong. The message comes back. There is train trouble. He must drop us all off. Another train will come.

Everyone unloads. And stands. A crowd. Not in so bad spirits. But I feel more worried. Many pull out cell phones. I open my plastic bag that I hastily loaded this morning. Within is: a Baltimore Gas and Electric turn off notice—you know when they send you the pink one with no return envelope? It's for two hundred dollars. I also include an old bill with an envelope. And my checkbook. If you send it to them right away, it will be all right.

And there are all my notes for data entry at work, and typed notes I refined for myself. One page I wrote in a parking garage, yesterday. And a whole mess of Temp Agency papers. One to get direct deposit. A letter. A pamphlet. A form to fill out to get paid. I need to figure this out today at lunchtime. But no number to the office. No card. I couldn't find the card with the person's name on it at home when I looked. No phone number.

A train comes from the opposite direction. Without direction, the silent crowd wonders. Then slowly filters in. It doesn't seem right. I am one of the last who remain outside. Why get on a train in the opposite direction? Is our track down for good? I exchange looks with another of the last holdouts—and then board with the rest. It doesn't feel right to not follow the crowd. But then an announcement must have come out because everyone gives a collective sigh and gets back off.

The crowd stands. I ask one lady near me, in the crowd, who pulled out her cell phone—if I could use it. I must call the temp agency. I have been frantically looking through the paperwork. I read that being late without calling in is grounds for being fired. She agrees, but will not let me make a call to information. She says I should use a pay phone. I run up and find one. I look in my bag. Dollar bills. Not enough change. No pen. And I have a horrible head for numbers, to remember it. I start to panic. I ask the only person near me, a young man in The Crow make up—if he has change for a dollar. He looks amused, happy to be in face paint, happy to talk to people. I say I am freaking out and don't make sense.

I see the train coming. So I run back down, on the other side of the rest, the doors won't open. I run around and get in. I look at someone's watch. I am now 40 minutes late. Come on. Come on.

The train gets to my Baltimore and University and I jump out. Look around. See a Rite Aid. Run into it—run down to grab a pen to purchase, to get change—I will call the temp agency first. In line I am surprised to be behind old homeless men who purchase small flasks of alcohol for one and a half dollars. The whole shelf behind the cashier is alcohol. I never saw a Rite Aid like that. The first old man is friendly. The second snippy. Black and Tan—between those two flasks there. "I knew it's there, I just thought you wanted a pint." "NO, a half , I said a half." The cashier seems tired. I try to be very polite. And some change. Thank you very much. But I shoved my pen in front of her before she even finished with the man. She doesn't seem to feel my politeness none.

I run off. Good shoe choice. Wednesday's good conservative footwear cut me in the back of my feet and the blisters are raw. But these shoes I can run in. I run down Baltimore Street. There just aren't pay phones anywhere. Is this like when it's a bad part of town and they get rid of all the phones so drug dealers can't use them?

I'm already at the Greyhound Station. This area is very seedy, intense characters around here. I watch a woman spit a fat white stream out her mouth, like it's in slow motion—as I run by. I am shocked kinda, the roughness of the neighborhood that I am suddenly in after I exited the train. Because I am moving so fast in uncertain surroundings, the contrasts hit all the more trippy. Baltimore has always been strange like that, how things can change block to block. The visible and invisible barriers of race and class. Just like how "The Block" (Baltimore's famous old strip joint area) is just one block from the Main Police Station. It's funny like that.

I never saw a phone on my run. So when I see the Greyhound station I run in and grab the pay phone. I pull out my new pen, it's a cool sharpie type. I had no idea. I call in. The man is friendly and understanding at the temp agency as I spit out what has happened.

I keep running. Up to my floor. Almost run into my supervisor. She looks at me with disapproval so heavy I can feel it on me like a slap. She is angry and disgusted and on her way out of the office. I come down. Sit in the cubicle. Tiff says "I wondered where you were." I put down the roses. She doesn't care for them. It's not an office you

"The Next Pink Slip Could Be Yours!"
(from a Protest during the Republican National Convention NYC, 2004)

Children drawing w/ chalk on the side walk (Clinton St. LES NYC)

bring fresh flowers to, I figure. Space is tight and work is constant. I try to clear my mind and start work. Just survive this day.

When I got home I had a phone message saying not to return to Provident Bank on Monday but to call the temp agency instead. I got fired (well not actually fired, since I was never actually hired). I'm in shock. I've never been fired before.

It's Just Salad

When I went in for the salad bar job interview and they told me how hectic things could get around lunch time; asked how I would handle the stress of customers asking me for things while the salad was running low; and what would I do if I ran out of spinach? I thought to myself as I gave the appropriate answers (I would remain calm, answer questions with a smile, do one thing at a time, find the spinach) Yeesh, its just salad!

I was surprised to find out how hard the job really was. Most days I kept on my feet running to fill up the various bins of salad as well as to keep the bar stocked with numerous utensils, containers, condiments, napkins, sugar, honey, half and half, lids (for the soup, the coffee, and tiny ones for the salad dressing cups) yet always being asked for something that wasn't there: "where are the sticks to stir my coffee?" and items that were in other parts of the grocery store.

Sometimes people got very angry when they couldn't find what they wanted. I was surprised how rude people could be over "just salad".

Inevitably people spilled everything, often even spilling their entire salad or the whole container of salad dressing and walked away without a second thought. Somehow the salad bar was a special place where one was not inclined to clean behind themselves. The tiny bins were hard not to spill from and I wiped around them with my rag and pushed the piles back into order (with the spoon placed on the right) as compulsively as one checks their email for a crush's reply. Keeping the salad bar full and clean was like building sandcastles by the seashore—endlessly knocked down and endlessly I built them up again.

My presence was often not noticed: wearing a baseball cap, name—tag, and white cook's shirt turned me into an invisible class that was to fetch and clean like some kind of "magic elves". This is a very different experience than being a waitress. But then again, your waitress brings you your whole dinner and dining experience. This was "just salad".

And when I worked my butt off on a good day with the pride and satisfaction of keeping the Lettuce, Mixed Greens, and Spinach piled high all day—it was still "Just salad". What have I actually done with my life? And how can this job take so much out of me that I lay on the sofa on my day off, unable to move—body aching, mind numb, glad to be out of work, regretting going back tomorrow?

Letter From Brother

Hey China,

Welcome back to reality. I'm sorry that that the salad job isn't all what you expected. Christina had mentioned now and again that I don't have to work in an office, and could go back to baking pizza, but you really get spoiled by a job that has more creative/andor/professional aspects, not to mention the money. I know what you mean about not being able to create after working a long day, it's a problem I've struggled with a lot myself. I find that I'll do nothing for months on end, then somehow I find the energy to work on something. Once you get started then it goes on for awhile, but then I run out of steam and just flop around after work. Now it seems that my to—do list is endless, professionally, personally, and with my family. I don't think about it too much, just kind of do what needs to get done most at the moment. Things have a way of taking care of themselves if you just get the major important things done, and keep in mind what is important. Well, you can always look for something in graphic arts again. A lot of people say you have to have a job in something that you like to do, but I always thought that was like selling out. You can never really do what you want on a job, and you are being used by the system. But I see now that there are other subtler aspects that make that partially true. First, you gain experience in something you like, and you learn discipline. That was what working at Merit really gave me, being forced to work every day not only honed my skills, but now I find it much easier to motivate myself to do my own personal stuff as well. Second, you get contact with people that are related to the field. That's the real value, networking. When you don't work in your field (by field I mean that thing you like to do), you are an outsider. But when you have a professional job in something related, then you make contacts and people take you seriously. I now know people around America and Germany through Merit that know and respect me, and would help me if I asked. The real trick is to blend your day—to—day life together with your whole life. A lot of times when you think about what you want to accomplish with your life it's depressing, you can't do it all now, you have to do it in bits and pieces and that's frustrating. You try to do something today and know it can't be finished and that is depressing and drains your energy. But then once in a while something actually gets accomplished and you see how things are progressing as you get older, and that somehow makes it worthwhile and gives you the energy to go on. You just have to have one clear goal, and when things get tough, and it seems you are going nowhere, you have to center yourself around that goal. One thing I think about a lot is to have something for every aspect of myself —Mind, Body, and Soul. You can't work efficiently unless you balance those parts of yourself. I'm not lecturing, I just got on a roll. Anyway—back to my reality. Christina is sick and still sleeping, and I have to change Laura's diaper. Love you—Chris

Toyota Paid In Full Eastern Seaboard Division

I called in sick today—only my 10th day on the job. The thought started in my head yesterday. It seemed a lot of people take off and they don't get mad. Why not me? I had been feeling dizzy. My eyes twitch at the end of the day with eyestrain. This is upsetting. I was hoping to organize my time into responsible productive writer mama life now that I had a job. I leave the house at 6:30— get to work at 7:00—pretty much keep a steady pace with a few breaks when I need them—leave at 3:30—pick up daughter on the way home which is nice— get home at 4:00. That's still early. Time to put a little writing into my life—work towards solid goals. After all my dreams of being a writer that is going to be my future—not this temp job.

But so far I haven't done any productive writing. Writing towards a project I can submit to be published. Don't get me wrong. I write a bit during the day: a line or two. A page at lunch. Some in my diary at the end of the day. This is what I always do. My "compulsion". But it's not

structured enough and its loose—apt to get lost— ideas sketched out that I never finish. I want to get more disciplined about shaping my writing into something.

I don't know if I ever have had a pattern of steady writing and working. It seems feasible. If you are disciplined enough. I think I get more writing goals accomplished when I am unemployed. It used to be that when my mother took my daughter for a whole weekend that I could bang out a zine. Finish writing up the notes and thoughts I had—lay it out—and zerox. Now it seems its more like the unemployed months when I get stuff done.

Projects. Zines, essays. That kind of stuff. Full stories. Because I am always writing notes: notes from the playground. Notes about being a mom. Outlines for projects I see in my head. I always feel there is no time to write so I write what I can. Then my "notes" began to be about work: waitressing, nursing school, formatting scientific text, copy editor, granola girl, salad bar lady... These aren't all my jobs. I am writing something about grocery shopping too. And about when I was an art model. I wrote something about my old street being destroyed by the airport. I always say that, don't I? I have a great story but I can't quite shape it up and I don't know what to do with it.

Monique and Star by Fred Limbaugh

❧ **Art Model** ❧

But when I get home after work—well, I am sooo happy to be home, but the time flies. I feel accomplished when I make supper. I feel good like I am supporting and loving my daughter. Because at 16 she can cook herself and in this house—mama doesn't always cook and when she does you say "thank you" in real gratitude. But I am starting to cook supper almost every night now because my daughter has a lot of homework and I want to nourish her. Be maternal. The dishes are never all clean—but I do a load or two as I cook and try to get rid of anything that is rotting or overflowing.

I eat and talk to her and watch television and check my email. Sometimes I talk to people, run an errand or work on an accomplishment.

But I am doing very little. And I feel wiped out. By nine o'clock, sometimes even 8 o'clock, I am literally not good for anything. That is a time to read a good book or watch TV or relax.

Still it seems like there must be writing time in all this. My job seems to be a job that doesn't emotionally or physically drain/kill me. Thank god. The dumb job I have always wanted. But just the fact that I put in that 8 hours (its really 9 hours with the driving. And I feel lucky for such a short and easy commute)—5 days a week—is pretty big. I feel like such a whiner—this is what everybody does, you know? And the cooking and cleaning I do is part of "my time"—even though everything is always embarrassingly dirty, I do these things.

As a single mom I play the role of both mom and a dad. My parents help out a hell of a lot. I would be lying if I didn't bring that into the equation. But it often feels like I am a failure, and it's embarrassing. Like last year when I was in a big unemployed phase for the second time—my dad told me that he would not pay my mortgage forever. That at a certain point, in so many months, he would take in my daughter and support her and turn his back on me. I mean, that's a harsh thing—you know? I knew I would get a job before that time limit was up, but just the fact he is thinking like this, I have definitely gone beyond any imagined line of being a loser bum daughter for sure.

But I was depressed then. That's the thing about being unemployed. I don't want to be so classic—like all the office workers that don't know what to do with free time and just wake up late and watch too much television and eat food and plummet downhill. But I do, I get depressed and isolated. The time spreads out into a vast boundless thing and I don't make good use of it. I don't know my future, how I will support myself. And I don't have any money but what my parents give me, or I charge on my credit card, or the tax money I had stored away. So it's all running out. And looking for work— GOD—is the most sucky thing in the whole world. You look at strange jobs listed in the paper and try them out for size in your imagination: Could I do that? Be a prostitute— dress up as duck—give ghost tours—convince someone I am a graphic designer in this hard job climate? You know? And job interviews. Oh my god. Not when you are down and unemployed—to go in and try to smile and be judged like that—all the while just knowing you are not going to get the job.

Sometimes I ignore that whole thing and just get into my writing. Although I have no future and things are desperate, I have some money to eat with now and the bills are sliding for right now (you can get away with a month like that, a month and a half). That's when I get some of my best projects done, I think.

But I blow a lot of time when I am unemployed. And being depressed sucks. I just realized I haven't thought about killing myself once since I got this job. It used to be a thought that popped up in my head about once a week. What am I gonna do? What am I gonna do? (End it all—the voice whispered.) In the end I didn't even really feel parental guilt about that voice. The life I had given her was bad enough—it might just be better with me out of the picture.

So many times I get writing ideas and start to build on them but don't finish and the time passes and they get swept away and never done. So I was thinking—I would just seize the moment while I still feel fresh to the idea and want to write—and call in sick. Cuz what's more important? Putting mail in boxes, the mail that never stops, that will never stop. This job that is not going to get me anywhere? Or to take the time to write.

I still believe there must be a way to do it. Just one time, one book, one strategic start, to get me out of this. Or to progress a little bit as I go onto the next project, the next struggle. The writing

Photo by Victoria Law

❧ Goat Fighters ❧

(In Guilin there are goat fights, where business men and tourists bet money on the outcome. The goats are led into the ring, a dusty square really, on leashes. A female goat in heat is led in as well and the two male goats fight over her. Once it is clear who has won, but before the winner can finish the other off, they are pulled apart and led away. Goat fighting is not a common occupation these days.)

never stops, you see. But can it be—something? And not half done/never seen. To hold down a job and be a mom and be a writer. I am always looking about how to do it. Is it part—time work? Is that it? I don't know—I am trying now to do this. To support myself and my family and that means full—time. Well, there's no real way—as much as you plan and scheme in and out of employment. There is just what is. So I think I will call in sick. I'm scared to because I hate to lie and my tendency is to care about my work. But I am tired. And I need to take care of my needs and myself. This job will get me nowhere. Maybe if I stayed with it, it would get me up to a higher and better paid 40 hour a week box with benefits.

If I stayed home—I could do so many things! God all you can do with a day. All the things I keep meaning to do. Weekends go by fast full of domestic obligations with the sweet feeling of sleeping in but also the late Sunday panic of time running out. Weekdays zip by. BUT a sick day is regal. It's the true time to do the things you need to do—it's stolen time.

But I'm scared of fucking up cuz I need this job. And not only that, I'm scared my writing isn't good enough. I'm scared it's not worth it. That I will get all stuck up mentally when I actually try to go sit down and write what I thought I could.

I was supposed to leave 5 minutes ago. But here I am. Writing this.

Car Company Bill Mail

Sort the mail into the proper slots: 006 Baltimore, 118 Richmond, 021 Midtown, 022 Boston, 127 Pennsylvania, 128 Connecticut, 129 Persipany (New Jersey), 140 another Virginia one, 171 down south. A slot for the mail that is Mid or West Coast. Put mail that is for Leasing in an envelope.

Sometimes the numbers will be on the envelopes. Sometimes you have to look inside. Sometimes there is no account number and you look up the Vehicle Identification Number on the computer. Sometimes you can't even find that. The mail is rolled in twice a day—twice a day you sort the piles of mail and make sure the piles are ready to go back out.

After sorting all the mail for the department, you work on your own division (002)—and make piles for Processing; Customer Service. You open up Pay off letters from individuals, dealerships, banks, and insurance companies; and make sense of what you see. You type down the account number, pull up the name, and go to the notes. tab a tab tab c c c tab p tab ctrl v cut out the address and insert another in your basic saved entry. Add if there is an enclosed envelope: EE. Or to send it to the customer CUST or if there is an Odom reading or other special notes. Definitely note if its been signed by the customer or not. The signature is the most important thing.

Enter. Get a top sheet. Paper clip. Write down the customer name and number and off the document goes to scanning. Make big piles of this in its own box to be lifted onto a roller and pushed down to scanning, by the same mail delivery people who deliver your piles of mail you must sort each day. Click click click goes the sound of my fingers on the keys. I am learning my number keys and urge myself to go faster—enjoy learning and checking my process. Faster. Click click click click ten numbers tab tab tab type type type tap paper clip write turn face down in the pile continue.

An hour gets the morning mail put away when I am rolling. Then I can spend the next three hours trying to catch up with sorting the Boston mail and entering pay off letters so we know where to send the title. This is just a part of what we do, but all I know to do. I have sorted out contracts and titles from fast tracks before, putting them with a cover letter. Typed up cover letters with numbers that I add 700 and 0001 to the beginning and end of the customer numbers and then cut and paste and enter them. I don't know why.

The car company bills move fast. Sorted and transported by humans. The information entered into the system. Moved. Sent back. The mail moves in steady streams like traffic. Like cars themselves. Like commuters. A steady stream of numbers run under my fingers, letters pass through my hands. Looking for the facts, the forms change. Only sometimes do I get a letter meant for customer service. "I was in Puerto Rico for a family emergency. I value my car but I value my family more." Or a death certificate with an insurance pay off. One letter was written by the father. It says that clearly, twice. "I am her father". I read

the death certificate, curious and sad. She was ten years older than I am, married but divorced, to a veterinarian. Who knew all that was on a death certificate?

I look at the seal; the old fashioned way of wording it, recording death. I think of the people who processed the certificate. More people like me. People everywhere taking in bills, numbers, with information fast flowing by them. Clerks, data entry, mail, phone calls. Toll booths in a very big system for the papers accompanying the purchases and official proof of human beings.

Only sometimes I get a hand written letter from a "person" and I value it. The only other personal markings I see are signatures, which I find very interesting. It is something we all scrawl so fast, over and over again. What it becomes. One was a series of loops, one after another then coming back to connect all the loops. Some are glorified two letters. Some angular, others round. Really beautiful actually, a signature. Such freedom—such diversity. I can understand why someone would study handwriting. I often wonder about the people who signed them—can almost see something about that person. Certainly it is a place for the eye to rest among all those forms. It is important. Without it, the paper is not good.

Other times I chuckle at the letters people send. Not in a mean—spirited way: misspellings are also a breath of fresh air for me—some personality. Some people do not read or write very much—this is the basic kind of letters literacy allows for. The letters with high standards of grammar come out polite but a bit too form letter like—as if the person themselves is so proper that they can pull out their own form letter for every interaction.

The mail keeps coming in, twice a day. Men come and go with boxes. A cart is rolled up from the filing room below. Everyone is always falling behind. People had voluntary overtime when I first got here, if they didn't catch up there was going to be a mandatory Saturday workday. The mail keeps coming and going and when I switch tasks, and move down an hour through my day I feel good to get it done—and then oh the mail is there again. "Just like at home!" says the woman says sitting next to the mail cubbyholes. What does she mean? Like how there are always dirty dishes to be washed? Or that woman's work is never done?

In conclusion:

I also wound up passively-aggressively losing my Toyota job because it was driving me crazy and I didn't freak out this time but quickly began looking for work before what I had done would set in. This time I was lucky and got a job in my neighborhood working in an antique store. I'm their one and only employee—it's a small independent business. I really like it a lot.

I only work four days a week—which I have discovered is the ideal amount to really have a good full balanced life—around 30 hours a week, sometimes less. That's not enough to support us though, so I am kinda surfing by on that at the moment. I don't really think too much on it, or a lot of things, that are stressful, that are too much for me. Like I don't have the kind of household where everything is done and paid and taken care of.

I think that my writing is the thing, the thing that I am about. I met Ariel Gore and she gave me much encouragement, coached me on writing book proposals. I also helped edit her last new book. But I kind of disappointed myself by not jumping on writing a book proposal and mentally being afraid and perhaps incapable of writing novels at this point in time. She still, such a kind friend, believes in me and thinks that all of this is like "whatever." So, of course I still need to work on it

Motherwork

"Work—once something to avoid, in my life it has become a leisurely vacation compared to the demands of taking care of my kids, AND it pays!!!!! The hard part is finding/paying for childcare so you can do it, finding something interesting to do since most of your paycheck goes to childcare anyway, and being hired in the elusive part—time category because you really can't stand being away from your kids that much right?"
—*Madre Zenith*

A study released by the Department of Labor (in Sept. 2004) has found that the average working woman spends roughly twice as much time caring for children and on household chores than the average working man, confirming that divisions of labor based on gender still exist. The study also found that almost as many women as men have

❧ **Parade Balloon Seller** ❧

(The Mayors Christmas Parade, Hampden Baltimore)

❧ Small Business Owner❧

jobs, with 78 percent of women employed relative to 85 percent of men, the New York Times reports. At the end of the work day, however, two—thirds of the women surveyed stated what women's rights activists call their "double day," preparing meals and performing chores around the house. Comparatively, only 34 percent of men reported helping with meals, and only 19 percent reported doing housework.

"Indeed, becoming a mother is the single best way a woman can elevate her risk of living in poverty—a truth that ought to be the unwavering call for action of the feminist movement."
—Caitlin Flanagan

3 in 5 preschoolers have their mother in the labor force

1 in 2 will live in a single parent household at some point

1 in 3 children will be poor at some point in their childhood

1 in 5 children are poor now

1 in 6 households with children lacks access to enough food to meet basic needs
(from the annual report on hunger by the U.S. Department of Agriculture which delayed releasing the information that "food insecurity" has increased until after the elections which is part of the Bush Administration's dismal practice of withholding key information from the public)

Women are 40% more likely to be poor than Men (gap closes at college graduates)

Raising the Minimum Wage to $7.00 an hour would benefit many of the 12.1 million American children living below the poverty line
(Children's Defense Fund)

Income inequality in the U.S. is far greater than that of all other advanced countries, as is poverty, particularly of children

In March 2003, about 13% of the workforce were low—wage workers (defined here as those earning between $5.15 and $7.99 an hour)
(The State of Working America 2004/2005)

Where are the voices of the single mothers? With a third of us in poverty I am not hearing too much. It's just not about a man and a woman—it's about society and power dynamics. I feel there is so much I'm not saying/including in this issue of my zine. ARG!

Question: What are all the everyday invisible unpaid or underpaid forms of Labor that go on around you and behind the things that you take for granted?

Avedon And My Cousin

John LaConte took this photo of Richard Avedon walking down the street in NYC outside of his MET exhibit in 1978. The little girl in the corner is his daughter, and my cousin, Michelle Laconte. This picture captures my imagination heavily.

First of all, we have Avedon, a master of iconic portraits (having taken every persons picture I can think of: Marilyn Monroe, Jean Genet, Pablo Picasso, Robert Oppenheimer, Frank Lloyd Wright, and Mae West and that striking fashion shot that stood out for me so much in my youth of Natasha Kinski with the boa constrictor)—just walking down the street like anyone else. And now he is the subject of another native New Yorker photographer—one who also takes pictures of the people of his day: Jimi Hendrix, Andy Warhol, Lou Reed: but this photographer remains unknown, his pictures never published (until now in my humble zine)—waiting for the right moment and maybe a sponsor or a promised show.

John sent this picture to Avedon and even once saw in a photograph of Richard Avedon with his desk in the background—that this very picture was laying on it!

Significant in this photo is the depth: City in the back, photographer in the middle, child in the forefront. I like the composition. His child is making eye contact with us, showing off her book. This picture, and I hope I get the story right as family stories always tend to go astray in the retellings, caused some hurt feelings. You see the father cropped his daughter out of the picture; excited to have the picture of the famous photographer he thought his child's presence (and oh how our children are always present, jumping in our photographs that are not even about them, interrupting our phone conversations, and hands in our mediums often "messing" them up) was not important to this picture.

How would he know, thoughtless as we parents often are to the small things that might hurt our children, that his daughter was mortified to find she had been eliminated from the picture: their memory of their day together? For who is Richard Avedon, really, compared to Michelle Laconte — daughter, forefront and first: hello!

In later years he reprinted the picture in its entirety, as the original, child with book in the corner. And lo and behold — it was a better picture for it. This seems to be to be of some kind of moral or significance to me. Like to say—our art is better with our children, with the surprises, the real life and serendipity of it all. And so I like the picture very much.

I love my cousin Mich! (And her wonderful son Quinlin!) I came to her wedding last year and to visit with my Aunt who I hadn't seen for so many years as she had cancer and I might never get to see her again. I wound up learning a lot about a more distant part of my family, my dad's side, and seeing these amazing pictures that Michele's dad took. My Aunt did pass away this year but my mind is always full of the amazing bonding time we had together and her presence remains with me. I want to write much more about my Aunt in the next issue. New York bohemian, artist, model and single mom in the 60s. My beautiful mysterious aunt who I take after in some ways.

the future generation
P.O. Box 4803 Baltimore MD 21211

This picture—like most of Laconte's photographs of the hipsters he was hanging out with (Andy Warhol, Lou Reed, Marlo Thomas, Jimi Hendrix in the 60s and 70s)—has never been published before. And it's not allowed to be reprinted without his permission. I hope he has a show one day.

The Sea Of Life

Today my 16-year—old daughter dropped out of High School. "Drop out: that sounds so negative—it should be called ending a chapter of schooling and diving headfirst into the sea of life," said my daughter as we walked into her high school together to sign the papers.

"That's too long a description," I laughed and agreed, not wanting to go into the office and tell them she is "dropping out" but perhaps homeschooling? Going on to other things?

She was a Junior at an all-girls magnet High School in Baltimore. A really good school. She used to love it. But one day she totally shocked me by telling me she wanted to drop out.

"What?!" I mean this is my daughter: the kid who always wanted to go to school and then onto college. She made me buy her the most expensive school ring, the platinum one! Dropping out is more my style than hers.

I remember when she was an infant: I told people on the subject of schooling, "Look, I wouldn't even have a child if I was going to turn them over to the public school indoctrination system—what's the point?" I was pretty adamantly anti-school. I still have a fat file about this subject: Paul Goodman, A.S. Neill, Frantz Fanon, Ivan Illich, John Holt, George Dennison and such. I thought I would write a column about it one day but by the time I got around to it my daughter was pretty deep into the school system and I was more ambivalent about it. I mean, I learned a lot of stuff when I went back to college and she was learning stuff in her schools. The truth is you can learn a lot anywhere you go—in or out of a school.

Sometimes school can be a supportive environment. Her high school, for example: it had a lot of unity and school spirit. She had the same chorus teacher for the last three years and she was the only teacher whom she hugged, crying, when she said goodbye. She had some good teachers there, her American Government teacher last year encouraged her to debate controversial views in class and speak her mind. He was engaging, with the oratory style of a minister. She never could figure out his position exactly—but oh, he did have them learn this political system inside and out. My daughter once smirked at a story I told her of anarchists playing a drinking trivia game at the Wharf Rat and losing because the subject was American government. (They should have won. Know your enemy.)

She was so excited to be in the larger world of a big school: Dances, Sports, School Paper, Traditions, Revel, Pennies for Poe, Big Sisters and Little Sisters. (Their marching band—a combo with the school next door, Poly—was one of the best in Baltimore.) It was like a sorority, in a good way, and was preparing the girls for college.

Bluntly, to have a school that pushes you, inspires you, in a poor city, means something different than within privileged circles. These kids weren't spoiled, just proud and strong. (Hell, this is the year that Baltimore City School kids walked out and protested in order to try to save their schools with all the drastic budget cuts going on.)

And as a poor single mom, I can tell you, a good school can be a blessing. It gave us more structure, support, and help than I would have on my own. It made me feel good to know my daughter was happy. It was everything. I know I'm not the only anarchist who has found a happy middle ground with a public school. My friend Vikki has her toddler in Head Start in New York City. She likes that her child can be part of a larger world away from her and that her child's classmates are Chinese which is the half of her cultural make up that she is less exposed to. She feels that a New York public school education exposes you to different kinds of people instead of being in your own little niche. She's told me about people expressing a negativity to her on this choice—that unschooling or being in radical communities is the only way to go or something.

Fuck that. Make your own choices as you go along in life.

Originally, I felt I had no support in my own community that my daughter had to be turned over to "the system" when I first put her in kindergarten so that she and I could get a break from each other. It wasn't what I believed in. That was the first thing I did as a parent that I really felt shitty about—not just the school but the control from the state that begins there. I immunized my child so she could go to school (which I didn't believe in, and if you don't, sign the religious objection forms!). I researched all the options in Baltimore and came up with a private school that (surprise! How unlike me!) had school uniforms and church stuff once a week but was as racially diverse as the city (unlike Waldorf or Montessori which was predominately white) and they were located downtown and took a lot of field trips out into the city. Their approach to learning was creative and active. And I heard they had an openly gay teacher on staff.

I moved the next year—to Minneapolis—in large part because I felt that city would have more support for the subculture parent and healthier environment for children than Baltimore. My daughter went to a free school there for first grade. Totally free. A hippie punk kind of school started in the sixties. Kids signed up for classes they wanted to go to; attendance was not mandatory. The only thing that was mandatory was a weekly democratic meeting where kids held positions to call on people to speak, second motions, and vote on outcomes. This school was pretty awesome though at times a slacker school.

The next year my daughter wanted to go to public school because there were only two little kids in her free school (it was all ages from K to 12th grade—most of the kids were older) and she really wanted to ride the school bus with the kids in her neighborhood. So I let her. It was kind of rough. We lived in a rough neighborhood. My daughter has always thought I was wrong for protecting her, looking out for her. She is always trying to do the more "normal" or "standard" thing. Like, for instance, public schools.

Things got too hard for me at that point, and I decided to move in with my grandmother and go to nursing school so that I could play it straight myself and be empowered to never have to be so poor again.

So, with me going to college, I had to live with my grandmother in the suburbs and have my daughter go to suburban public elementary school. It took only a few times of bringing sprouts and tofu in her school lunches for her to learn to ask for white bread and what everybody else was eating. Yes, my daughter went over to the other side and she went over big time. Conservative daughter of the freak mother—you know the drill, right? Once we even argued about school. I told her if she insisted on staying in high school and immediately going into college that I wanted her to take a year off somewhere so she could explore her own interests and have time to find herself. "NO!" She said. "No soy milk. And No damn anarchy. I believe it's more effective to create change from within the system. And I'm gonna bottle feed my baby if/when I have one. Breast feeding is disgusting."

Our arguments seem very funny to some people and sometimes it seems as if we have reversed positions, she is the parent and I the child. I'm just saying: It is very possible to rebel from an "I'm giving you nothing to rebel against" parent.

I used to blame school, for this, but somewhere along the line things changed. College didn't exactly work out for me as I'd planned—I never did become a nurse, and I'm not even using my graphic design degree right now. We moved back into the city (Thank God! There is nothing as culturally isolating as being poor in the suburbs when you have been transplanted from urban living). My daughter went to an "alternative" school I paid for. Oh yes, you do have to pay for things like Respect, Experiential Learning, and other high falutin' ideals. But not too bad. This school started as a parents co—op and was maintained on that participation. My daughter loved that they were reading Shakespeare and that they had time to talk between subjects. I loved the idea of all the camping trips they would take, apprentice hours in the neighborhood, and graduating trip abroad (She went to Holland and France and Denmark). But still, my daughter didn't belong! Not because she loved avocados and mangoes and once wore two velvet skirts on top of each other in 2nd grade, but because she wore make—up and liked some mainstream culture. She wasn't "weird" enough and she thought the kids were too sheltered. By this point she had been expelled from middle school in the suburbs for fighting and suffered a disastrous homeschooling attempt that mostly consisted of me going to work and her staying home watching soap operas.

By the time she made it to high school, she was excited. This school seemed like a fit: Diversity, Smart and Fashionable! Still, she was an outsider. As the most white—looking half—Hispanic girl in the world, she was a bit of an outsider at her all African American table. It wasn't too bad. It was just her peers didn't invite her to go places on the weekend; made rumors about her after a party where they saw she could dance and danced with boys; and accused her of trying to talk black when she said, "You pick up the speech patterns of your friends."

She used to hold much disdain for the Hot Topic punks—as many of the white girls (who were in the minority here) at her school did fall into being fashion victims. "They're just being different, in all the same ways. I know your friends and this isn't what punk is about." Strange punk has gone on for so many generations now that my friend's daughter could say to her peers who accused her in middle school of not being punk

enough: "How can I not be punk enough? Ian MacKaye changed my diapers!" Anyway….

But then this year my daughter started hanging out with the grungy kids and listening to "alternative rock" instead of the R&B and Motown that she had been into for so many years. Weird. But I could see she felt at ease with making her own fashion creations and being her own self than when she had been hanging out with the very fashionable (need money to buy it, too) set. The downside was that white kids smoke. Ug! Yep, it all started going downhill when she started hanging out with the white kids.

The thing was: I had totally accepted that my kid was kind of straight laced. It was funny. I was proud. And I felt good, although stressed. How can I afford all she wants? And the way she sees life? The expensive cars, "good" colleges… how she sees I am poor because I don't do the right things. My daughter would go onto college, take a sensible path, work hard, and have money.

My daughter didn't drink or smoke. She had already been through stuff in her early adolescence and early teen years. That is not the kind of stuff my kid does!

But then one night she didn't come home and went drinking with neighborhood kids! Shit—she would worry me too death. She did this for a few weekends. I tried talking to her, grounding her (because honestly, I thought she really wanted me too, and perhaps this is what a good mother should do). And then I gave up. I am totally scared of her being drunk in the city streets with kids I don't even know. Look around this neighborhood!

And then she wanted to drop out of school! I thought it would pass. I'd gotten very comfortable with the role I had adjusted to, the daughter I thought I had, the daughter who liked school, conservative even if she was a hybrid of forces, open minded, the vice president of the Straight and Gay Alliance club, and radical in ways that didn't capture her attention because heaven forbid she be anything like her mother.

It happened so suddenly. I didn't like that. I felt pretty upset. I didn't want to hear the typical anarchist agenda or the typical straight ahead advice. No propaganda! What's right for us? How should I as a mother act? So I felt it out for a while. I talked to her. And I talked to other people.

I encouraged her to stay in school. I let her have a day off to think about it. She gave me all her reasons, that school was killing her soul; what is all this work all the time for? She wanted to work (she has had jobs before), explore her interests, get her GED, take some college courses. (For me — that is a must and the same conditions my mother put on me when I dropped out of high school. I, however, hated school for years and had to agonize before I was allowed to drop out.) She said she felt like me now; she understood what I had said about school before, that by the time you get out you don't even know who you are.

Right now she wants to work in a restaurant, be a bartender when she is old enough, and maybe own her own business one day. Last year she was considering being a forensic doctor. She's thought about different careers—lawyer, massage therapist, clothes designer, music technician—over the years. She still has time to explore, to try, and to change her mind. When does that ever stop?

But at least she'll have a head start on having the time and experience to explore her interests and get out in the world. Time to pull out all those unschooling theories. Maybe borrow a copy of the Teenage Liberation Handbook. If we are going to do this—and she never wavered nor changed her mind—I might as well get a positive attitude.

It's not an easy path. Looking for employment is depressing and there is a real danger of my daughter watching too much day time television and sinking into the social isolation that drop outs and the unemployed are inclined to. It's easier to go the societal-approved path. When I was in college, my dad bought me a car. Going to school gets you to wake up and finish more projects on time. But life is always what you put into it. I feel confident of all the skills my daughter has already gained: She's a great cook, extremely crafty, good at thinking, compassionate, secure in her independence, knows some things about life. I think she is going to grow up a lot this year and that's what she wants to do. There are some things I have a hard time imagining, such as my baby driving a car. Suddenly I am not on safe ground. It's as if what I thought was going to happen next year is happening this year. My kid is out of high school.

It was easier for me when she was in school—I could go about my own way knowing where she was. I was comfortable being negligent and, what the hell, my daughter had no interest in my interests anyway so I didn't bring them up. Now I feel I have to parent a bit more. I assist her with what she is interested in and get her out of the house. She is open to and likes my help now. I am fairly good at talking to people, I know what's up, and have connections out in the world (stuff she never took me up on before). I took her to Red Emma's Café to see an art show/Burning Man Slide Show and band, Mongoloidian Glow. I asked the owner of a local restaurant if he could hire her. I asked someone I know from seeing around if we could tour her workplace in the Bronze Casting Foundry. That field trip was utterly, intensely inspiring! After seeing the giant molds taken from clay sculptures and made into wax, the molten metal, the really cool woman who was welding together parts of this giant ape…We left with this fresh zest for life. "Want to go sign the papers at school now?" she asked me. "Yeah, I'm ready," I replied. I need to call back now and ask if she can apprentice and teach my daughter how to use a blow torch because my daughter said, "That is the best job ever." My daughter is shy but she went out on her own and asked a local arts store if they would buy the duct tape purses she makes (which are fantastic). She plays on her keyboard everyday and talks about how much she wants to learn bass. She is looking into taking GED classes on her own and has applied for jobs she hasn't gotten so far. She is ready for so much: to go to work, earn money, follow her interests. There are lots of exciting possibilities, living her own way and jumping into the sea of life.

—originally printed in *Slug & Lettuce* and *Hip Mama*

Rad 17

Sometime last year my daughter started becoming more radical. I wanted to document it, but I didn't and now it feels like the transformation has crept up on us: My 17-year—old is really rad.

Last year, when she was a sophomore, school spirit mingled with new alternative interests. She started really doing her homework for once which made her grades rise. And her musical tastes changed. She made her own T-shirts with slogans on them like "Fuck Labels" and collages from magazines she found lying around the house like *Adbusters*. She planned to make a duct tape prom dress in order to try to get a scholarship for college.

She went to her first protest of her own volition—a school walk—out to protest budget cuts. Most kids went back inside the building when the teachers told them to, but my daughter managed to get to the downtown demo with only the dollar in her pocket. (She had to hop the light-rail to get back home). She told me later, "I knew you would be alright with it." Of course!

But this year, she really changed and grew rapidly—becoming more radical than before—especially after she dropped out (or "rose up") from high school. And everything was on her own volition, which made me feel really good—to see her use initiative, to see her secure with making her own choices, to see her self directed. I have opinions, I guide and suggest, even scold and praise at times—but you can't make a teen do what they don't want to do. So I just run back up.

She enrolled herself in Community School, an alternative storefront school for dropouts in Remington, and then dropped out of that. Both choices were good for her. She was lonely and they were a little family there, but then she tired of repeating the standard curriculum and felt prepared for her GED. She applied to take the GED herself, sending in a money order she got from the 7-Eleven. She did apply a little late, and I did ask about it a few times—but that's OK.

She looked for work and wound up with a full time job as a prep cook and waitress. She felt proud. "Nobody tells me to wake up, nobody tells me to go to work everyday, I just do, I'm like a grown up." It made her feel good to be independent. I started to feel differently about her too, see her as more grown. I enjoyed our easy friendly interactions, how we checked in with each other, but did our own thing. Soon she'll be living on her own for real, so for this last leg of parenting, I wanted her to benefit from living with me and having her freedom.

It was funny. I'd documented my teen daughter's conservative rebellion from her rad mom, and suddenly the apple wasn't falling so far from the tree after all. She dyed her hair blue—black! She bought a vintage Bauhaus shirt! She's still different than me, but I can relate to her better. We're really similar in some ways. She's started to explore new interests, Ian bought her a bass, Maggie gave her lessons, both of them burned her mix CDs to give her a musical education—the background to what some of her indie bands are derivative of. Then she started to write screenplays.

Man, if she stayed in school, she couldn't be growing like the way she is now. This is the unschooling people talk about, the radical education she wasn't interested in when she was younger. Back then, she wanted to go to school like the other kids. This is the real world education. She works hard and I can relate to her waitressing stories. She handles normal restaurant stress with composure. I'm truly impressed with her abilities to deal with a cook on crack, a late grumpy owner, rude customers—all of it! She's a great cook and considered going to culinary school at one point. Her natural creativity comes out in garnishes, kitchen skills, and problem solving. A fellow waitress (much older) purposely took me aside to tell me how wonderful my daughter is to work with, how amazingly mature she is, the way she handles things. And what a good person she is. She told me, "you did a really good job raising her." That made me feel great! 'Cuz really, we parents of teens are there for the hard times, for the least-celebrated times, for the fucked up times. It's nice when things work out.

My daughter told me one day about the people she waited on—"real people." They were a family, the mom and dad had tons of beautiful tattoos—the father was a talented tattoo artist who works from home and she got his telephone number. ("Maybe I'll get a tattoo from him when I am eighteen.") They were nice, joked with her, and weren't "snobs". The kids reminded her of how she was as a wild child. She let them change diapers on a chair when she really shouldn't have.

So now we're at the point when "real people" are the freak culture she has come from, she isn't rejecting her subculture background, so she's being enriched by it. It does have a lot to offer. But she found her own radical interests for herself. I started keeping my mouth shut a long time ago: Letting her do her own thing, supporting her interests no matter what they were.

This year my daughter started hanging out with me sometimes. (She'd stopped having an interest to go anywhere with "mom" when she was eleven.) I took her to little record store shows. It felt good, that my daughter would hang out with me. I have so much to show her—things I think she'll like; things I think will inspire her as they inspire me.

When we ate at the Golden West bar on half price burger night, she said, "being in a bar reminds me of my childhood, I remember my head coming up to just under the bar." When we ate breakfast at Pete's Grill I remembered how we had eaten there when she was little, and she took the plastic rat that hung out at Normal's Bookstore with her and had it under her arm. A little girl who loved to play with a big black plastic rat. It gave an old man a scare. I told her the story.

I remember some of our first shows (Crash Worship in San Francisco was our first real show, not just being a friend's band playing at a party, when she was one and a half or so. We only went in for a few sets.) Together, this year, at Atomic Books "I Hate the 80s" anniversary party, after being a wallflower for a bit she dove in and made new friends, enjoyed herself up front with the bands. We had a good time together, doing our own thing then sometimes circling back to hang out together or check in with each other. My friend Lauren told me how great my kid was, how interesting to converse with; how she was so proud of her, how not shy she was. "Yeah, that's how she used to be. Used to dance at shows and make friends everywhere. This feels familiar to me."

So people know I have a kid again! Some are surprised I do and a 17-year—old one at that. Others see her around town "I know your mom"—she can't escape my shadow, she says laughingly.

She goes to shows on her own, too. She saw Le Tigre at Sonar with her Aunt and went to the WHFS festival on her own and paid for it herself. I felt scared to leave her at the big stadium for an all day show—scared of weird drunk guys from the suburbs—but when I dropped her off and saw a lot of those kiddie faces, I knew my kid could hold her own. She had a great day, even got in the mosh pit and experienced the crowd, falling down, being pulled up, others' sweat drenching you.

And then the night came. She went out with a new friend to the International Drag King Festival (in DC, she didn't tell me that part) and didn't come home. And for the first time, I didn't worry about her. I knew she was having fun. I felt fine about her company. And she had a great time, she met a new household of people, young creative working adults. She found her "niche" she told me. She helped one of them paint her bedroom red and work on a fish pool in the backyard. She read books at their house, listened to music, ate with them and laughed. She didn't come home for three days.

I remember the time I went to a party at this house and wound up moving in. You know that feeling of meeting a new group of people that open the world up to you? So I started fearing she might move out sooner than I thought and all of a sudden felt a horrible and unexpected feeling—the "Empty Nest Syndrome"! I like my kid! I just like her presence around, coming and going. After all these years, who could have known that it wouldn't feel like freedom when she leaves (I'm already free to do what I want, write for days, not come home at night, go to a party or even book tour for a week) but just emptiness? Who would have known that kids get so nice to be with—right before they're ready to take off. One last little you're-fucked-parenting-surprise, just so it hurts when they go.

I mean I really don't worry about my kid anymore, I believe in her. Yes, life is a fragile thing for us all and anything could happen at any moment. But I have confidence in her—she's a great and cool person. I'm gonna miss her! So, believe me you, when she came back I was happy to have her around again. She dragged me to Sowebo Fest (a yearly street festival in southwest Baltimore) after work on Sunday. I didn't want to go but she was antsy and it's hard to get across town for her so she wanted me to drive. I wound up having a good time!

It was beautiful weather, and I saw some people I knew. I hadn't been there for so long. It used to be fun once upon a time ago. I'd drink and enjoy friend's bands and look for the one other rad mom with a kid for Clover to play with. So we walked around and I saw a few teenagers I'd last seen as babies.

We saw a new puddle of punks lying on the ground together. How many years it's been since I've lost touch with what new generation of punks was coming up! Well, I saw one of them: the young punk kids I knew are now all 30. I told that to Clover.

Both of us thought the punks were cute, though, begging for beer money with a ukulele, going to put on a little song and dance show, a friend passed out on the side walk with a sign "dollar for a kiss" and a bucket to throw the money in. Two of the guys reminded me of guys I'd known long ago, friendly jokesters with the crowd.

Sitting on the curb with an old friend of mine and his girlfriend, nephew and nephew's friend, we talked about my column in *Slug and Lettuce.* And I didn't go to the punk picnic yesterday. "I'm too old," I said. "Funny, I'm not a punk anymore. You know. But I write for *Slug and lettuce."*

"And you're not much of parent either, you've documented every step of my life and now I'm on my way out," said my daughter.

We all laughed. I shrugged my shoulders.

Yeah, what am I going to write about? I tell you I have a lot to write about—but is this column done? This zine?

Preparing to take her first Greyhound Bus trip all by herself—to Wisconsin—I realized that my daughter feels pretty secure and not scared to go into the world. She's been exposed to it over time; it's no big surprise to her. She's not led a sequestered existence: she's been poor, had money, experienced rough times, has been talked to like an intelligent being, and had bites of independence all along the road. I feel good about that, that I did raise her right. I let her live out her own choices yet protected her also in the right balance. She agrees with this assessment, says so herself.

I know I shouldn't take the credit exactly, and I'm not. I'm just saying when I was seventeen I felt a lot more scared of going out into the "real world" than she does. Things are changing so fast. I'm feeling proud these days and my daughter is treating me with respect, love, and openness in return.

I'm glad my daughter has become more radical in some ways, because I hope she finds strength and inspiration there—instead of in the envy and depersonalization of being a slave in "The United States of Marketing." Trying to live up to mainstream middle class visions of life is very anxiety producing. And I'm enjoying the positive changes in our relationship as she grows past early teenagehood. It's more important to me, the way we have been getting along, than the fact that she's more similar to me than she thought.

I am not saying that everything is the same for everyone. I am just saying that teenagers rebelling from their radical parents isn't an aberration. It happens. It can really hurt to see them reject and be angry with you for your closest held ideals. But in the end, I think they will find the values they have been raised up with serve them well—better even than some of the material things they lacked and wished they had as a younger teen—and they find a familiar home (and heritage) within the counterculture.

The spirit lives on!

Afterword

by Clover

Oh, hi there. It's me, the prodigy daughter born from the cracks in the cement that my mother cracked with her sledgehammer. A green weed growing freely in the chaos my mother built before me. Screeching halt. I have been built equally from the environment that surrounded me and my defiance against it. Less a wild weed and more of a planned and carefully placed piece of street art like the Legos built into the holes of a building wall.

In the early days we laid spread out in the grooves of the carpet with highlighters, crayons, and markers coloring in the pages of *The Future Generation*. It was in my head that the children's book themed cover was especially for me. I learned a sense of self when *The Future Generation* was getting laid out for printing. The floors were a real-life "lava" game, and I skipped from safe spot to safe spot until I reached solitude in my own activities. The rooms outside of my play area weren't fun until it was time to color in the covers. I didn't know or care about how much about me wasn't or was within the pages. I cared about privacy, sure, in the ways kids can, asserting themselves in the small life choices they can make. I was always and foremost able to make my choices within a world of tolerance only radical parenting can provide. At the end of the day it was OK to be naked, but OK not to be naked if I didn't want to. I could be a pirate or a king and have trucks if I wanted to, but nothing was wrong with wanting a purple-haired doll from the thrift store that resembled a Ziggy Stardust David Bowie. I felt free to understand sexuality as a concept and explore it when it was time but felt no pressure in one way or another from society. There were these problems like how people treated me outside of my mother-daughter relationship—a sort of disdain of our kind of existence—and problems like money and security. I think I was like a weeble-wobble back then: no matter how the earth shook I had this weight in my feet that kept me grounded.

As time progressed and I entered puberty and suburban society, being the object of my mothers writing felt like I couldn't breathe without a mistake or argument becoming the topic of someone's story. My mother has always been a rebel and like her I yearned to break free from the structure I was born into. How does one rebel against rebellion? Normalize. I daydreamed of pantsuits and biweekly paychecks. Her zines were nothing more than creations made from my nightmares. I felt like my story would never be my story because I was now a topic of someone else's story. I think China tried to pull back, the way that a documenter of life can. Change a name here and there and leave pieces out to not make it seem so cruel. There are pictures in these pages that tell a thousand words that no one would know from reading this book. Like how the picture of me blowing out the candles on my cake was also the birthday when I farted in front of all my friends at the same moment I blew out those candles or how I was in love with my best friend who emotionally abused me until I was 17. I stopped coloring in those pages, I become wild and angry about having an expressive mother, and I coiled into my own universe. Certainly there was more to me than these stories and this background, and no one would understand any of it in my new suburban world, so it was better to just fit in. I think there is a period in growing up when you are so inexperienced with the flood of existential and romantically complicated feelings you start to have all at once that you speed through your day to day a ticking bomb for anyone who lights your fuse.

What happens when you take a free bird and you put them in a cage? They start pecking at their own feathers. I had been this radically raised free child, but through my own request I entered the school system, and it tore me apart feather by feather. I had the desire to meet others, be educated, and experience what a regular school was like. Instead I was met with bullies, adults who gave up on us before we even walked in the door, and zero-tolerance policies. I felt so attacked and hated in middle school that before long when I looked into the mirror I saw a new bully in my reflection looking back at me. I screwed up in my first year of middle school and ultimately was expelled for punching a girl after being coaxed by my peers.

After my expulsion and recommendation for Juvie, mom refused to let me fall further. Society deems that when someone is hurting and lashing out that we punish them further, which only nourishes the demons inside more than extinguishing them. She found an independent school that saw something still salvageable inside me. I flourished in radical education; The GreenMount School in Baltimore offered me some calm oasis between public schools. It wasn't until I found out I could never be a regular kid that I found some happiness and built a stronger and more radical relationship with my mother. I dropped out of high school at 16 because I was probably going to fail out, all my friends failed out, and I felt like everyone there hated me. They were regular, reasonable 16-year-old reasons. My mother had always allowed me to make my own choices in life, the real serious choices, and she allowed me to make this serious choice. I finally ended a 6-year abusive and toxic relationship that poisoned my relationship with my mother. I made my own zine, *Dildo*, where I documented nothing and found humor in everything, I tried some more school but mostly just found things I loved like film, music, and painting. My awakening brought a new era of mother and child. At 17 I became my mother's "Rad 17," almost as if my political and personal revelation was what she had been waiting for, a payoff for the last 6 years of trauma.

As the dust settled from the very public announcement of my weirdness via the zine, this became the physical monument to my lack of privacy and failure to embrace the magic in my anarchist upbringing. How could I come from something so cool and be so dull? I had to make my own story and find out what it meant to be both myself and the pieces that made up my past. Appreciation for what my mother made grew in me as I allowed myself to really see how *The Future Generation* was a generational outcry to open the doors to communication, to express thoughts, feelings, and ideas rarely shared in print. It grew in me as I learned how courageous it is to yell on a mountain or on paper that you are poor, depressed, and having a hard time being a mom. Maybe we aren't supposed to care about our parents' feelings before we even understand our own. Underneath the documentation in *The Future Generation* of the Clinton era is the story of how a mother and daughter grow together, hurt each other, and heal each other. The story of having a teenager going through these phases was hers, and the older I get the more I see the beauty of the two stories living parallel in time instead of somehow villainizing or stealing from the other.

My early twenties were an odyssey sparked by my own personal cry out for independence and the yearning to feel, express, and love. What am I doing now? I'm not leading the revolution; I'm not raising some cool chill kid with a kick-ass grandma. I work, have fun and have friends, and try my luck in comedy. I made a lot of mistakes and continue to make a lot of mistakes. I'm at the crossroads on my twenties and thirties, living my story. I'm the child of someone with depression and I too have fought with my depression and anxiety. I'm afraid of the world constantly; I'm living in the Trump era, when destruction is not only a possibility but also almost a guarantee. In the promise that my mother was honest with her reality in her zine I will be honest with my reality. We aren't a TV version of mother and daughter where the mom makes a book and we become rich. We aren't *Gilmore Girls*; all that junk food made me fat and I developed an eating disorder. My mom didn't marry the business owner down the street; he turned out to be a jerk after all.

Life is messy, and if you were hoping for a fairy-tale ending this is it, honey. The fairy-tale ending is that I love my mother and we made it. We are still here despite the crushing weight of the patriarchy. Our relationship never went backwards—we never let it. We fight and we evolve like maternal Pokémon, becoming fiercer and stronger in each battle. I was the future generation, but now here we all are, living embodiments of the hopes and dreams of the generation before us, and we live in the now—the current generation. I sat across from my mother in a cafe in Hampden, Baltimore, and we chatted about a Kickstarter that would later turn into an Indiegogo (to support the reprinting of this book), how this second edition could be different, and what would help bring *The Future Generation* of the past into the future. I felt the urge inside of me to now voluntarily contribute to her writing in a way I never wanted to before. Here is the current voice of what was at one time *The Future Generation*. I look forward to "our future generation"; they are growing up in such a revolutionary time despite the political hardships that face us. All that was once radical isn't as radical as it was; being gender queer and acknowledging our privileges aren't something you have to shuffle through zines to find out. It's everywhere, and we are linked together through the Internet to communicate to each other about our struggles and dreams. *The Future Generation* is an empathetic historical account of radical motherhood and a yearbook of my youth.

If you came here for some sealed envelope of the story, I leave you with water that pours through the cracks of your fingertips. The story continues running off the pages into the daylight. There will always be another future generation, and as fast as we run towards it, the future runs away at the same exact speed. Some problems still exist and are timeless while others have made strides. New hot topics get added to the bill but one thing never changes: everyone is a critic. This book is a bulldozer that pushes critics aside. It is a safe place for the voices of the radical subculture that at the end of the day have one message: you are not alone.

May 31, 2017
Baltimore, Maryland

ZEN Anarchy

I'm a buddhist. I'm like an organic gardener - I want my natural child with a few bugs and all. I want her to know I'm gonna love her no matter what she do - its ok to be real + authentic + express herself. She means that much to me. I believe I might not know the scope of her being, I better give her a chance cuz in some situations, she might be right and I might be wrong and I would limit our existence if I ruled it by only my intentions without consulting and talking to her. I respect her as a being since day one.

I do respect myself and am understanding of my own "bugs" - I mean I don't have no christian whip around here cracking on our backs to strive for perfection by driving out demons. I try to live in a balance. Yin and Yang.Tao. All that deep stuff.
And you know what? Respecting kids is a good thing - cuz you can trust them and its alot easier than being the Boss of everything, all the time. You can be honest with each other, even if you are confused or having a bad time.

I trust in nature, in humanity, in myself - basically that we don't have to be watched,regulated,controlled, ruled , to be good citizens. People all want love and approval and need to work together to accomplish stuff. I'm more into co-operation than being anyones slave or master. Thats what Anarchy is about - No government, trusting yourself,working together. It's about political and social justice. Its about earning respect not gaining it through fear. Its about looking at the root of problems instead of treating symptoms - or trying to manipulate and control behavior on a surface level. She who rules least, rules best.

Anarchy can get a little utopian or christian for me, so I like to mix it with taoism and Zen. Thats about compassion. How the good and the bad, positive and negative forces mix all around and transcending duality. And again, like Anarchy, its a free form thing, it comes from inside yourself. No authority can teach you zen, you just get it. Cuz words aren't truth.

Read Alan Watts. He rocks. I read him when I was pregnant. The Way Of Zen and The Wisdom of Insecurity. I just mix up a bunch of different influences. Psychology and anthropology and experiences. Im not saying I never say "Because I said so Damn it, I'm the adult". no bodys perfect,theirs no Right Way all the way every day thing. I'm just going bla bla bla and now I've run out of words. But I don't need a reason either, for everything I do. I wouldn't hold myself back from experiencing life by being too pc.

Acknowledgements

Deep and sincere appreciation to everyone who preordered this book, helped with getting the word out, asked family members to preorder too (!), and donated to help make this second edition possible. Here are some of their names: Charlie Hughes, Andrew Bresko, Davida Breier, Lauren Logsdon, Lynne Buggy, Trace Ramsey, Megan Cooke, Lynda Martens, Nadja Martens, Heather Schultz, Amy Ongiri, Megan Trelfa, Mike Jones, Carly Toepfer-Gaver, Jeanine Malito, Milo Miller, Robin Markle, Joel Cahalan, Ariel Gore, Victoria Law, Judith Morris, Sara Morris, Lucy Morris, Norma Marrun, Megan McShea, Cecilia Caballero, Billy Janes, Kara Desiderio, Cara Dudzic, Alisa Johnson, Renee Maxwell, Amanda Frevert, Crystal Guengerich, Adela Nieves, Celia Perez, Karina Costa, Sue Stroud-Speyers, Jonathan Rochkind, Shannon Drury, Brieanne Buttner, Karen Su, Jo Penney, Mariah Boone, Katie Kaput, Michelle Gudz, Megan Weber Jeske, Parag Khandhar, Katie Kuhl-Adorno, Jodie Zisow-McClean, Jenny Hayes, Gabriela Rodriguez, Lainie Duro, François Villeneuve, Stacey-Marie Piotrowski, Lisa Harbin, Stephen Thomas, Elise Temple, Bhavana Nancherla, Katy Otto, Muffy Bolding, Eleni Diamantopoulos, LaMesha Staples, Elaine Doyle-Gillespie, Jacob Klippenstein, Dylan Morison, Evan Henshaw-Plath, Erica Deaton, Stephanie Sylverne, Kimberly Wiman, Jessica Mills, Adrienne Brown, Sarah Cummings, Terry Hiner, Melody O'Seadna, Courtney Gardner, Rhiannon Theurer, John Eaton, Meghan Wilson, Winnie Looby, Andrea Lomanto, Victoria Law, Nicole Kibert, Wooden Shoe Books & Records, Lisa Factora-Borchers, Caity Pittenger, Normal's Books and Records, Atomic Books, Amber Yada, John Hughes, Traci Quigg Thomas, Sabrina Adams, Christopher Simpson, Jessica Thrift, Sasha Luci, Scott Feinstein, Zoë Williams, Holly Nochimson, Joyanna Priest, Zoe DeHart, Lisa Peet, Lauren Smith, Chelsea Earles, Nic Riesen, Miki Takata, Erica Deaton, Meg Novak, Lisa Gray, Starri Hedges, Rebecca Fish Ewan, Jenny Forrester, Jonathan Dudley, Jessica Varsa, Theresa Columbus, Lesia Waschuk, Brittany Shannahan, Annie Kaufman, Nina Packebush, Laurie Bezold, Karina Lizotte, Amy Hamilton, Jen Silverman, Gerald Ross, Katherine Arnoldi, Layne Russell, Tracey Kenyon Milarsky, Jessica Hoffmann, Coleen Murphy, Ian Nagoski, Lisa Morgan, Autumn Brown, Sal Talbot, Gina, Julia Janousek, and Nic Ramirez Riesen.

Special thank you to Samuel, for being a cool kid friend I'm lucky to have gotten to know this last year. Also to animal friends (other people's pets) Yoshimi, possibly the world's best dog, for the moral support while on tour, and Waffle, for Waffle time. To Andy, for hanging fliers with me, although no one ever responded to them, and many other helpful acts like encouraging me to try harder and helping me get places. Shout out to Sheep's Hill Farm for the vegetables and last-minute editing. Sara and Megan, you are both so awesome! Love to my cousins Jane Williamson and Michelle North. Acknowledgment also to my grandmother Doretta Law, who passed last year and now is hopefully with her mother/my great-grandmother Elsie Farinholt; and Connie Murillo, writer comrade who passed all too soon. Most of all to my mother, always a phone call away, and my daughter, in the next neighborhood over from mine: I'm lucky to have y'all. We have a good time together. Clover, you are a wonderful daughter and human being. This is a happy ending, in a grown family kind of way, if you ask me.

Samuel

Yoshimi

China Martens was born in St. Agnes Hospital (across from the orphanage where Babe Ruth lived) in 1966. Her mother, who read to her as early as one month old and fashioned cut-and-paste picture books for her as a toddler, was her original zinester influence. Her first book, *The Future Generation: A Zine-Book for Subculture Parents, Kids, Friends & Others* (Atomic Company, 2007; PM Press, 2017) is a compilation of 16 years of her first zine. She is a coeditor of two other anthologies, *Don't Leave Your Friends Behind: Concrete Ways to Support Families in Social Justice Movements and Communities* (PM Press, 2012) and *Revolutionary Mothering: Love on the Front Lines* (PM Press, 2016). She is also a zinestress extraordinaire, producing titles such as *BWI Spy*, *Supermarket Supermodel*, *Zen Bride Doll*, *Dust Bunnie*, *A Little Book of Short Stories*, *Monster Stories and Tales of Horror*, and *Catbird*. She participated in all four issues of the collaborative mama/papa zine project *Mamaphiles*, was a columnist for the DIY newsprint publication *Slug and Lettuce* (from 1994 to 2004), and won *Baltimore City Paper*'s "Best Zine" Award for *I was . . . a Student Nurse!* Ms. Martens still lives in a formstone row house in a now-gentrified neighborhood in Baltimore. She hopes to publish her novel *Shopgirl Metaphysics*, about working in an antique store on the avenue, next.

PM Press was founded at the end of 2007 by a small collection of folks with decades of publishing, media, and organizing experience. PM Press co-conspirators have published and distributed hundreds of books, pamphlets, CDs, and DVDs. Members of PM have founded enduring book fairs, spearheaded victorious tenant organizing campaigns, and worked closely with bookstores, academic conferences, and even rock bands to deliver political and challenging ideas to all walks of life. We're old enough to know what we're doing and young enough to know what's at stake.

We seek to create radical and stimulating fiction and non-fiction books, pamphlets, T-shirts, visual and audio materials to entertain, educate, and inspire you. We aim to distribute these through every available channel with every available technology—whether that means you are seeing anarchist classics at our bookfair stalls; reading our latest vegan cookbook at the café; downloading geeky fiction e-books; or digging new music and timely videos from our website.

PM Press is always on the lookout for talented and skilled volunteers, artists, activists, and writers to work with. If you have a great idea for a project or can contribute in some way, please get in touch.

PM Press
PO Box 23912
Oakland CA 94623
510-658-3906
www.pmpress.org

FRIENDS OF PM

These are indisputably momentous times—the financial system is melting down globally and the Empire is stumbling. Now more than ever there is a vital need for radical ideas.

In the many years since its founding—and on a mere shoestring—PM Press has risen to the formidable challenge of publishing and distributing knowledge and entertainment for the struggles ahead. With hundreds of releases to date, we have published an impressive and stimulating array of literature, art, music, politics, and culture. Using every available medium, we've succeeded in connecting those hungry for ideas and information to those putting them into practice.

Friends of PM allows you to directly help impact, amplify, and revitalize the discourse and actions of radical writers, filmmakers, and artists. It provides us with a stable foundation from which we can build upon our early successes and provides a much-needed subsidy for the materials that can't necessarily pay their own way. You can help make that happen—and receive every new title automatically delivered to your door once a month—by joining as a Friend of PM Press. And, we'll throw in a free T-shirt when you sign up.

Here are your options:

- $30 a month: Get all books and pamphlets plus 50% discount on all webstore purchases
- $40 a month: Get all PM Press releases (including CDs and DVDs) plus 50% discount on all webstore purchases
- $100 a month: Superstar—Everything plus PM merchandise, free downloads, and 50% discount on all webstore purchases

For those who can't afford $30 or more a month, we have Sustainer Rates at $15, $10, and $5. Sustainers get a free PM Press T-shirt and a 50% discount on all purchases from our website.

Your Visa or Mastercard will be billed once a month, until you tell us to stop. Or until our efforts succeed in bringing the revolution around. Or the financial meltdown of Capital makes plastic redundant. Whichever comes first.

DON'T LEAVE YOUR FRIENDS BEHIND
**Concrete Ways to Support Families in Social
Justice Movements and Communities**
Edited by Victoria Law and China Martens
$17.95 • ISBN: 978-1-60486-396-3

Don't Leave Your Friends Behind focuses on
issues affecting children and caregivers
within the larger framework of social justice,
mutual aid, and collective liberation.

REVOLUTIONARY MOTHERING
Love on the Front Lines
Edited by Alexis Pauline Gumbs,
China Martens, and Mai'a Williams
$17.95 • ISBN: 978-1-62963-110-3

Inspired by the legacy of radical and queer
black feminists of the 1970s and '80s,
this anthology centers around mothers of
color and marginalized mothers' voices.

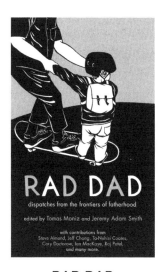

RAD DAD
Dispatches from the Frontiers of Fatherhood
Edited by Jeremy Adam Smith
and Tomas Moniz
$15.00
ISBN: 978-1-60486-481-6

The best pieces from the award-winning zine
Rad Dad and from the blog *Daddy Dialectic*,
two kindred publications that have tried to
explore parenting as political territory.

RAD FAMILIES
A Celebration
Edited by Tomas Moniz •
Foreword by Ariel Gore
$19.95
ISBN: 978-1-62963-230-8

Rad Families: A Celebration honors the
messy, the painful, the playful, the beautiful,
the myriad ways we create families.